IMAGES
of America

REDWOOD VALLEY

3

Constitution and By Laws of the Redwood Valley Improvement Club

The name of this organization shall be the Redwood Valley Improvement Club

The purpose of the organization shall be to advance any interest which will result in benefit to the farming community of Redwood Valley and Mendocino County

The membership of this shall consist of those men, residents of Redwood Valley, who are actually engaged in agricultural pursuits, together with their wives and their daughters above the age of sixteen years.

The officers of this Club shall be a President, Vice-President, Secretary, Treasurer and an Executive Committee of five members.

Officers shall be elected for a period of six months, the first election to be held immediatly upon the adoptio[n] of this Constitution.

On election of officers, or any other business coming before the Club, a quorum shall consist of ten members in good standing, and a majority shall elect or decide.

Shown here is the front page of the constitution and bylaws of the Redwood Valley Improvement Club adopted on January 3, 1912. Dues started out at 25¢ per month, and most valley residents joined. (Authors' collection.)

On the Cover: The one-room Calpella School is pictured here in 1912–1913 with teacher Tom Jameson. The next year, Jameson became the rural-route mail carrier, a position he held until his retirement in 1952. Note the boys in the forefront are barefoot. The outhouse is located to the rear of the building. (Courtesy of Lucille Rovera Neese and Susan Neese Mathis.)

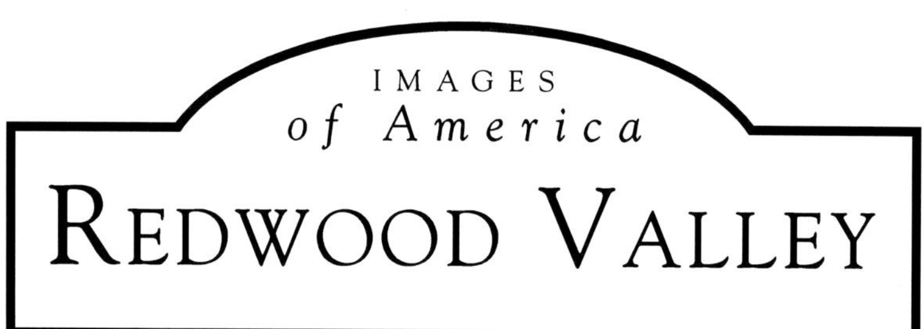

Marvin and Linda Talso

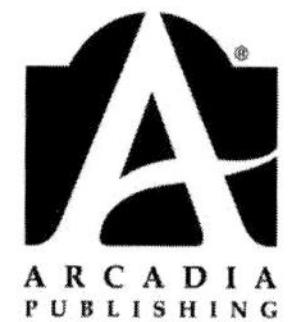

ISBN 978-1-4671-3450-7

Published by Arcadia Publishing
Charleston, South Carolina

Printed in the United States of America

Library of Congress Control Number: 2015938959

For all general information, please contact Arcadia Publishing:
Telephone 843-853-2070
Fax 843-853-0044
E-mail sales@arcadiapublishing.com
For customer service and orders:
Toll-Free 1-888-313-2665

Visit us on the Internet at www.arcadiapublishing.com

To our children, Justin and Mariah, and grandchildren, Chris, Lucy, Caleb, and Brooklyn—this is your heritage; now the future is yours.

Contents

ACKNOWLEDGMENTS

We would first and foremost like to thank the staff at the Held-Poage Memorial Home and Research Library for their assistance with obtaining many of the photographs used in this book. Unless otherwise noted, all images appear courtesy of the Mendocino County Historical Society. The society is performing a real service for the citizens of Mendocino County through its members and many volunteers, as they preserve the history of our area.

Our sincere appreciation to the residents of Redwood Valley, past and present, who contributed their knowledge and photographs: Leo Bleier Jr.; Janet Marsh; Julie Soinila; Marsha Johnson Isbester; Linda Phelps-Wilson; Marston Gillette; Lewis Martinelli; Marguerite Gowan; the late Marvin Ford; the late Delbert Phelps; Cheri Blacklock Weatherly; Kay Testa; Ruth Carr; Marie Fix; Lucille Neese; Greg and Sue Mathis; Ralph McDill; Nancy Jameson-Lapic; the late Lowell Near; the staff and volunteers at the Redwood Valley Calpella Volunteer Fire Department, the Russian River Cemetery District, the Redwood Valley County Water District, and the Local History and Genealogy Reading Room of the Library of Congress; Bruce Brunell; Jim McCleary; Ed Bold; and Ukiah High School librarian Chris Douthit.

INTRODUCTION

Redwood Valley is a small community two hours north of San Francisco on Highway 101 in Mendocino County. Surrounded by beautiful hills, its first outsiders came in 1857, before Ukiah, located 11 miles to the south, was incorporated. The valley seemed like a paradise to the Native Americans, the Pomos. Each year, they burned the valley floor; as a result, the majestic redwoods thrived. The Pomos had several villages in the valley, and they often moved their villages because of the seasonal flooding of the West Fork of the Russian River, which flows down the center of the valley. They had subtribes, and the boundary of these groups was the waterfall on Forsythe Creek where steelhead were often caught. On December 24, 1858, a military fort was established at the head of the valley, named after California's governor John B. Weller, but it only lasted until September 1859. No trace of it remains.

As their numbers increased, settlers had to adapt to the wild environment, which included the grizzly bear. They scratched out a living by raising livestock: cows, sheep, turkeys, hogs, and horses. Crops were added, including hay, grains, and corn, as well as grapes, pears, apples, blue plums, and later, hops. A March 17, 1913, article in the *Ukiah Dispatch Democrat* headlined the following: "The Redwood Valley Improvement Club Accomplishing Splendid Results by Concentrated Action and Progressiveness." "Grape growing is perhaps at the present time one of most important industries of the valley, with hundreds of acres in vineyards and several important wineries in active operation." Each family had its own family garden to supply it with fresh fruits and vegetables—many still do today.

Homesteading, or the ability to buy land for $2.50 per acre, attracted immigrants from all over the world, including, Finns, Italians, Germans, Scots, and Greeks. The Scots and Finns staked out their own colonies and went about making a living. In the long run, the colonies did not last, although it was not for the lack of hard work.

Valley folks began to form a community, which included many cooperative ventures. The Redwood Valley Improvement Club was started on January 3, 1912, for the purpose of bringing more citizens to the valley as well as petitioning for road improvements, bridges, postal service, a fire department, electrical service, and even a dog catcher. The club built a clubhouse, which was used by the fire department as its first headquarters. The clubhouse eventually became the sanctuary of the local community church. In 1917, the Grange was established and soon became the center for social activities, dances, and plays. Four one-room schools dotted the valley. High school students, however, had to go to Ukiah. They usually boarded in town and returned home on weekends. Churches sometimes used the schools for events and services on the weekends.

In 1937, a poster was displayed in the downtown area and in local businesses emphasizing the need for fire safety. In part, it said, "It is time for everyone to do his best, no one can shirk or pass the buck to his neighbor. It is a community hazard and the community must meet it. Everyone for himself and for his neighbor." The $1,250 of needed funds were rapidly raised.

Charcoal kilns were built just north of School Way and east of the railroad by the Noble Electric Steele Company of San Francisco, which manufactured charcoal from World War I to 1943. When a fire broke out at the plant, local volunteers formed a bucket brigade under the direction of Finnish leader Alex Kauhanen and saved the kilns. The farmers and ranchers would deliver wood cut to length to the kiln during the off season to supplement their incomes. The first fire truck was parked there so that everyone would know where to assemble in case a fire call was made. Cy Goudge, the first fire chief, was in charge at the kiln. Later, a system of long and short bursts of the fire horn alerted the volunteers to the location of a fire. This system was needed, as many of the volunteer firemen were out in their fields working during the day. A fire horn still sounds each day at noon. The Noble Electric Steele Company also operated a manganese mine from 1914 to 1917 in the Skull Mountain area.

Another project showing community support was the formation and funding of a water district for the citizens and farmers of the valley in 1975; its limited source of water is the nearby Lake Mendocino formed by Coyote Dam.

From the beginning, the valley was a religious community. At first, there were visiting preachers who rode from town to town. A community church was set up in the Redwood Valley Improvement Clubhouse, which eventually became the church sanctuary. A community Sunday school aid society was formed by a group of Christian-minded ladies. The Calpella Community Church was established in its new building in 1925. Later, a small Baptist church was built on West Road by the father of Pastor Richard Warren, author of *A Purpose Driven Life* fame. Warren lived in Redwood Valley and graduated from Ukiah High School. Sadly, Redwood Valley became the headquarters of the Peoples Temple. The Reverend Jim Jones controlled a large congregation and attempted to buy up many of the holdings, both personal and business, in the valley. When his devious ways surfaced, he quickly left for Jonestown, Guyana, and the rest is a tragic history.

In the olden days, a May Day picnic was held at Laughlin's Homewood Park. The program included a ball game, piano and violin solos, and an auction of picnic baskets (made by the valley ladies), the proceeds to go toward a community endeavor. Redwood Valley is a place where young people go to the T.M. Jameson Arena to compete in rodeo competitions. This arena hosts the Redwood Riders, a locally organized horseback-riding group. Drivers will occasionally come across horseback riders along the country roads. Youth organizations such as the 4-H and Girl and Boy Scouts are also activities for young people. While the hunting is not what it used to be, bucks are still taken during the season. Today, fishing is restricted on all of the valley's creeks and rivers. Bicyclists use the valley's roads for competitions on weekends. Folks power walk along the roadways. The schoolyards are open to fly a kite or have a friendly game of baseball or soccer. The Lake Mendocino Lions Club Park is available for family gatherings, birthday parties, picnics, sports competitions, and a farmers' market. Each year, the Fourth of July Black Bart Day parade winds its way through downtown and out to Lions Club Park. In June, the Redwood Valley Calpella Volunteer Fire Department Beef Barbeque is hosted at the Delbert Phelps Firehouse to fund needed equipment and supplies for the fire district. Over 1,000 are often served at this event. A sense of community lives on in Redwood Valley.

Redwood Valley has a rich history of a diverse group of people brought together in a beautiful area to make a living and to create a community. As the flyer said so long ago, "Everyone for himself and for his neighbor."

One

Pomos and Pioneers

Before the first pioneers arrived, Redwood Valley was a pristine natural environment. Local Native Americans, the Pomos, burned the valley floor yearly so that only large trees, such as redwoods, remained, thus allowing the oat grasses to reach the height of a man. The Pomos interacted with their environment, gathering local acorns as one of the staples of their diet; they also hunted elk, deer, grey squirrel, quail, and grouse. Fishing for steelhead in the Russian River provided additional food. Eight distinct villages were located in the valley, from Mochatbida in the north to Chomchadila just south of Calpella. They have two reservations in the valley. Pomos are world famous for their basketry.

The first pioneer was a Mr. Veeder, who settled in 1857 near Calpella and became its first postmaster. B.F. Forsythe settled in 1858 in the area now occupied by the Broiler Steakhouse (previously Southworth's). In the valley itself, Wiley P. English settled in 1858 on land that became part of the Finnish colony. Dennis Quinliven, the Nuckolls, a Mr. Thomas, a Mr. Howell, William Jameson, Louis Finne, the Fred Finne family, and others came before 1900.

During the early years, the settlers faced a variety of issues in order to maintain their livelihood. They hunted wild game and had to contend with brown and grizzly bears, coyotes, and mountain lions. Most of the early settlers raised cattle, sheep, and hogs. The land was either homesteaded or purchased as part of the original Yokayo Grant.

Old-timers claim the name Redwood Valley came from two groves of large redwoods: one located at the base of Road M near the banks of the Russian River and the other to the southeast of Calpella.

Fort Weller was established in 1858, ostensibly for protecting the settlers from Indians, as bands of Indians were relocated from throughout California up to Round Valley. This fort lasted only nine months and was located on Rancho Mariposa. Before the railroad, there was a stagecoach service three times a week running from Ukiah through Redwood Valley over Tomki by a circuitous route to Covelo.

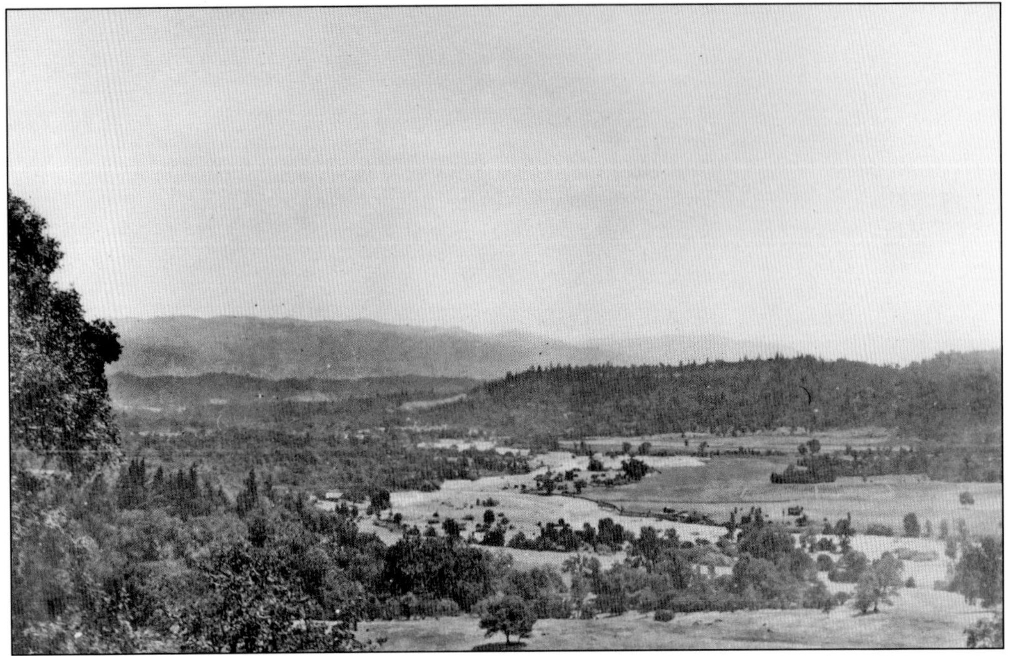

The earliest photograph of Forsythe Creek Valley was taken in 1907 from Redwood Mountain, looking southeast. Today, Highway 101 runs through this valley. A grape vineyard is in the lower right. (Courtesy of the Phoebe A. Hearst Museum of Anthropology and the Regents of the University of California, Photographed by Samuel A. Barrett, Catalogue No. 15-4018.)

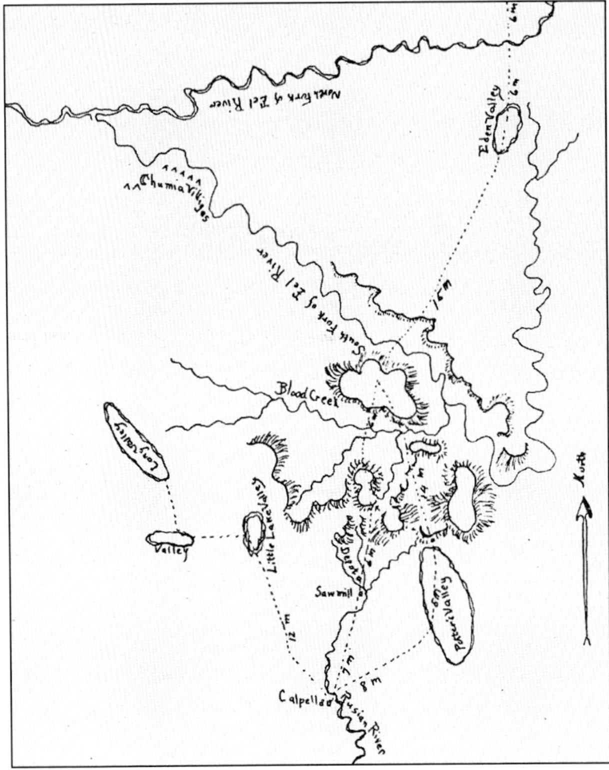

This is the earliest known map showing what was to become Redwood Valley. It was drawn by Bvt. Maj. Edward Johnson with Company D, 6th United States Infantry upon his return to Washington, DC, in 1859. The military fort that was established here was just north of the sawmill labeled in the center. Fort Weller was named after the governor of California at the time, John B. Weller.

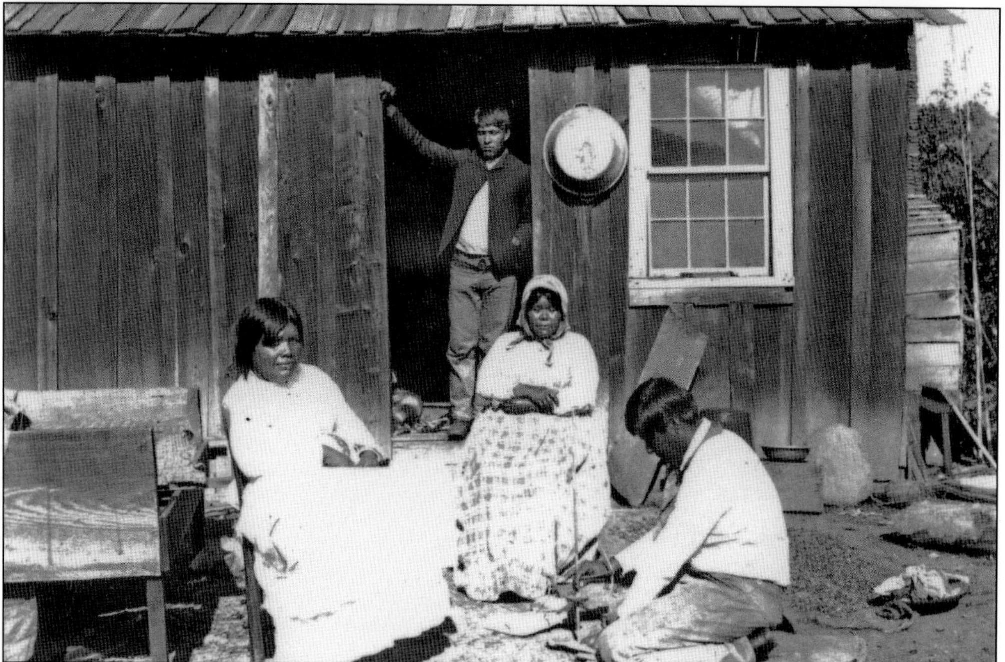

Pictured here in 1892 are the living conditions of the Pomos of Redwood Valley, perhaps on the McClendon Ranch. The woman on the left is Lulu, wife of Sam Burke; on the right is Minnie, her aunt. Lulu was the mother of Annie Burke, who in turn was the mother of Elsie Allen. All were renowned Pomo basket makers. Elsie Allen has a high school named after her in Santa Rosa, California.

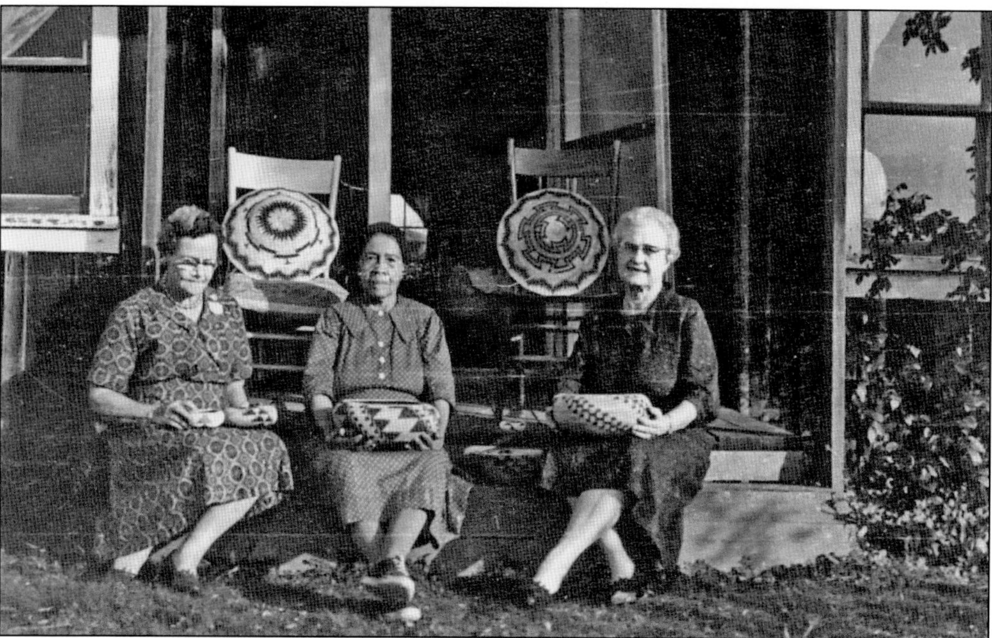

This photograph by George Ward shows ladies admiring Pomo baskets made by Annie Lake around 1960. Annie is seated in the middle. On the left is Evangeline Stanley, and to the right is Geraldine Ward. Baskets were used for different tasks depending on the size and shape.

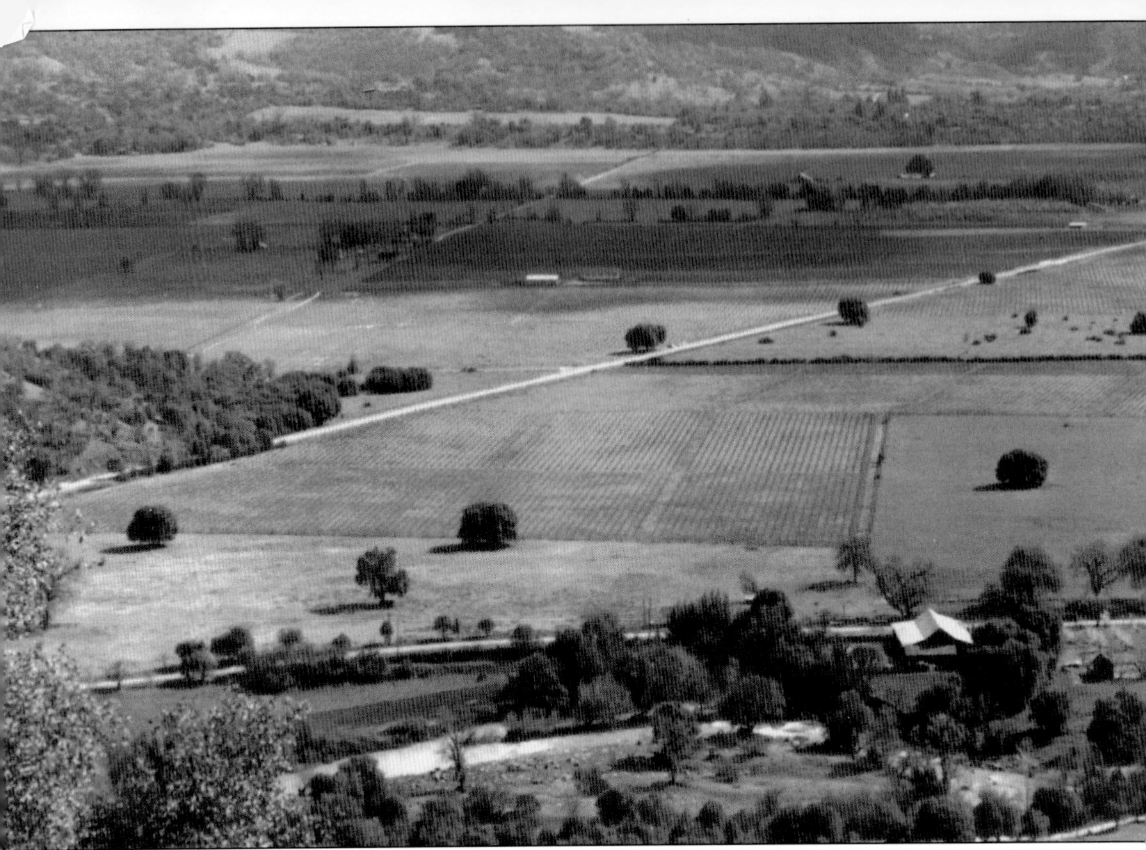

This is a view of the Coyote Valley before Coyote Dam was built; the area is now covered by Lake Mendocino. The Pomo Indians once occupied this land before it was settled and inundated. One of two in California run by the Corps of Engineers of the US Army, the lake is the most important source of agricultural water for Redwood Valley. (Courtesy of the Baptista Garzini family.)

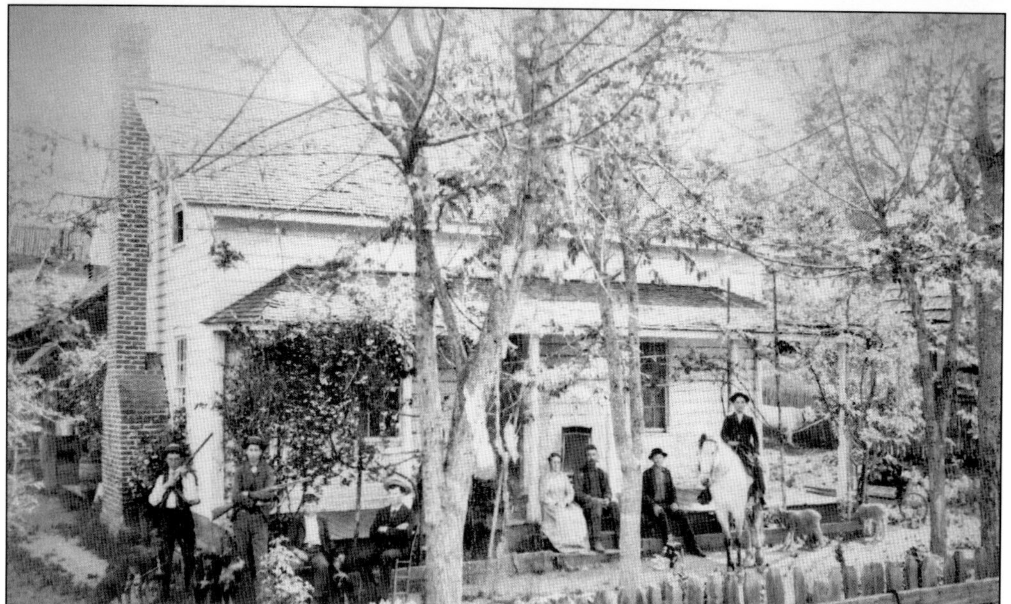

Referred to as the McClendon Ranch on later maps, here is the C.P. McClendon home in the 1890s. Pictured here are, from left to right, Harvey McClendon (holding a rifle), unidentified, Walter McClendon (seated), George McClendon (wearing hat), Zilda McClendon, John McClendon, unidentified, and Frank McClendon (on horseback). The ranch was located in the Salt Hollow area of Redwood Valley.

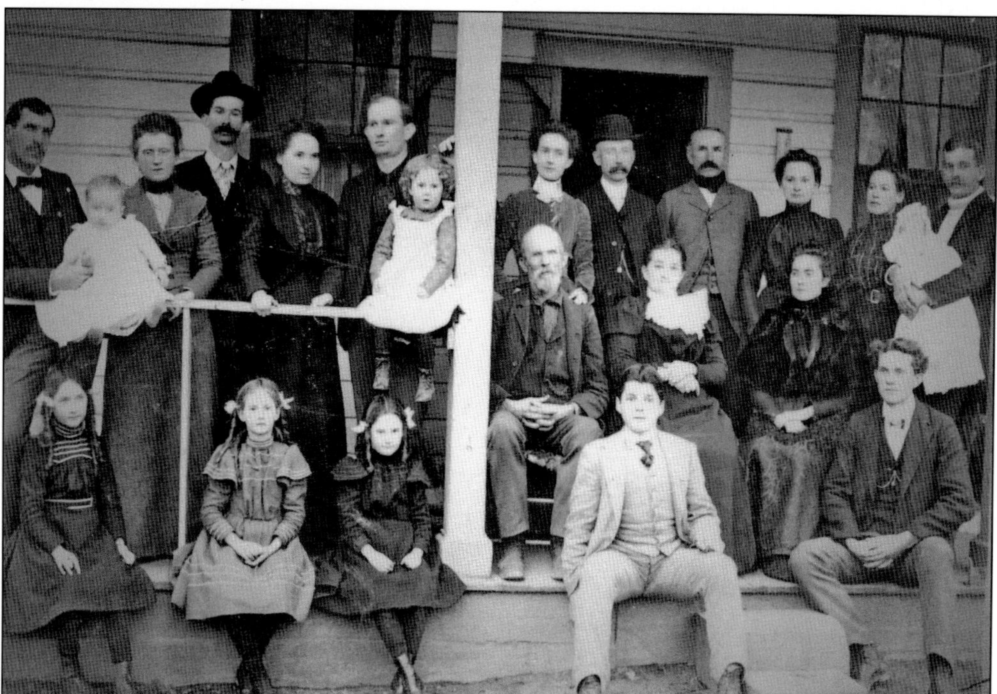

Here is a photograph of a large gathering celebrating the turning of the New Year, January 1, 1901. Wiley English is seated in the chair of honor as patriarch, next to the porch post. His wife, Hollis Neese English, is to his left.

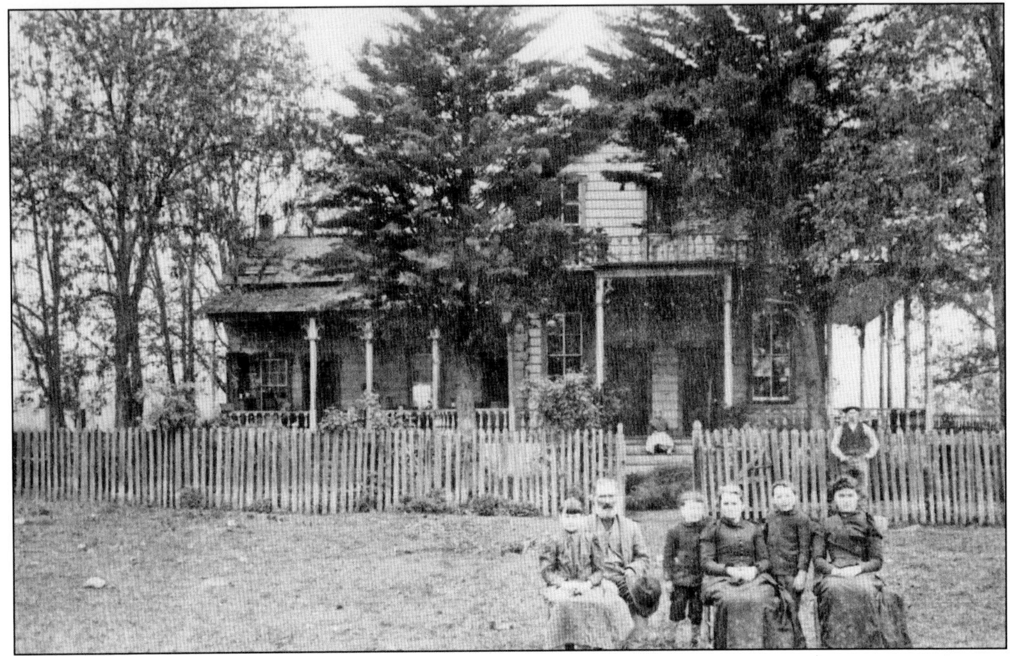

Pictured here is the English ranch house in 1910. Wiley P. English was one of the first settlers in the valley, arriving in 1858. His 1,400-acre ranch, which extended from the Russian River to the eastern hills, was sold to the Finnish colony in 1912. This house became "the Bungalow" for the Finns. It remained the first home for many of the Finnish immigrants.

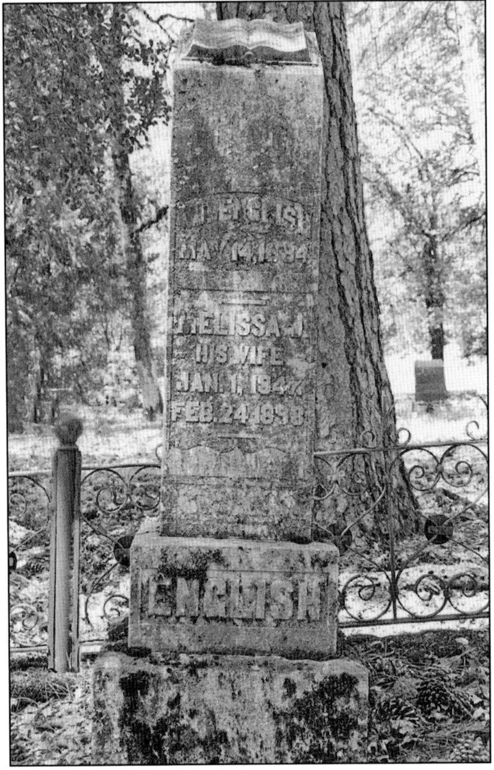

The Redwood Valley Cemetery was taken over by the Russian River Cemetery District, acting on a petition from the citizens of Redwood Valley in 1952. Here is the main tombstone of the English family; it is surrounded by an iron fence. Inside the fence are headstones of W.P. English, Gordon (infant son), James (two months old), Melissa (wife), and poignantly, one stone labeled simply "infant son." (Courtesy of Jim McCleary.)

Seen here is Frank P. Jameson, the four-year-old son of William and Nancy Jameson. These early settlers traveled all the way from Kentucky to settle in Redwood Valley.

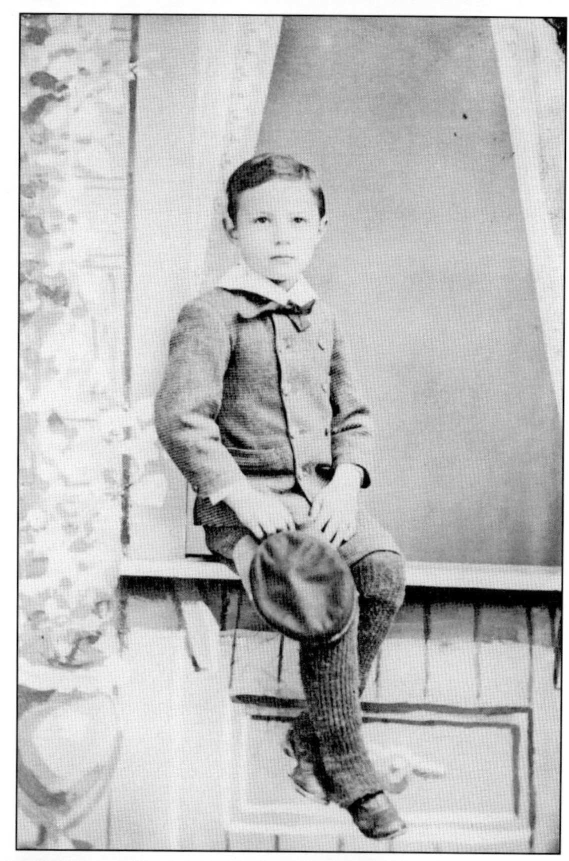

Olga Poma is pictured here standing outside of the Poma home with her children: Ann (being held), Emil, and Jane. Emil became a leading citizen of the valley. He attended the local valley schools as a child. Later, he acquired land on Laughlin Way, where his family lived and raised grapes and hay. Emil was very active in the Redwood Valley Calpella Volunteer Fire Department (RVCVFD).

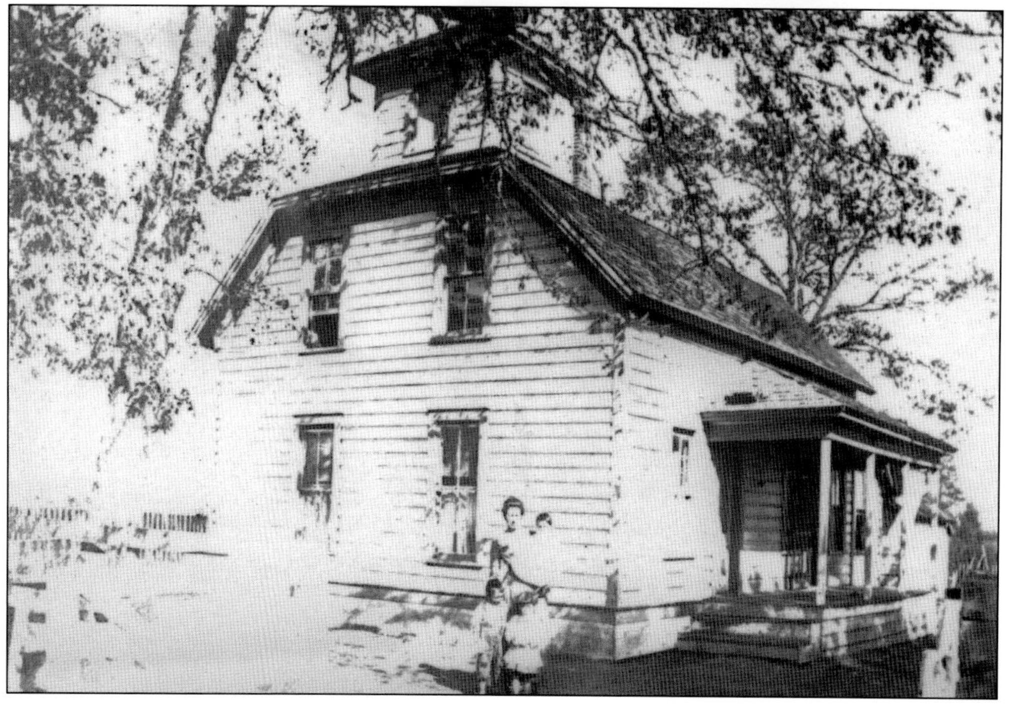

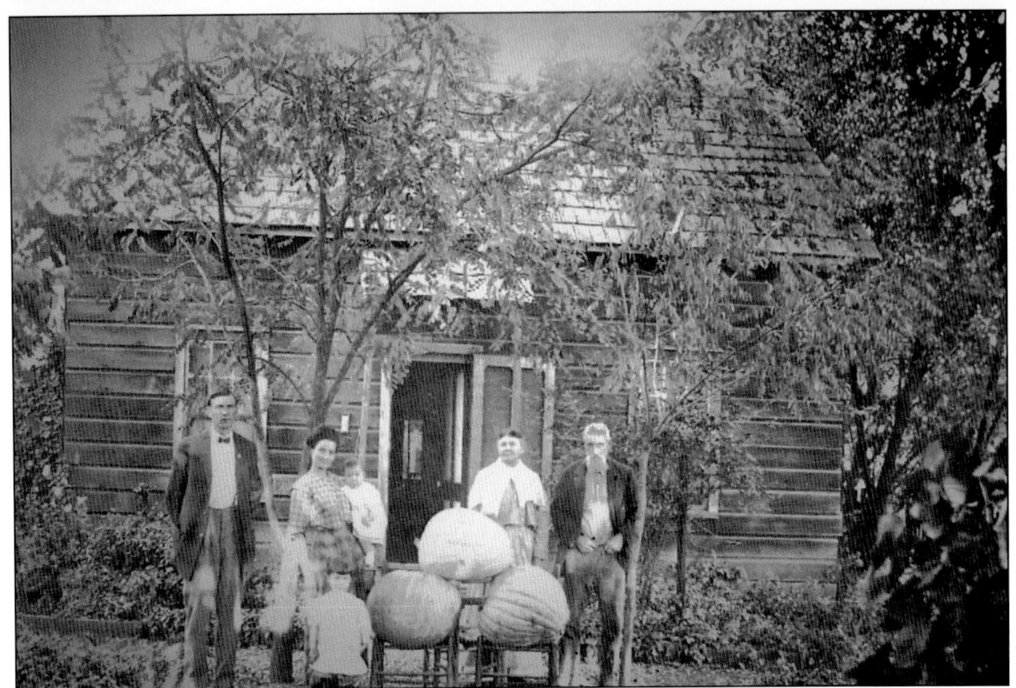

This photograph was taken at the Jameson home, with the family standing behind their prize-winning pumpkins; from left to right are Thomas "Tom" M., Rachael, Bobby LeRoy, infant Rachel Mariam, Nancy, and William Jameson.

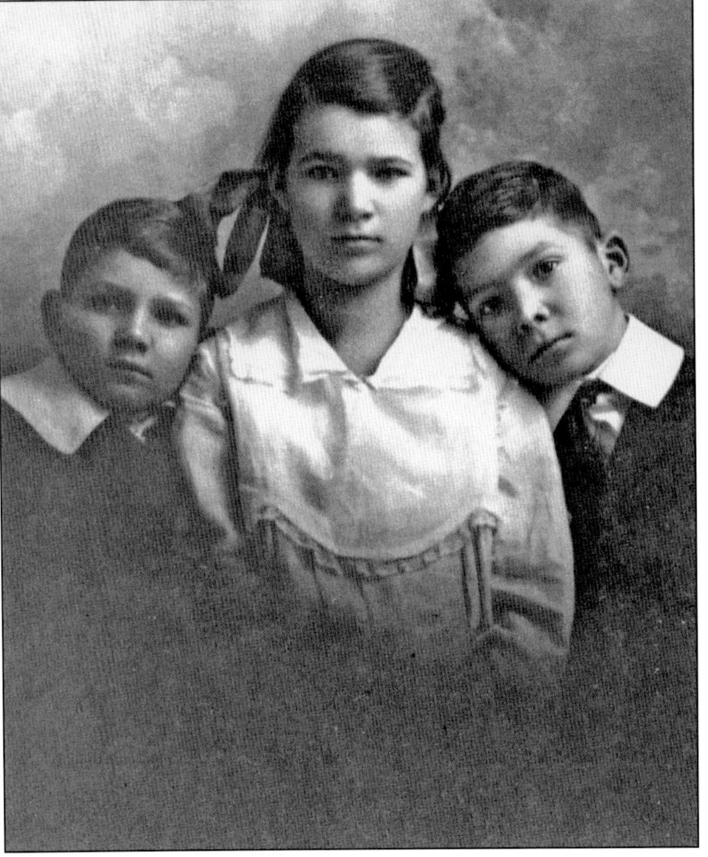

Pictured here are, from left to right, Thomas Lester Jameson, Rachel Mariam Jameson, and William LeRoy Jameson.

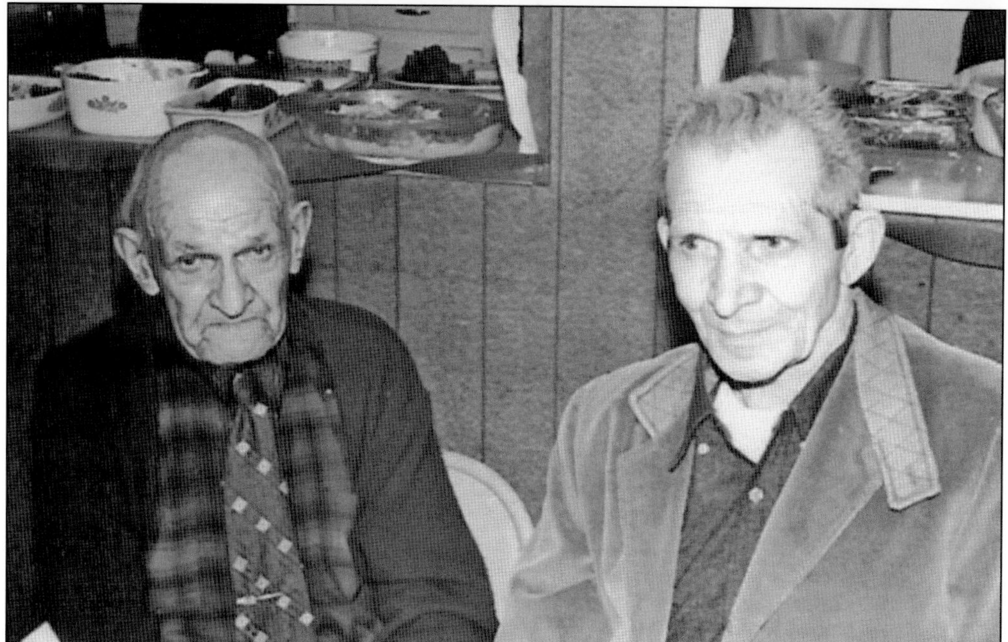

On the occasion of his 90th birthday, Tom M. Jameson celebrated with his son Bobby LeRoy (nicknamed "Pokey"). The party was hosted by the congregation of the Redwood Valley Community Church, of which Tom was a founding member. Tom left a rich legacy of personal notes and tape recordings of the history of the valley, which the authors reviewed many times in writing this book. (Authors' collection.)

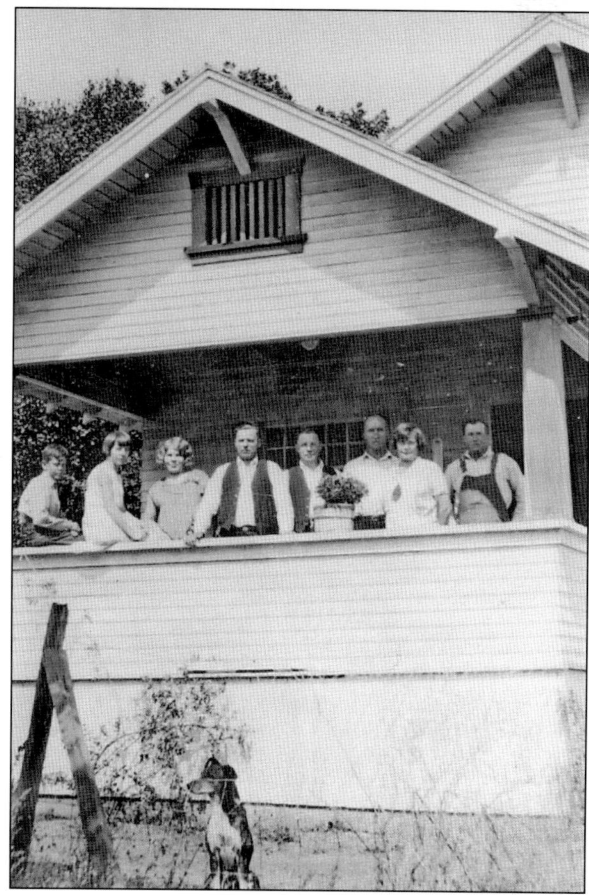

The Hietala family gathered around their home in 1929 for this photograph. Antti and Annie Hietala were part of the Finnish colony. They had six children on the colony: Mildred, Stella, Wolfred, Marjorie, Lorraine, and Norma. Notice the dog in the foreground; everyone had a dog in those days for hunting and herding and as pets.

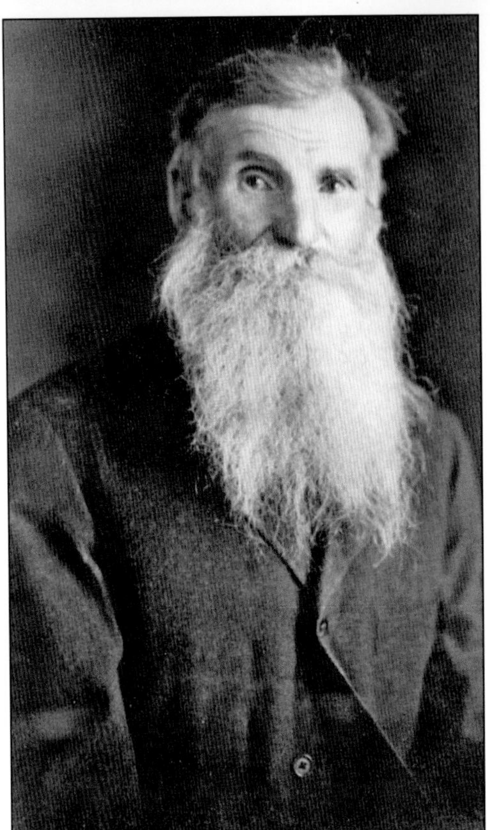

Matt Jacobson was one of the original members of the Finnish colony, who came to California in search of a place to establish a communal existence and a new way of making a living. Almost all of the men were miners, and many had been injured in mining accidents. He was one of several men in the colony who remained bachelors.

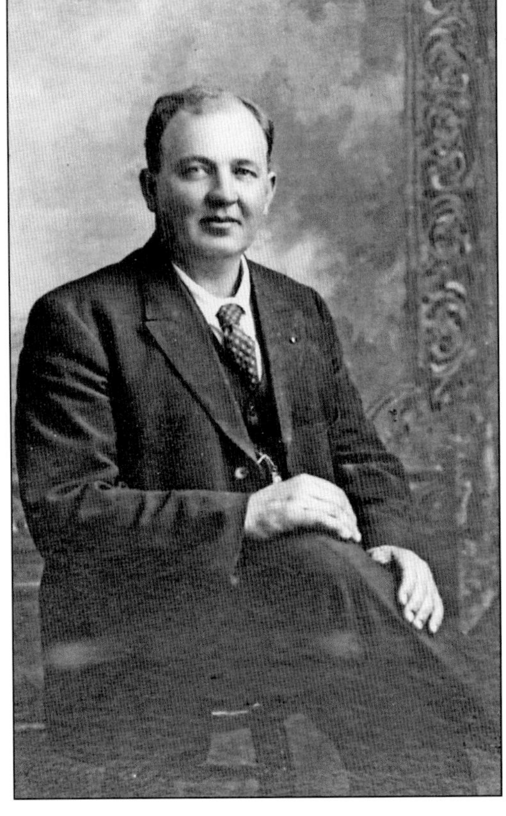

Alex Kauhanen was one of the founders of the Finnish colony. He was also one of the bachelors of the group. Kauhanen was a leading citizen in the valley, serving in leadership roles in the Redwood Valley Improvement Club, on the school board, and in many other civic endeavors. Kauhanen often took the Finnish colony children on trips; one memorable trip was to the 1939 Golden Gate International Exposition.

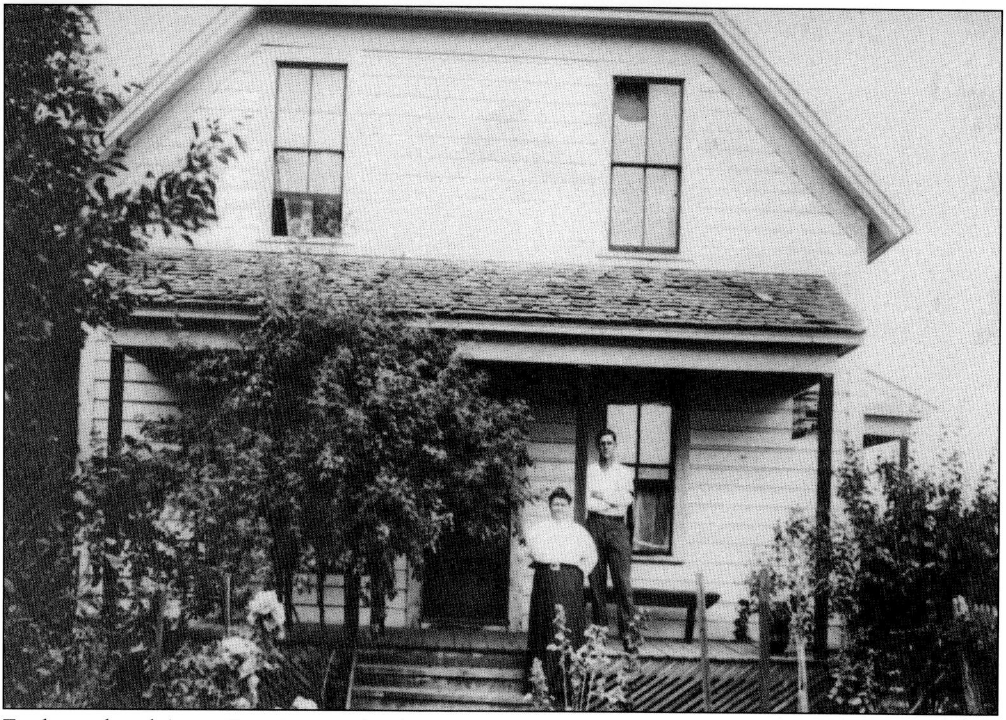

Ferdinand and Anna Faas Jr. pose for this photograph on their front porch. Before it was a home, it was the Forsythe Creek School, located on the west end of School Way. The Charles Forbes family owned the house after the Faas family, and then the Everett Witter family acquired the home. Elizabeth Witter conducted 4-H sewing classes for many years in the enclosed porch on the right side of the house.

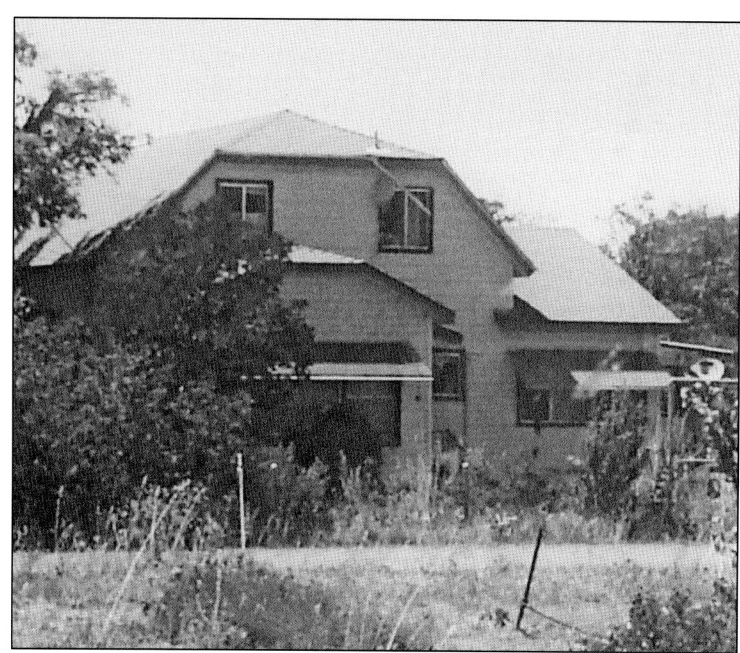

Pictured here is the Faas home as it appeared in 2015. (Authors' collection.)

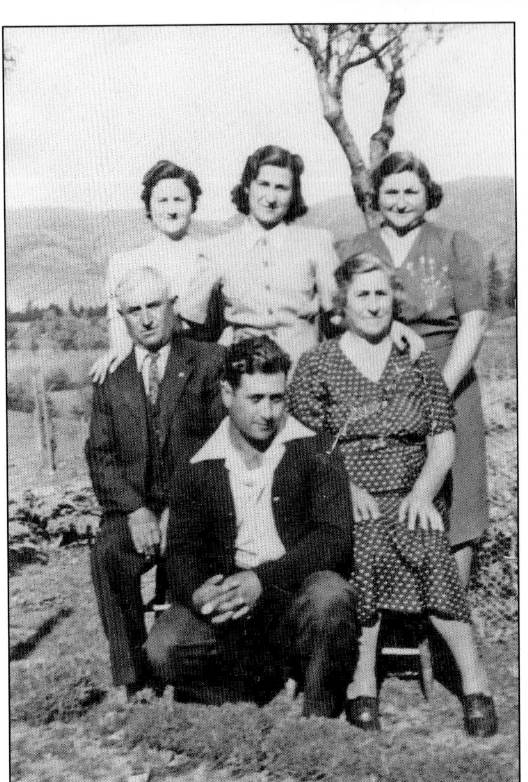

Martino and Amabile Venturi settled their family on the west side of the valley. Pictured here from left to right are (kneeling) Tino Venturi; (seated) Martino and Amabile; (standing) Norma, Zita, and Yolanda Venturi. This photograph was taken at their ranch at the eastern end of Road M in the 1900s. (Courtesy of Roselyn Lucchesi Pittelkau.)

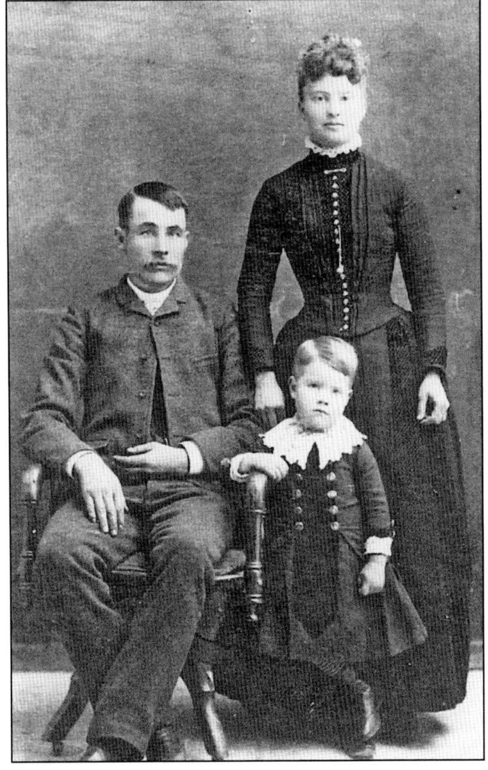

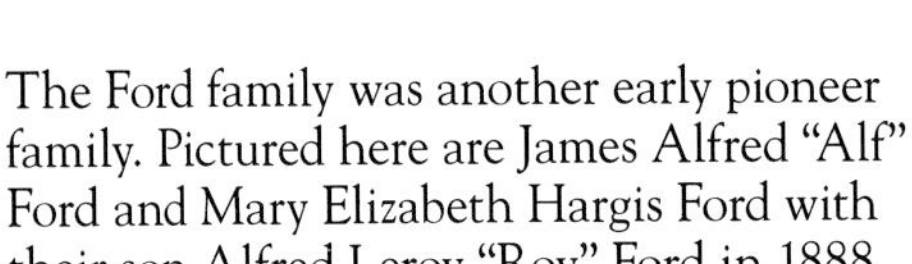

The Ford family was another early pioneer family. Pictured here are James Alfred "Alf" Ford and Mary Elizabeth Hargis Ford with their son Alfred Leroy "Roy" Ford in 1888.

Pictured here in 1915 is Hattie Mendocino Williams Ford with her children James (left) and Marvin. Marvin was interviewed by the authors when he was 88 years old, along with Marguerite Gowan, who was also 88 at the time. During a drive around Redwood Valley, they talked about each ranch or home they remembered a story about. It is tape-recorded and available at the Held-Poage Memorial Home and Research Library.

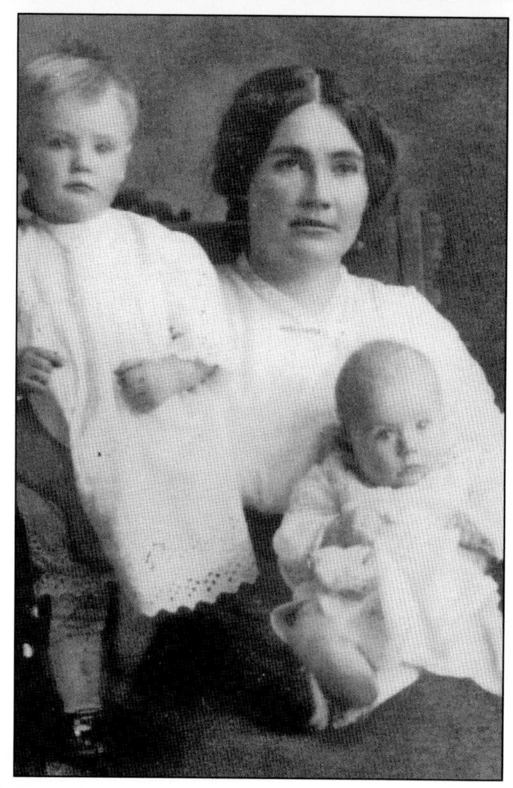

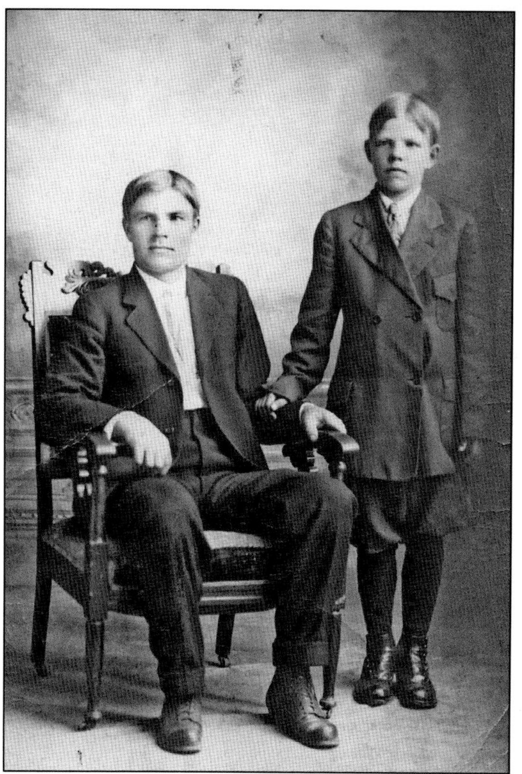

Knute Talso poses for this 1913 photograph with his son Arne. Knute was part of the original group of Finns who came to Redwood Valley from Butte, Montana, where they were engaged in mining, a very dangerous occupation at the time. He had lost his first wife to miner's consumption in Telluride, Colorado. (Courtesy of Julie Soinila.)

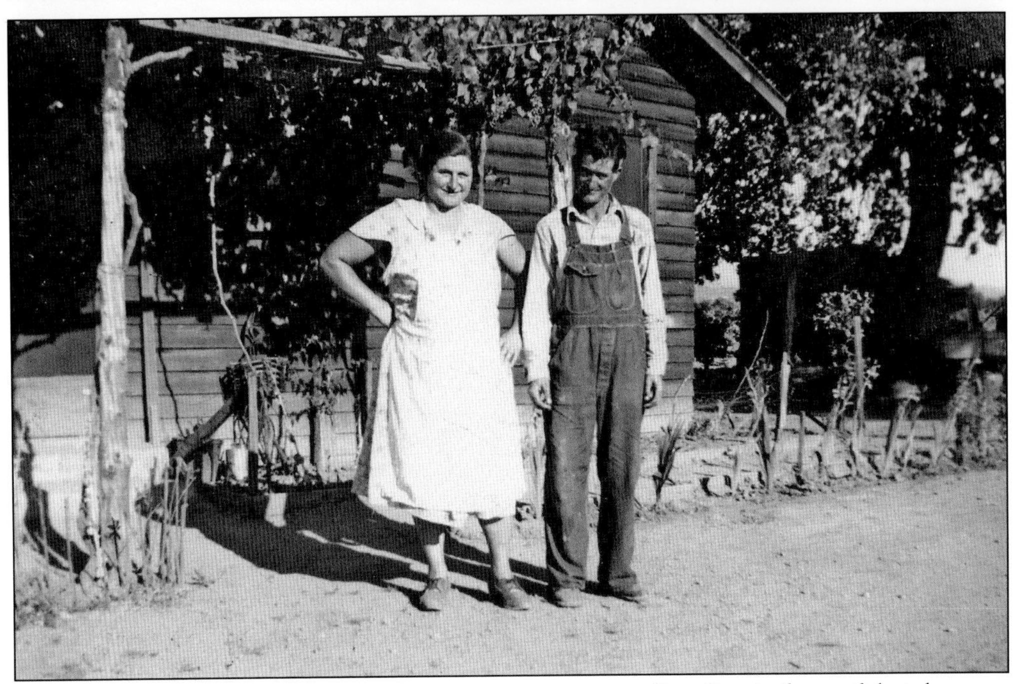

Standing in front of their home are Armando and Yolanda Lucchesi in the late 1930s. They had acquired their ranch at the east end of Road M from her parents, Martino and Amabile Venturi. (Courtesy of Roselyn Lucchesi Pittelkau.)

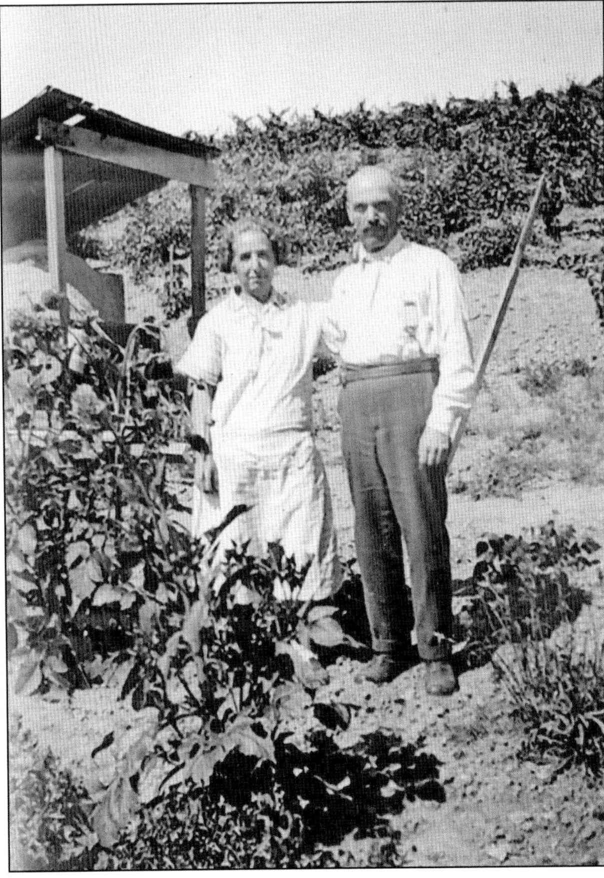

Pictured here in the 1920s are Calpella pioneers Giovanna and Agostino Penna. (Courtesy of the Testa family.)

Charles and Margaret Rovera are pictured here in the early 1940s standing in front of their home on Road D. (Courtesy of Lucille Rovera Neese and Susan Neese Mathis.)

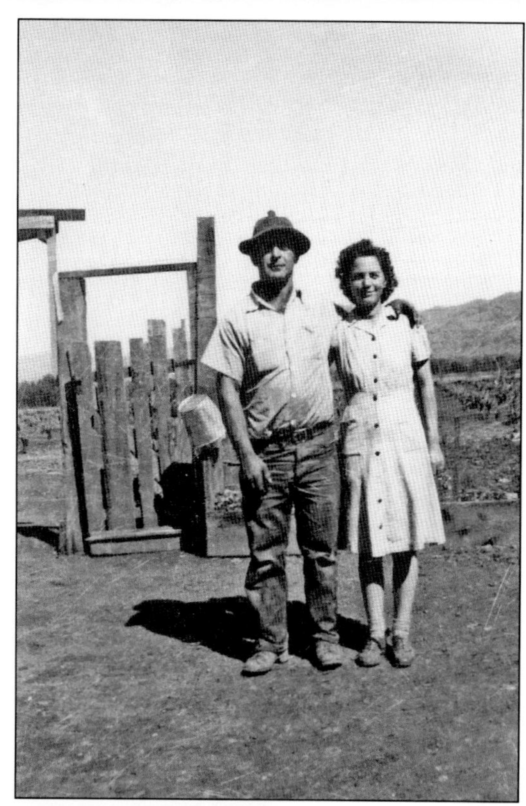

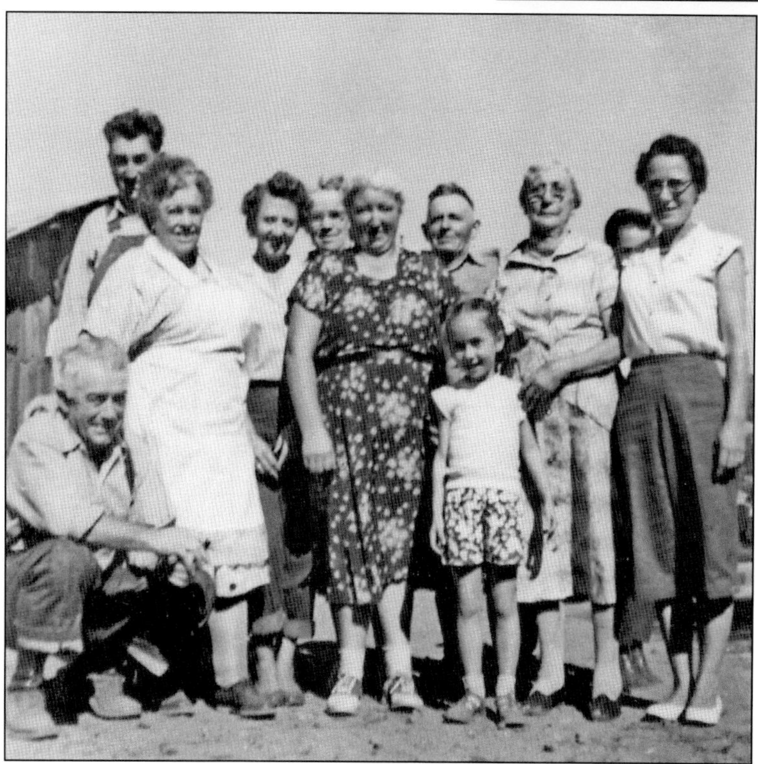

Pictured here in the 1950s are, from left to right, (first row) Charles Pedrioli, Inez Pedrioli, Katherine Villanova, Nancy Ricetti, unidentified, and Rose Ricetti; (second row) Emil Poma, Hilda Shultz, Olga Poma, Joe Villanova, and John Ricetti Jr.

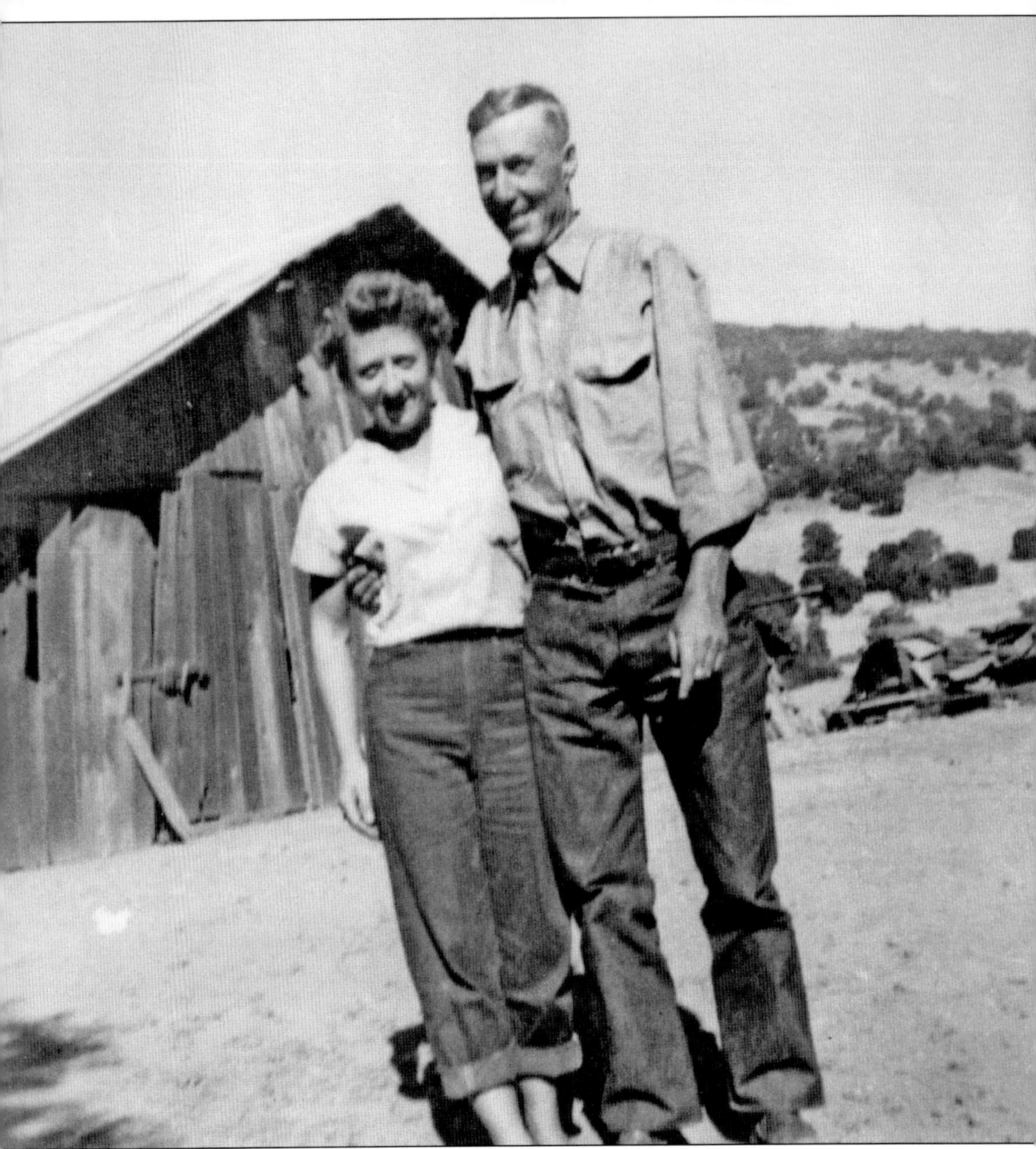

Hilda and Ray Shultz posed for this photograph while visiting with the Villanovas in the 1950s. Ray was probably interviewing them for one of the books he wrote about his time growing up in Redwood Valley. His books *Valleys of Mendocino County*, *Memories of Redwood Valley*, and *A Boy in the 1900s* are all still available at the Mendocino County Museum in Willits, California.

Two

Early Days around the Valley

After the initial influx of pioneers, the valley community began to settle into their new homes. Some of these original homes are still in use today. Citizens quickly saw there was need for improvements around the valley and came together as a community in several ways in order to address these issues. In 1912, residents formed the Redwood Valley Improvement Club, which petitioned the county, state, and federal governments for the construction and maintenance of roads and bridges and the establishment of postal and electrical services and animal control. The Grange provided leadership in the agricultural area and built a hall for social activities in 1918.

An annual May Day picnic took place at the Homewood Park, off of Laughlin Way, close to the Laughlin Post Office and depot. The ladies formed sewing bees as well as a community Sunday school aid. A community church was established in 1918, and used the Redwood Valley Improvement Clubhouse for Sunday school and Sunday services. Occasionally, Sunday school was held in the nearby railroad cars. The schools grew but maintained one-room multi-grade classrooms during this time. A fire department was formed after a brief call for funds and in cooperation with the State of California. Locals would gather downtown, where they could buy groceries and supplies as well as get their automobiles repaired. The post office was established in 1920 at Howland's store, with Calpella maintaining the rural route. The Improvement Club asked that the name of the post office be Pershing, but Redwood Valley won out. Members were concerned it might be mistaken for Redwood City in the Bay Area.

Tom M. Jameson had the rural route from 1913 until his retirement in 1952. The valley even had a female barber who had a shop out on the Redwood Highway, and she made home visits in her Model T coupe.

After the railroad came to the valley, the stop at Redwood Valley Station (sometimes referred to as Basil Station) and the movement of crops, charcoal, and passengers helped the valley grow. Redwood Valley was on its way.

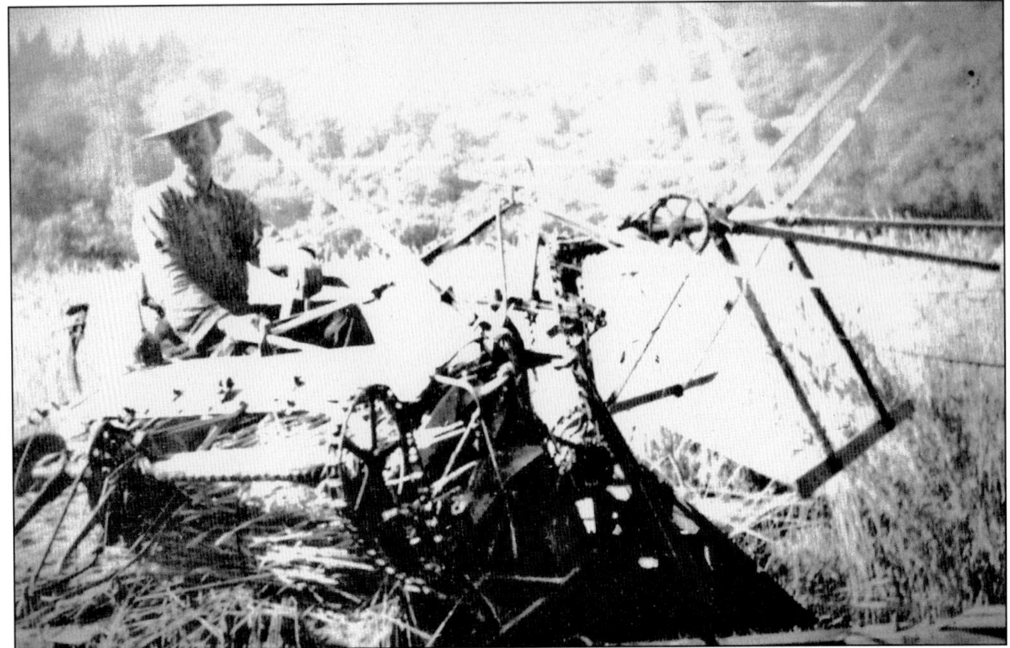

This is a close-up view of a straw binder from about 1913. This machine was used to collect and bundle pasture grass and straw, especially for silage transportation and storage. The machine was widely used in the farm and animal-husbandry industries. The photograph is believed to be of the Finne Ranch, now located off of Uva Drive on the southwest side of the valley.

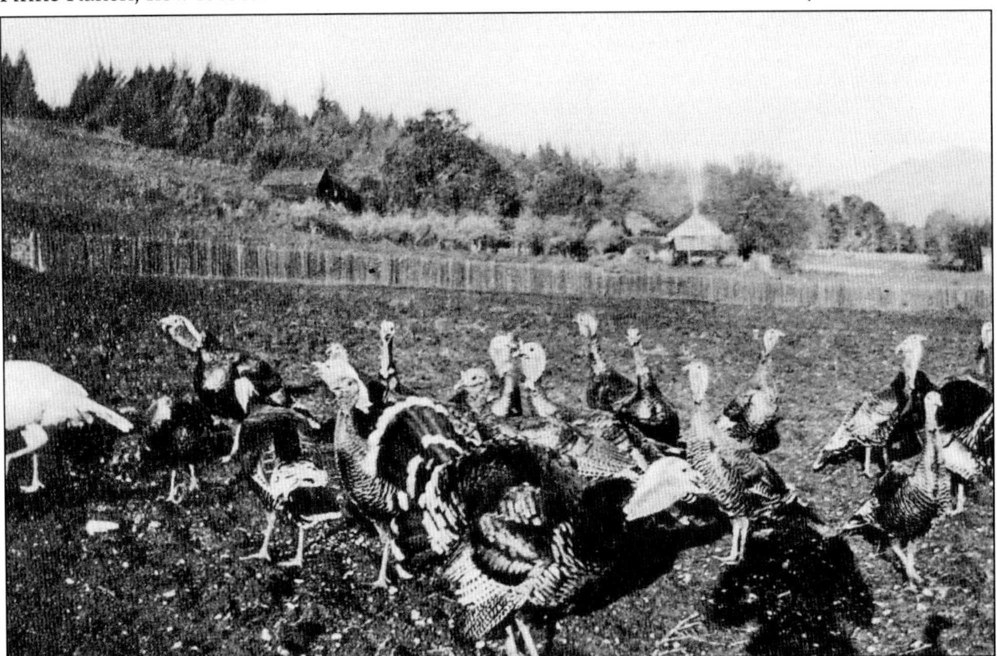

The Louis Finne Ranch is in the center, and the Peters home is on the right. On the hill to the left is the old Finne winery—the first bonded winery in the valley. It burned down in 1921. Finne first planted grapes in 1878. By 1914, he had 50 acres and limited his wine production to his own crop. His wines were said to be of the highest quality.

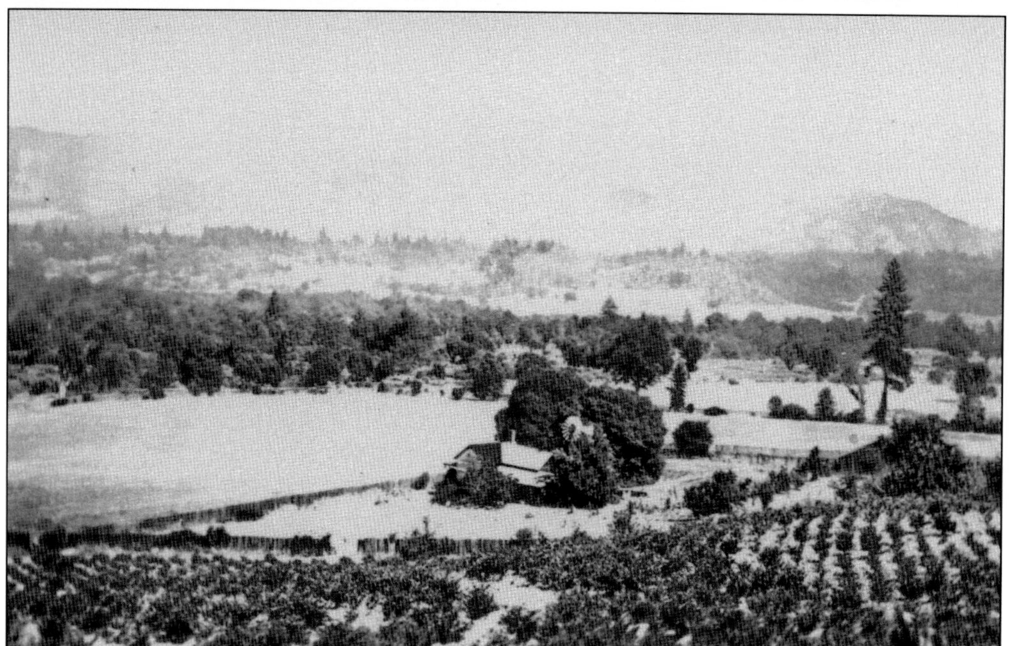

This is a very early photographic view of the Finne Ranch with a vineyard in the foreground, captured in 1916. In the background is the Forsythe Creek Valley. The old Redwood Highway 101 (now Uva Drive) runs from the left to right just below the ranch house. The present Finne Road was later located in the foreground.

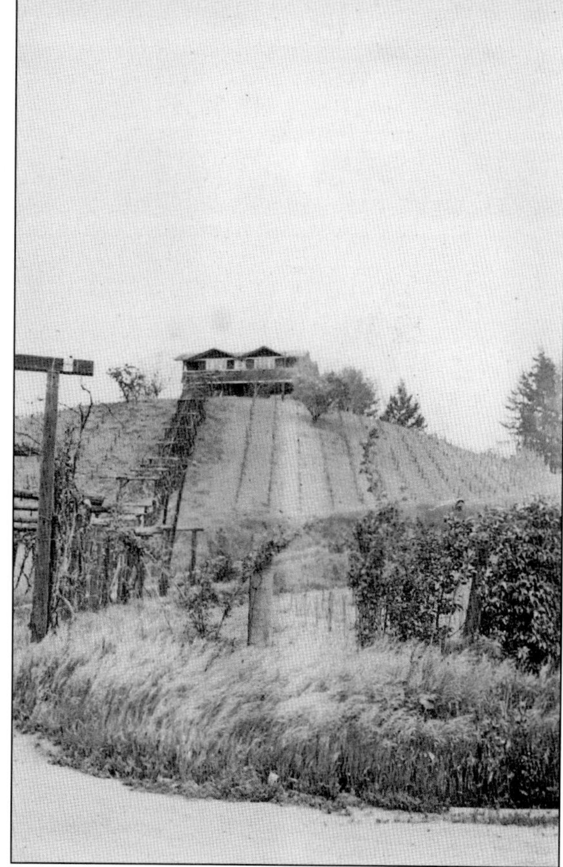

This photograph was taken from East Road looking east up the hill, to the Yarbrough place (formerly the Heilman place). The grape arbor was quite an attraction in its day; it is long gone. It was at this home in 1924 that the meeting that eventually led to the valley getting electricity was held. (Authors' collection.)

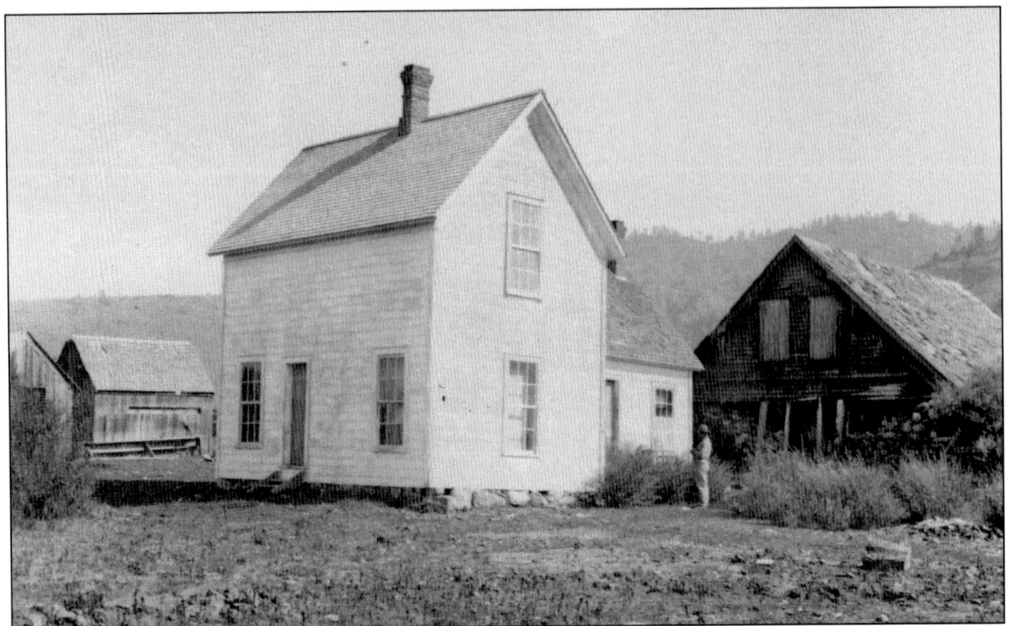

Pictured here is the Roy Ford home as it appeared in 1912. It is said to be the oldest home in Redwood Valley, located just north of Road J, across from the entrance to the Redwood Valley Vineyards. John and Doris Pringle lived here for many years. It still retains its original outline but is obscured with walnut trees in the front.

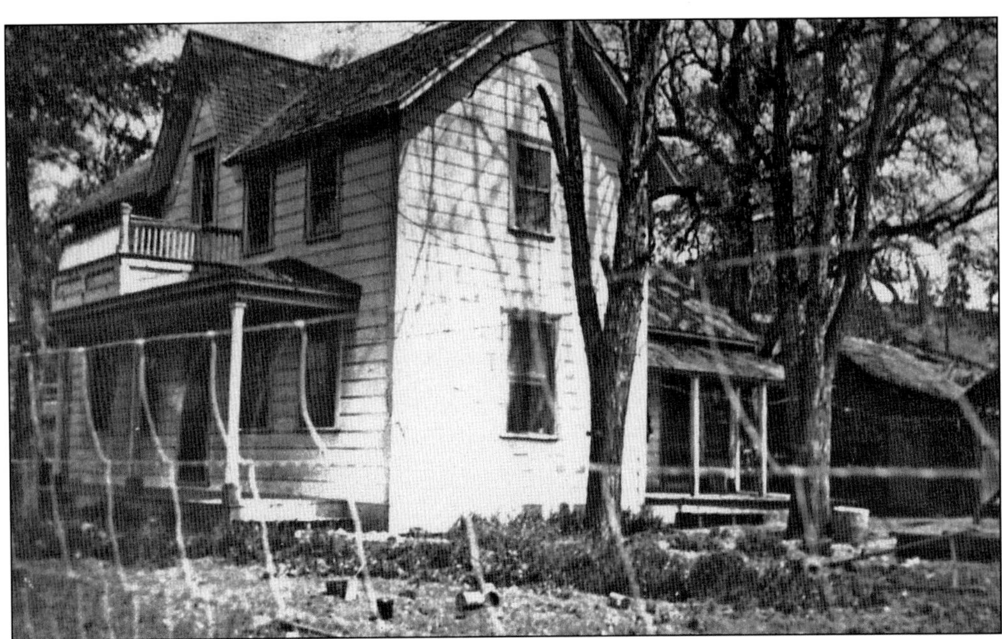

This photograph of the Wiley English home was taken before 1914. This house served as the first communal boardinghouse for the Finns of the Finnish colony. It burned down in 1914, and a replacement was built, which the colonists referred to as "the Bungalow." It was located off of East Road between Roads D and E.

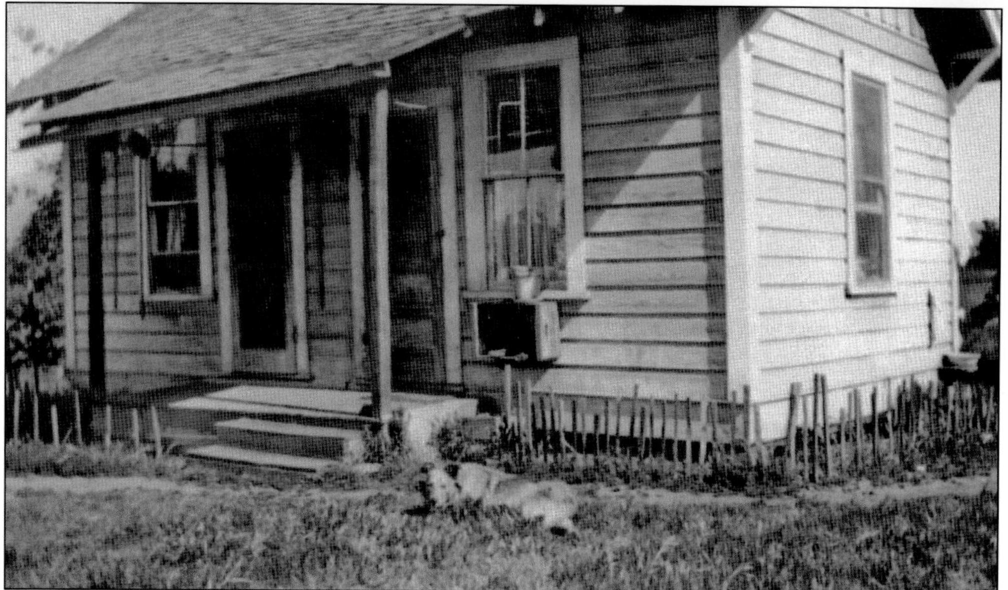

Pictured here is the home of the Rinta family in the Finnish colony. Matt and Ida Rinta were part of the original immigrants who came to form the colony. They already had three children when they arrived: Irene, Elmer, and Irving. This later became the Johansson home.

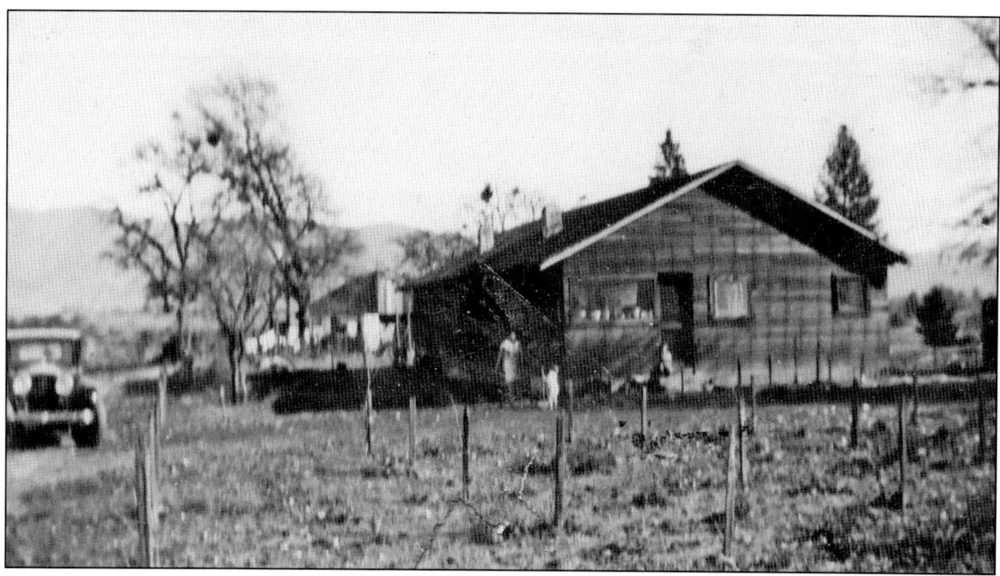

Located at the eastern end of Road M is the Venturi home, pictured here in 1928. The two trees in the background above the roof are part of the northern redwood grove from which Redwood Valley got its name. The first-growth trees were located near the banks of the Russian River and logged early on to build homes and bridges. (Courtesy of Roselyn Lucchesi Pittelkau.)

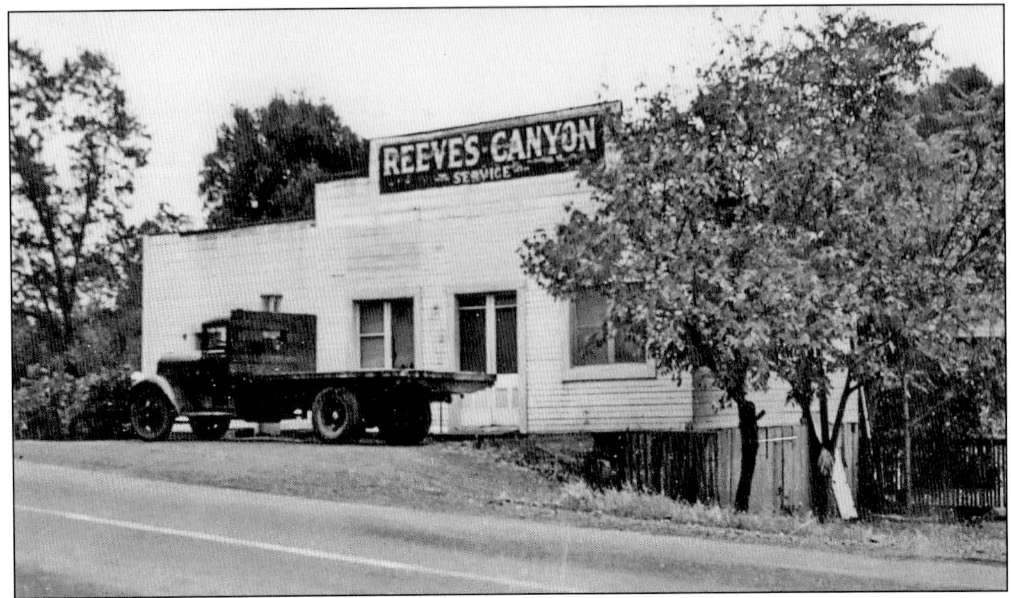

Pictured here around 1945, the Reeves Canyon garage was located at the intersection of Highway 101 and Reeves Canyon Road. Almost at the base of the Willits grade, it provided service to many a stranded motorist whose automobile overheated or needed repair after surviving the winding drive up or down the highway from Willits.

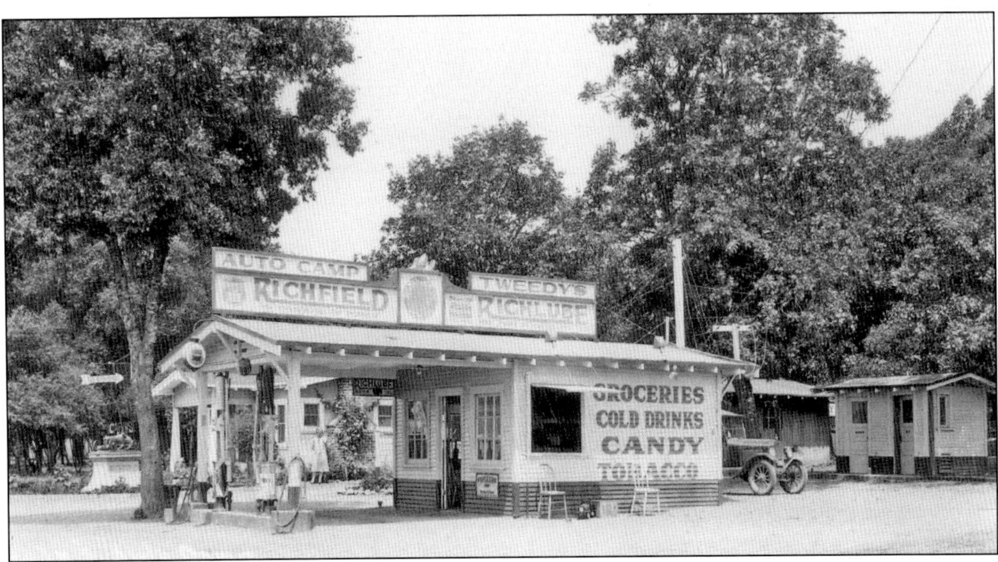

Tweedy's Auto Camp, service station, and cabins are pictured here in 1920 on the Redwood Highway at Laughlin Road. A close look at this photograph will reveal a race car statue just to the left of the tree. The outhouses are to the right. Lillie Tweedy is framed by the drive-through.

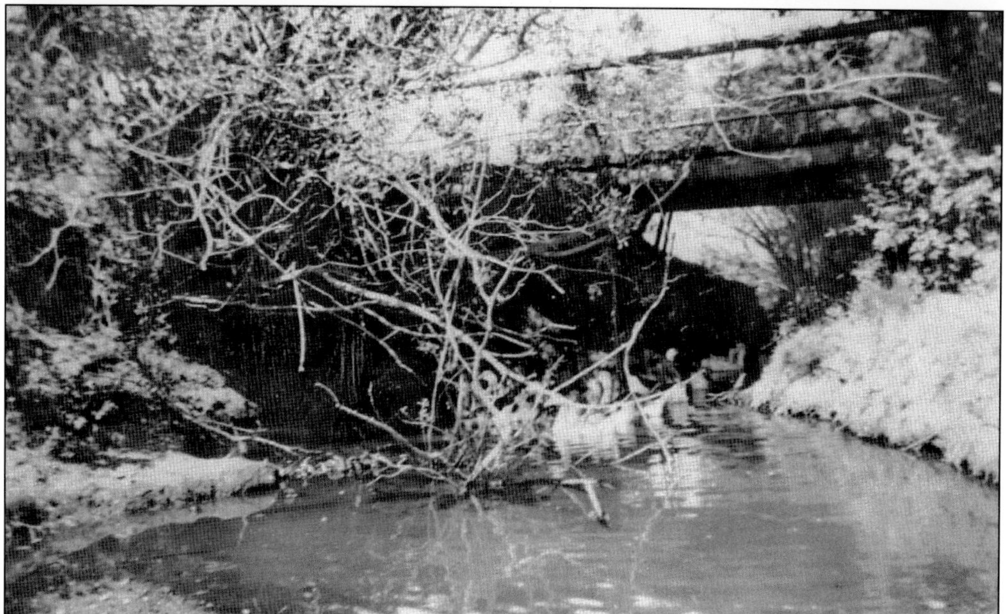

This is believed to be the original bridge at the bottom of the hill on School Way. The bridge was constructed of local redwood. A single lane with railings on either side, there are geese taking refuge under the bridge.

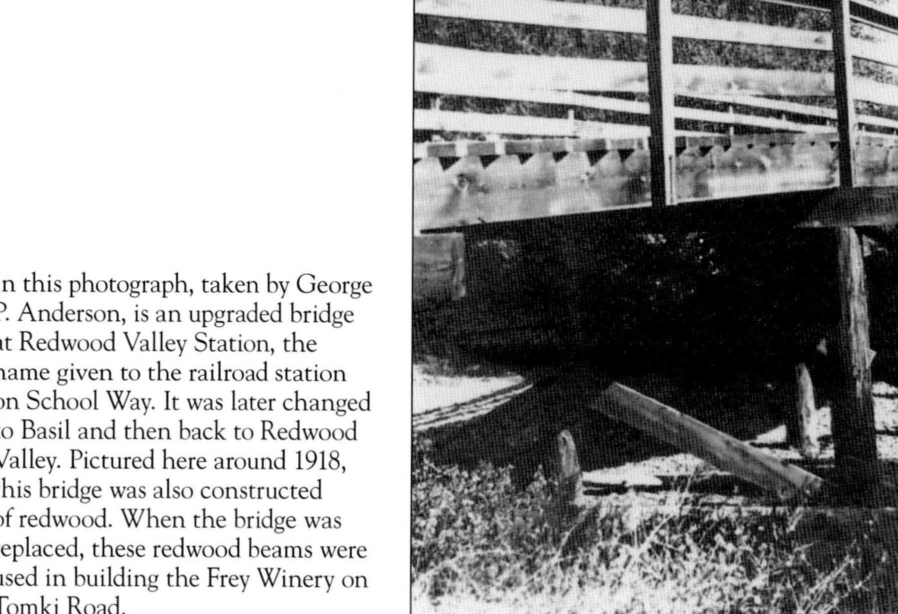

In this photograph, taken by George P. Anderson, is an upgraded bridge at Redwood Valley Station, the name given to the railroad station on School Way. It was later changed to Basil and then back to Redwood Valley. Pictured here around 1918, this bridge was also constructed of redwood. When the bridge was replaced, these redwood beams were used in building the Frey Winery on Tomki Road.

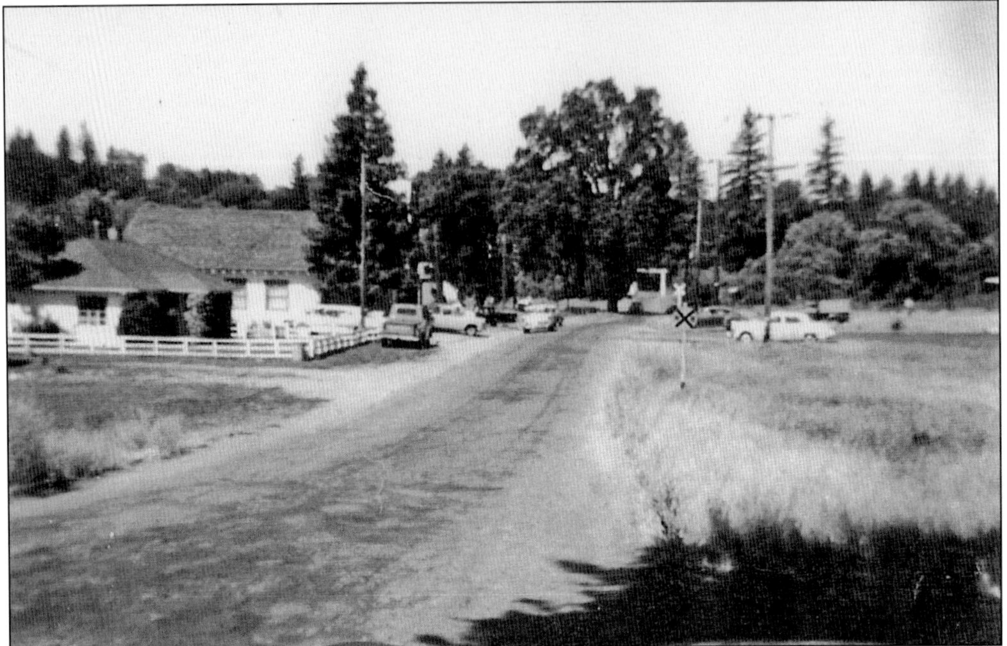

This 1950s view of the School Way bridge looks west from the shopping center. The bridge was wooden and had a white frame over the top just to the left of the railroad sign. The Redwood Valley Community Church is to the left. The redwood tree in front of the church is still there. The church sanctuary was formerly the Redwood Valley Improvement Club building. (Authors' collection.)

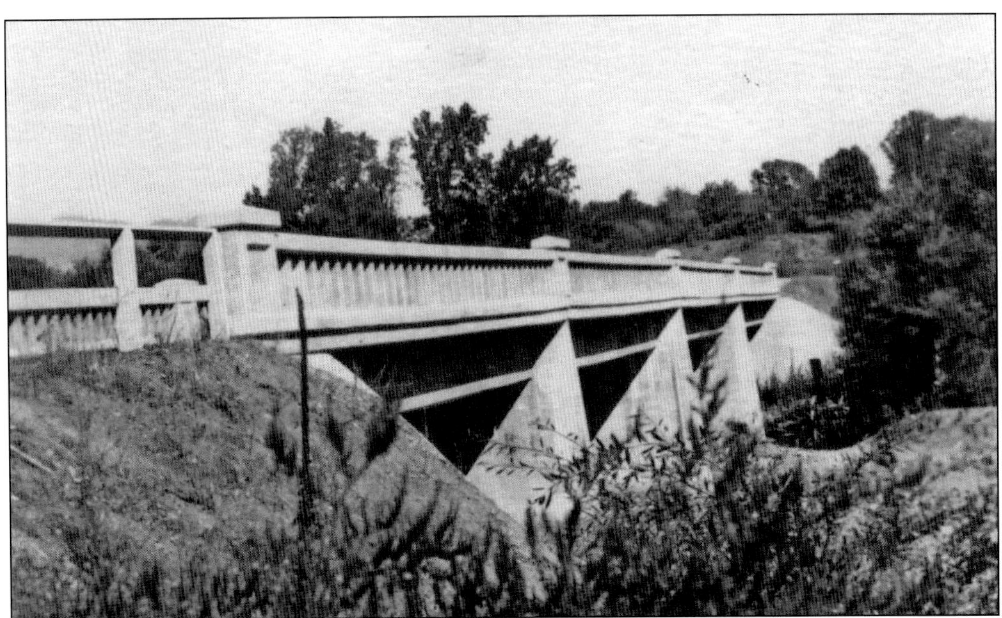

Many of the early pioneers related the difficulties they had in traveling around the valley. As a result of lobbying by the Redwood Valley Improvement Club, the Grange, and members of the Finnish and Scotch colonies, the roads and bridges were improved. George P. Anderson took this photograph of the first concrete bridge on Forsythe Creek.

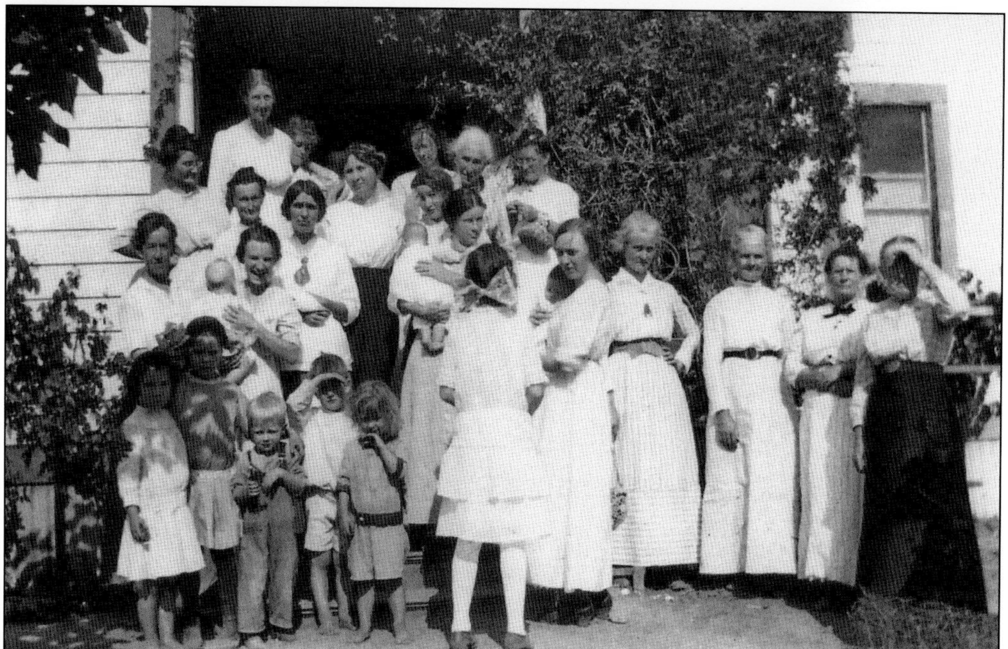

The valley residents knew how to have a good time. Pictured here is a gathering for a sewing bee at the Wells home. Notice the white dresses and the little barefoot children in the foreground.

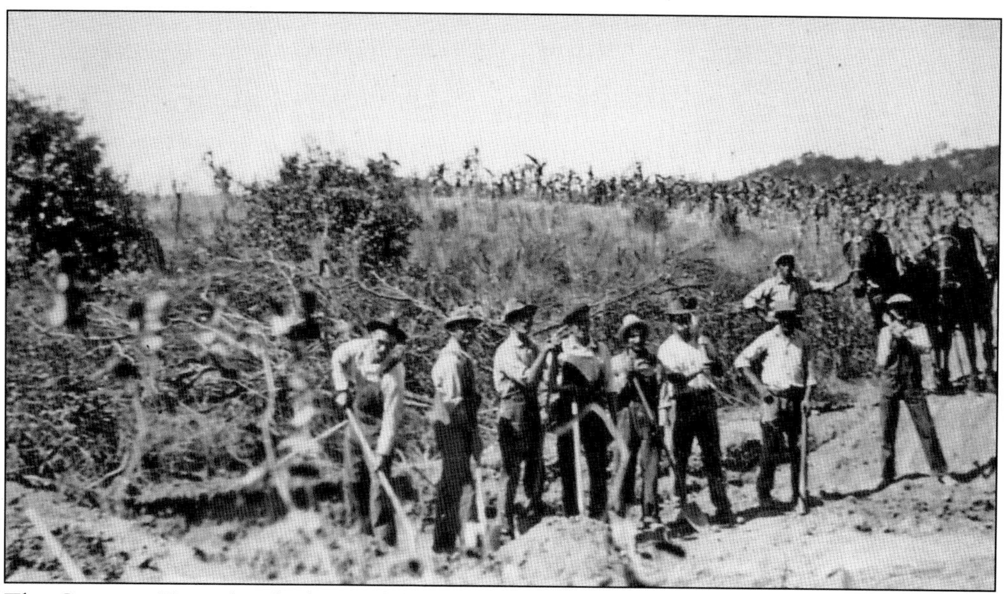

The Gaetano Testa family donated the land for the Calpella School. This group of men is leveling out the area at the top of the hill where the school building was to be constructed—a true community effort. (Courtesy of the Testa family.)

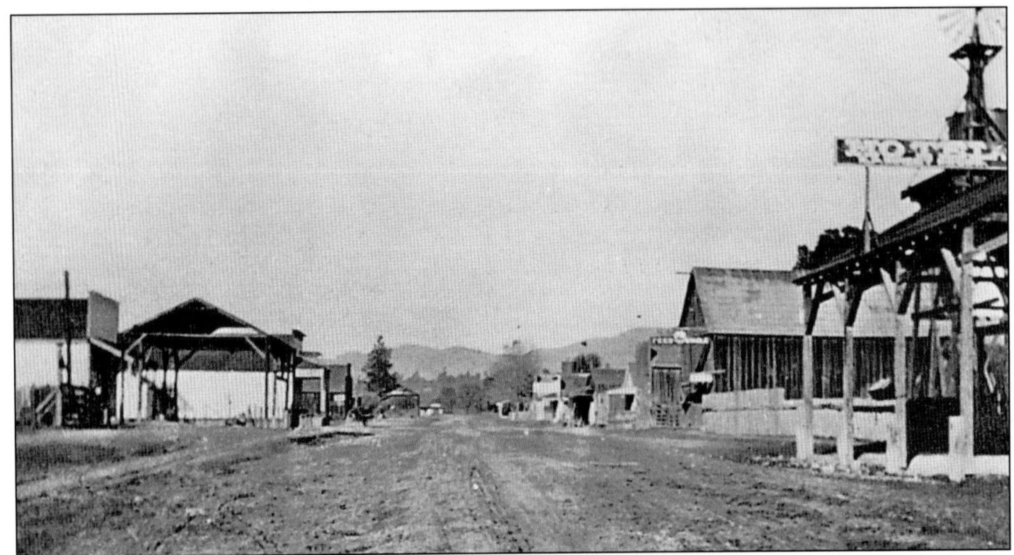

This early photograph shows the Main Street of Calpella. Some of the identifiable buildings are the Winsby Hotel, a feed and stable on the right, a garage, and a saloon on the left. The view to the extreme north is Redwood Valley. The redwood grove that includes Calpella as part of the valley is behind and to the east of the photographer. (Courtesy of the Testa family.)

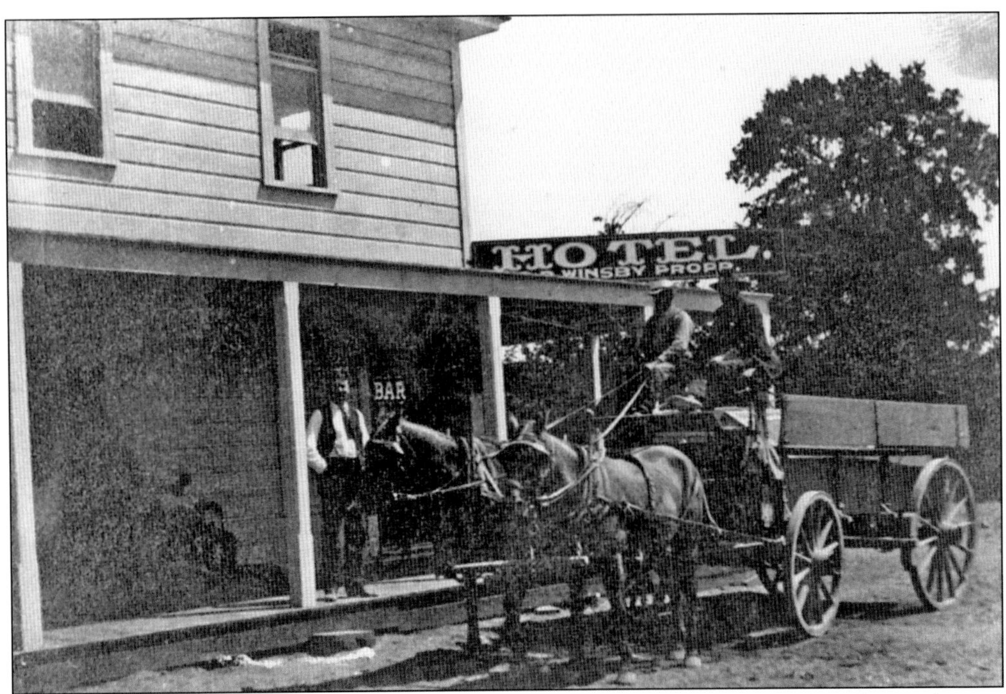

The Winsby Hotel in Calpella is shown here receiving supplies by buckboard. Jack Winsby was Delbert Phelps's grandfather, and he built the hotel in 1907 for his brother Richard, who owned it. The hotel was sold in 1910 and torn down in 1957. It was located on the southwest corner of the Club Calpella parking lot. (Courtesy of the Testa family.)

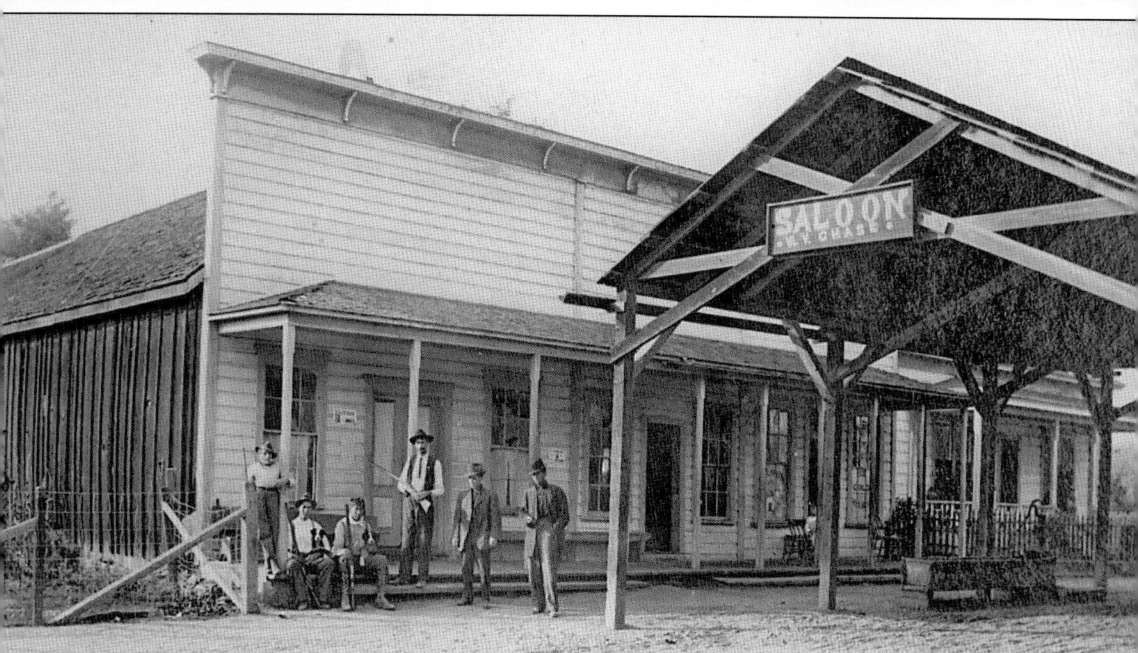

The W.V. Chase Saloon is a great example of the early days in Calpella. At least four of the five men pictured are armed with rifles. The store sports the false front of the day, and the saloon provided covered parking for horses or wagons for patrons. (Courtesy of the Testa family.)

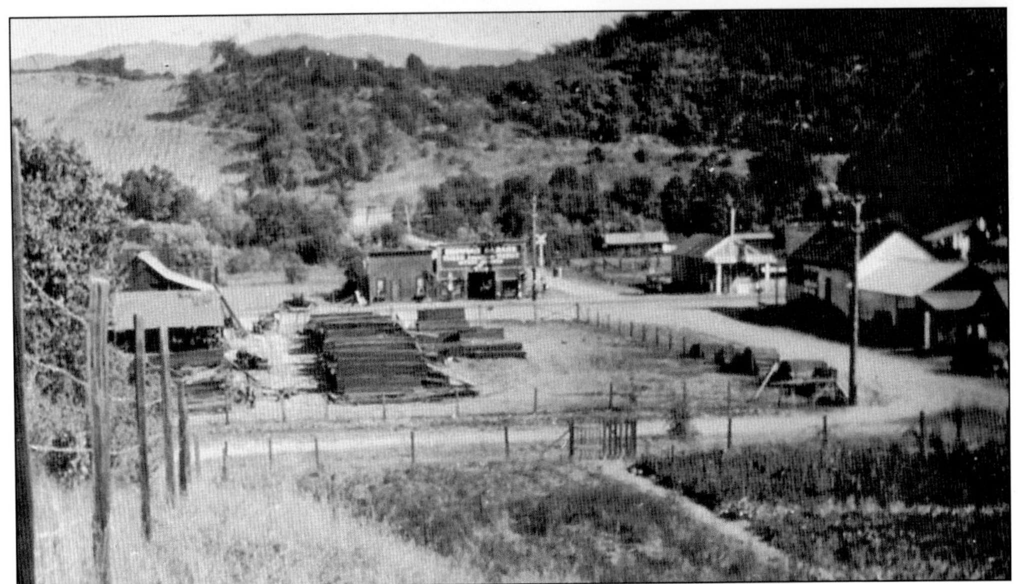

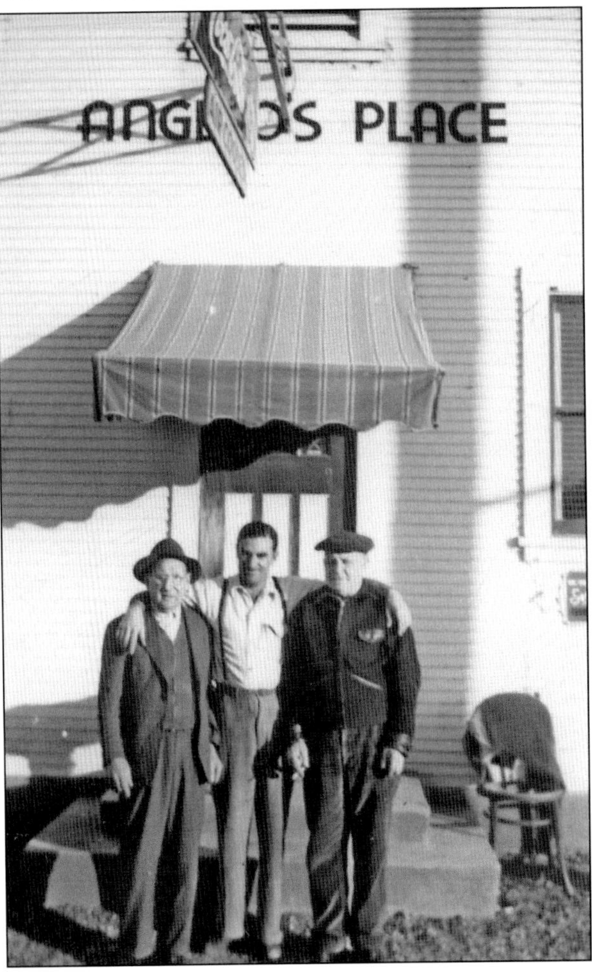

In this early east-facing view of Calpella is the intersection of Moore Street and Highway 101 (North State Street). In the foreground is a lumberyard, across the highway is a garage, and to the south is a store. The store is where today's Superette is located. Notice the railroad sign just before the Russian River Bridge and the vineyard beyond. (Courtesy of the Testa family.)

Angelo Poma stands in the center in front of his restaurant in Calpella, situated approximately at the location of today's Club Calpella. He also had a grocery store as part of this building, in addition to a service station. This photograph was taken during the 1930s. (Courtesy of Joyce Poma Myers.)

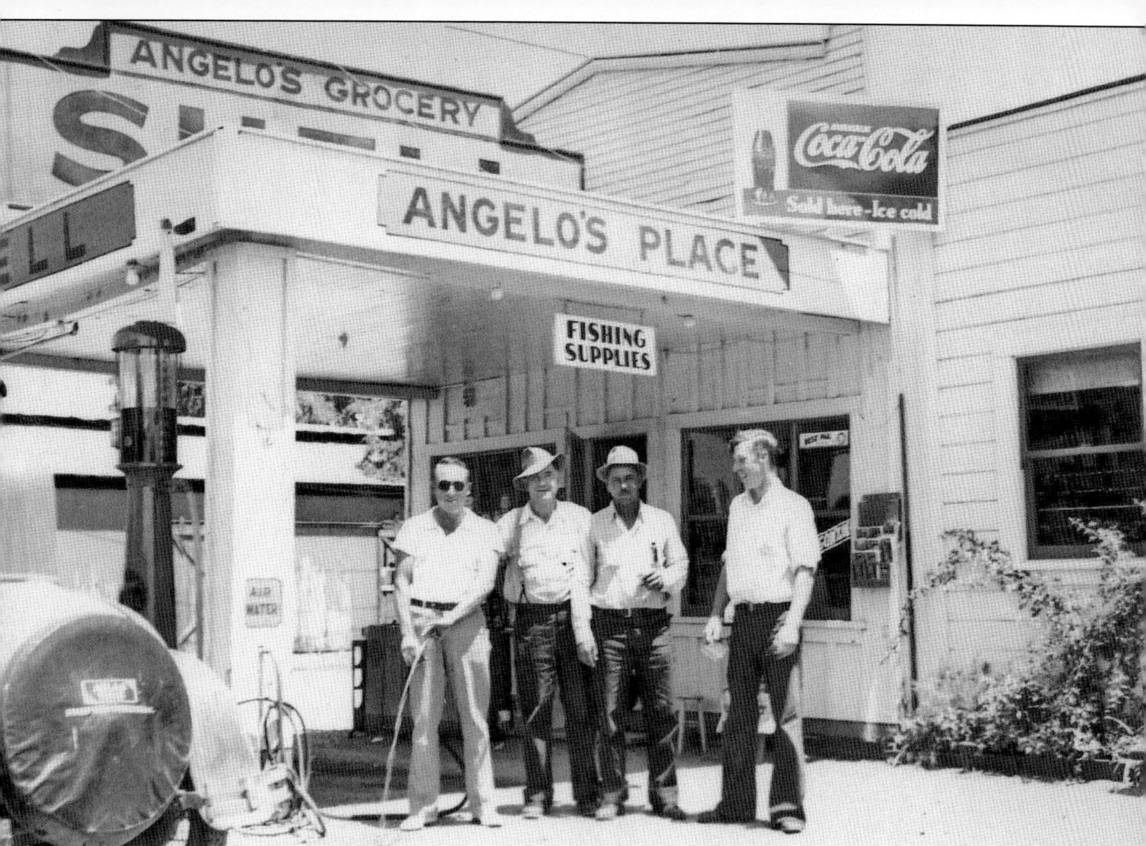

Pictured here are four unidentified men goofing off in front of Angelo's Grocery, restaurant, and service station. Note the gasoline pumps, where one manually pumped the amount of fuel desired, and then it would be drained to the automobile from the clear container above. (Courtesy of Julie Soinila.)

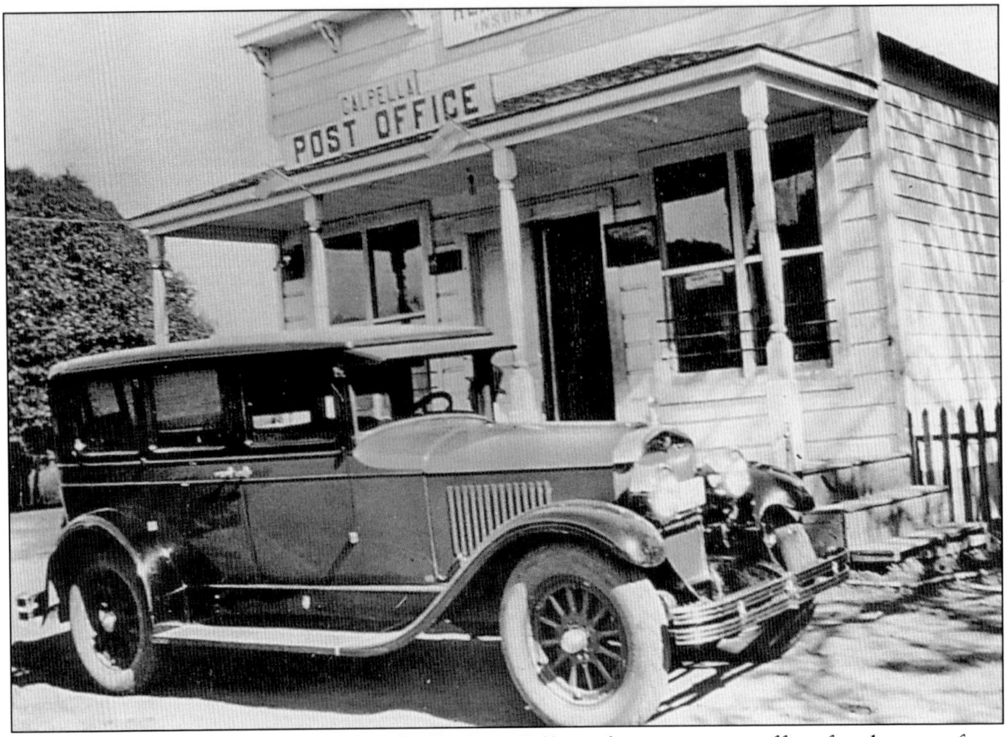

Pictured here in the 1930s is the Calpella Post Office, the main post office for the area for a considerable length of time. The rural route was run from here by T.M. Jameson from 1913 into the 1950s. Redwood Valley did not get its own post office until 1920, according to post office departmental records. Both offices are still in operation today. (Courtesy of the Testa family.)

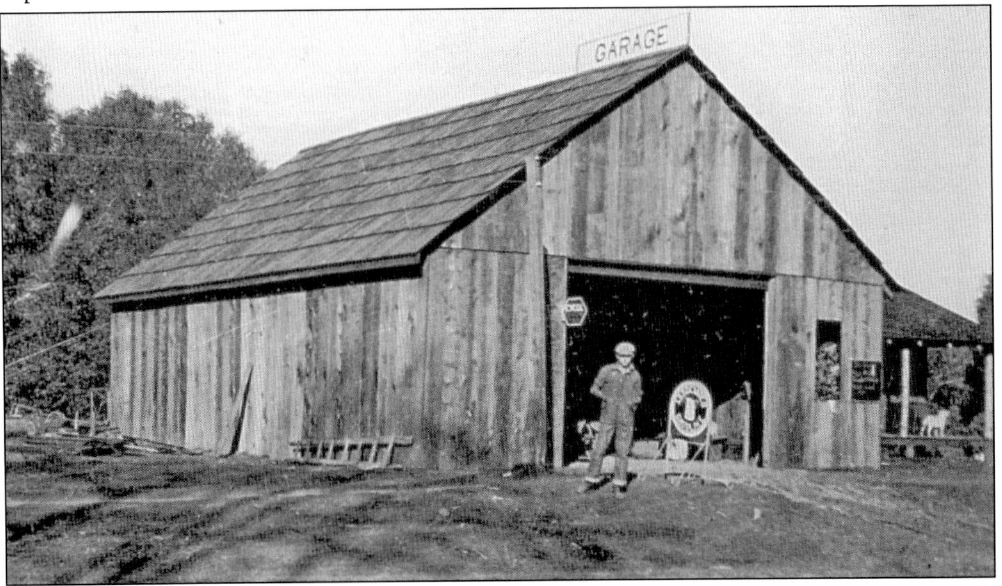

Shown here is Sam Newell's Garage on the west side of North State Street in Calpella, just north of the present-day post office. It sells Associated Gasoline products and has a blackboard posed to the right of the door to provide customers a look at the specials of the day. (Courtesy of the Testa family.)

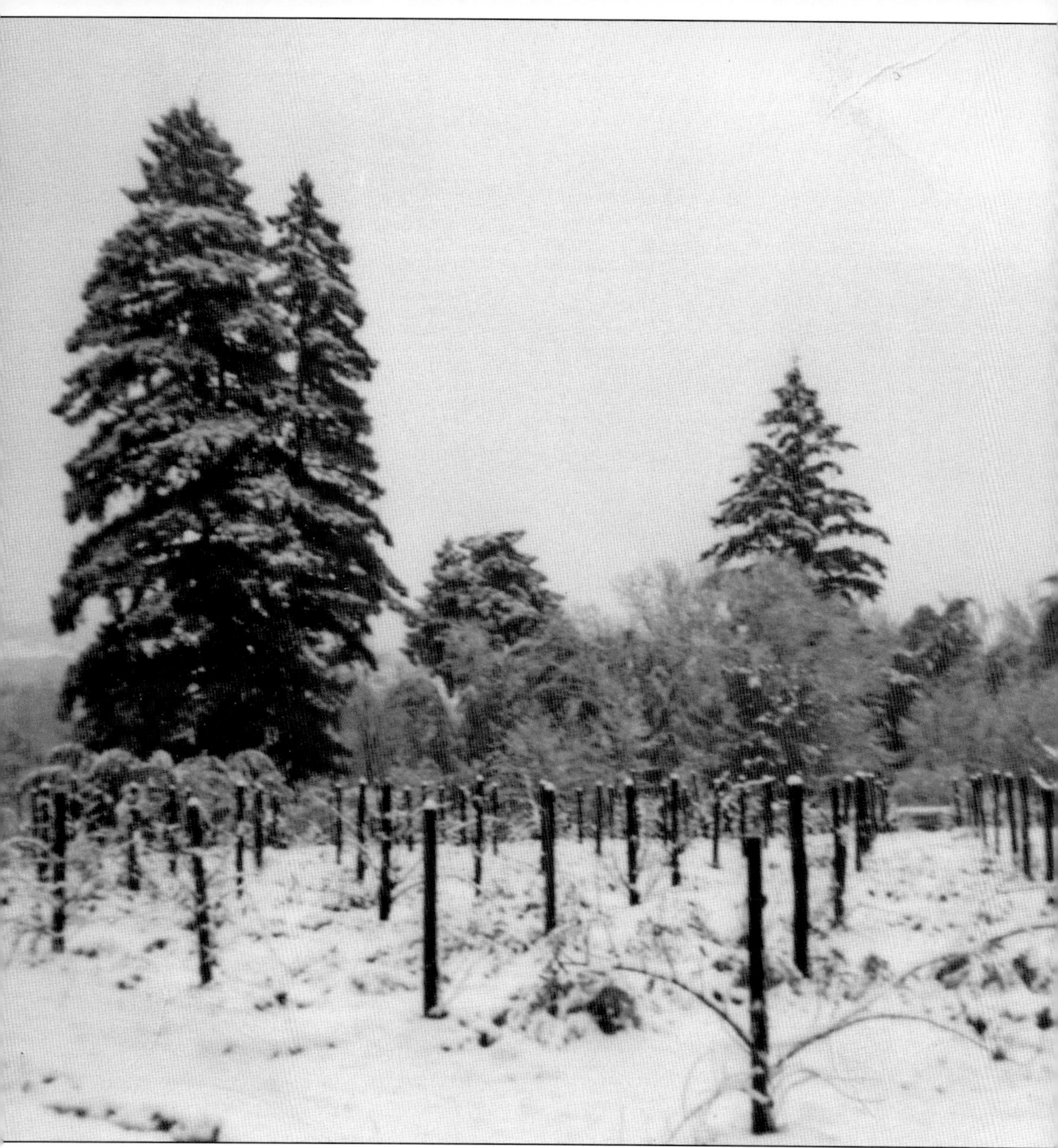

Pictured here is a stand of second-growth redwoods in the grove on Road M, which helped provide Redwood Valley its name. They are blanketed with one of the valley's occasional snowfalls. (Authors' collection.)

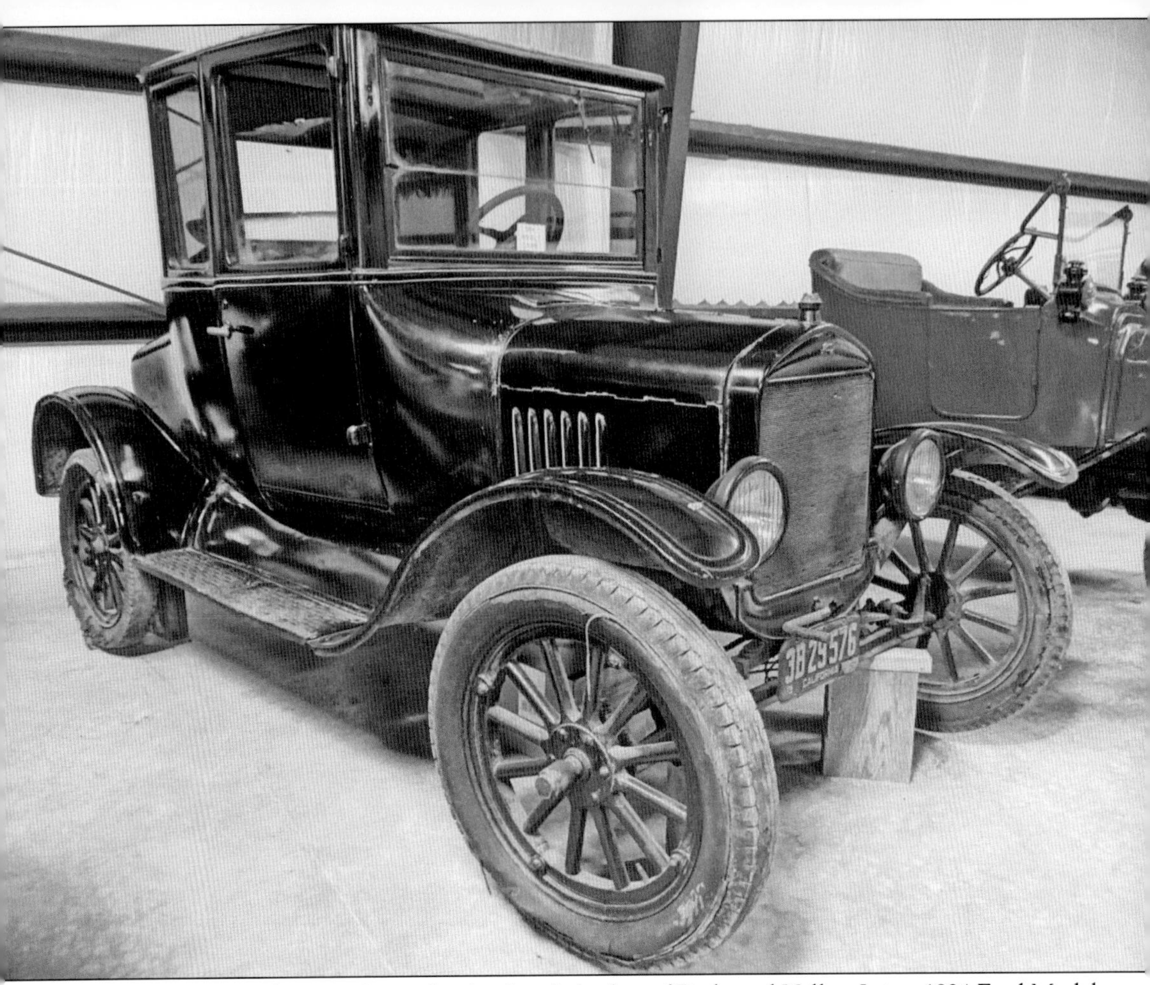

This is the car that was driven by the female barber of Redwood Valley. It is a 1924 Ford Model T last registered in 1952. It is housed in a wonderful museum at the Giuseppe Wines and Neese Vineyards' Tasting Room, located at the corner of School Way and West Road. (Courtesy of Lucille Rovera Neese and Susan Neese Mathis.)

Three

Downtown

Downtown Redwood Valley is located at the intersection of East Road and School Way. One of the first businesses was established by F.A. Howland, who came to the valley in 1915 and started a general-merchandise store as well as a post office in 1920. In 1928, the Redwood Valley Garage was acquired by Les Stansell; it was located where the fire department is today. Howland sold the store to Roy Williams in 1940, who became the postmaster. Elbert Lane started his barbershop in the shopping center building in 1944. In 1952, Williams sold to Leo Bleier Sr., who built a new shopping center in 1960. Upon his death, his son Leo Jr. inherited the business and ran it until it was sold in the early 2000s. Several other businesses occupied spaces at the shopping center: a café, jewelry shop, beauty shop, bakery, realty office, and a bookkeeper office.

Charles Cliburn's Redwood Valley Supply Company was established in 1960 across the street. In the 1970s, the Peoples Temple leased the property for their fleet of buses and used the building for meetings. Often, an armed guard could be seen watching over the premises. A mysterious 40-minute telephone call was made to Jonestown from this building on the day of the mass suicide in Guyana.

The Delbert Phelps Firehouse is on the east side of the intersection. Just to the north is a local icon, Vic's Place, established in 1950 by Veikko Soinila of the Finnish colony. The bar is still family owned and operated.

The charcoal kilns stood near the railroad tracks to the northwest of the town center. To the west was the North Sonoma Wines plant, which operated from 1946 to 1951. The Stolesen family ran the plywood fabricator plant during the 1950s and 1960s. This area became the present-day industrial park, which was reconstructed after a devastating fire in 2002. South and west of the railroad tracks stood the Lake County Fruit Exchange, a shipping point for pears.

The Redwood Valley Improvement Clubhouse was between the railroad tracks and the shopping center until 1952, when it was deeded to the local community church.

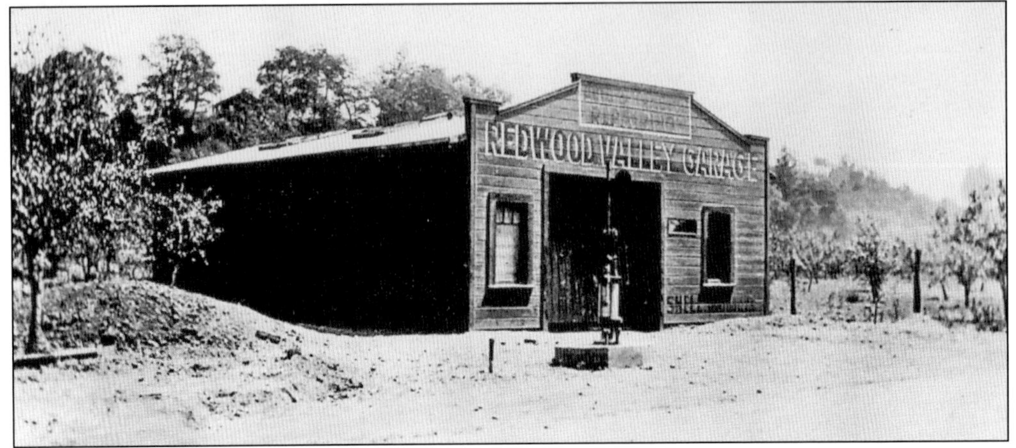

This is the Redwood Valley Garage prior to Les Stansell acquiring it in 1928. The signage reads, "Auto and Tractor Repairing." There is a single gas pump in front and practically no development around the garage at this time. A single house appears above the roof to the left.

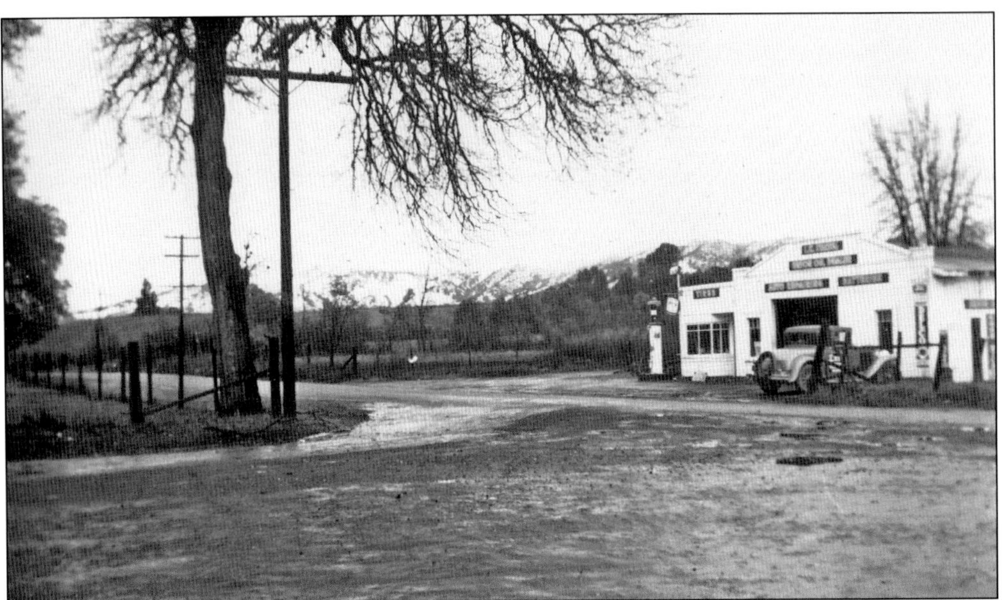

This view from the parking lot of the Redwood Valley Store looks northeast. While not named at the time, the street in front is School Way, and the road to the north is East Road. Notice also the snow on the far hills, which probably merited the photograph. (Courtesy of Janet Marsh.)

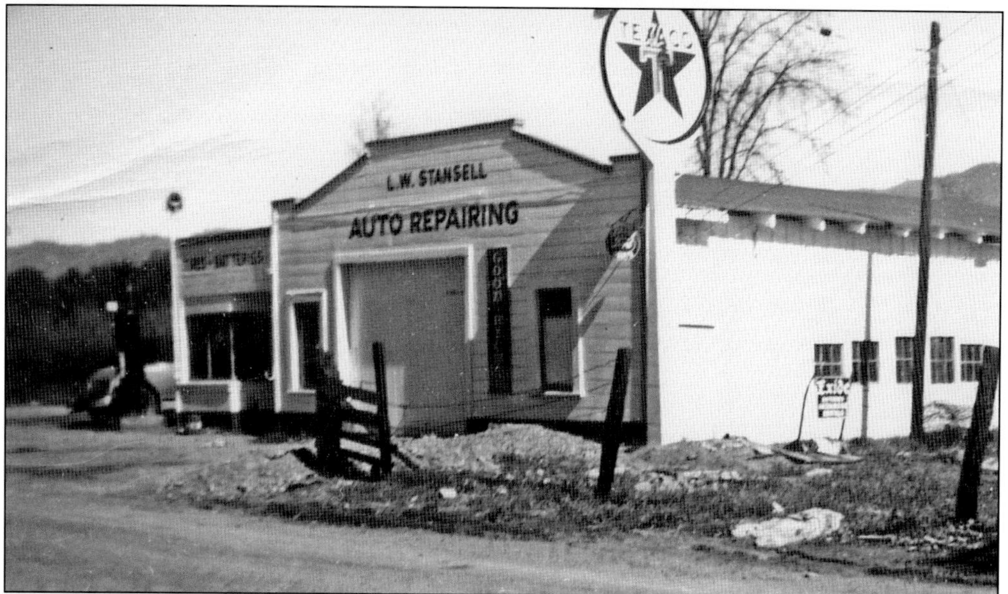

This is a view of the L.W. Stansell garage, which was located approximately where the firehouse is now. Notice that the fuel-supply company is Texaco; this changed over the years. The business also sold Goodrich tires, genuine Ford parts, and Exide batteries.

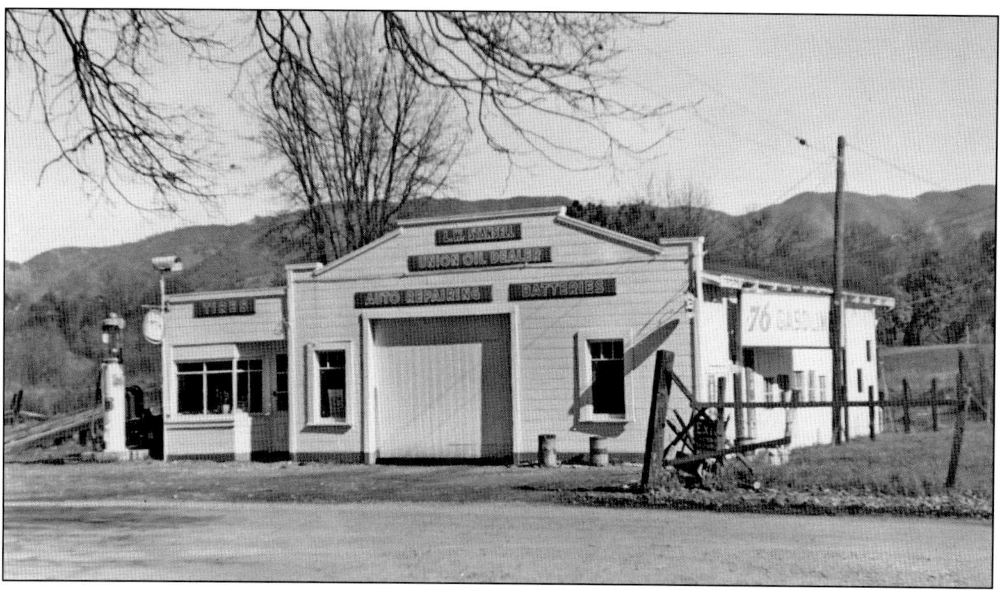

In this view, Stansell's has become the Union Oil Dealer for the area. The signage has been changed, and a paint job has spruced the place up. Stansell was a very involved community member, serving on the Redwood Valley Improvement Club board as well as volunteering with the Redwood Valley Calpella Volunteer Fire Department. (Courtesy of Janet Marsh.)

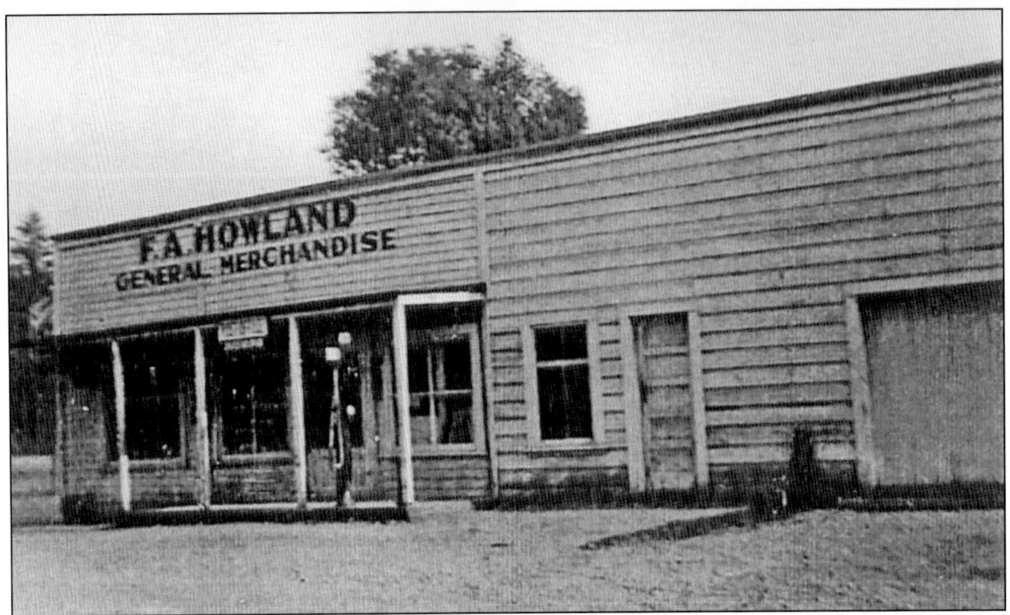

F.A. Howland came to Redwood Valley in 1915 and later established a general merchandise store. He became postmaster in 1920. Due to his ill health, Frank and Valeska Howland sold the building and stock to Roy Williams on May 14, 1940, and moved to Berkeley, California. Frank helped start the Redwood Valley Improvement Club. The photograph was taken about 1936.

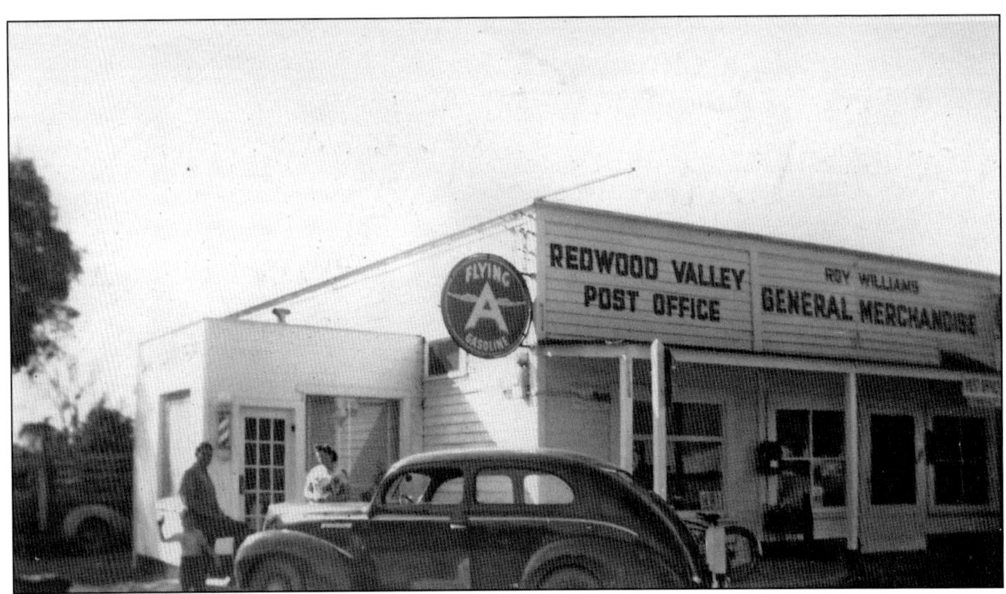

Tom Jameson is pictured with son Donald and Hazel Muir in front of the Redwood Valley General Merchandise Store. The car is the Ford owned by the Jamesons. The Redwood Valley Post Office was also inside the store; an old-fashioned drop box is visible by the door. Notice the bike behind the car; in those days, kids could safely ride around the valley. (Courtesy of Janet Marsh.)

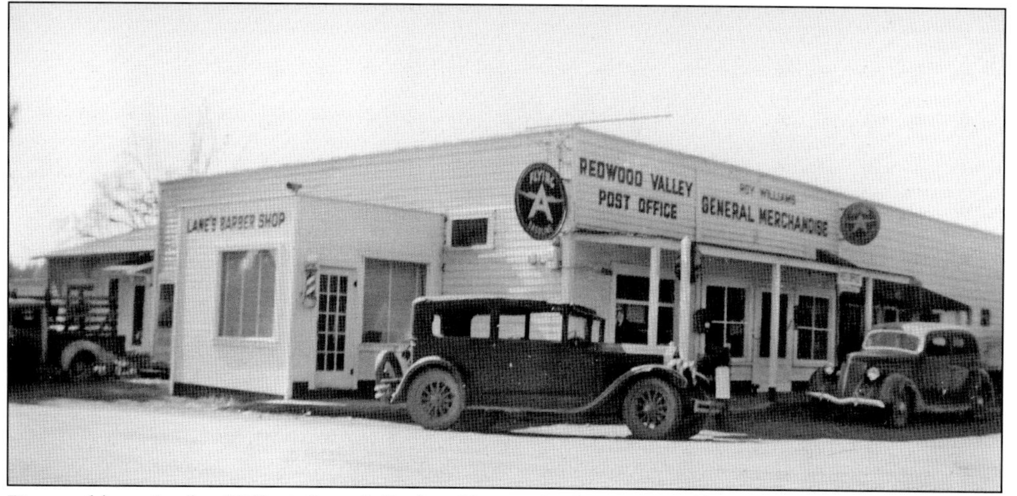

Pictured here in the 1940s is Lane's Barber Shop, which was an addition to the end of the store. Flying A was the distributor of the fuel products at this time. (Courtesy of Janet Marsh.)

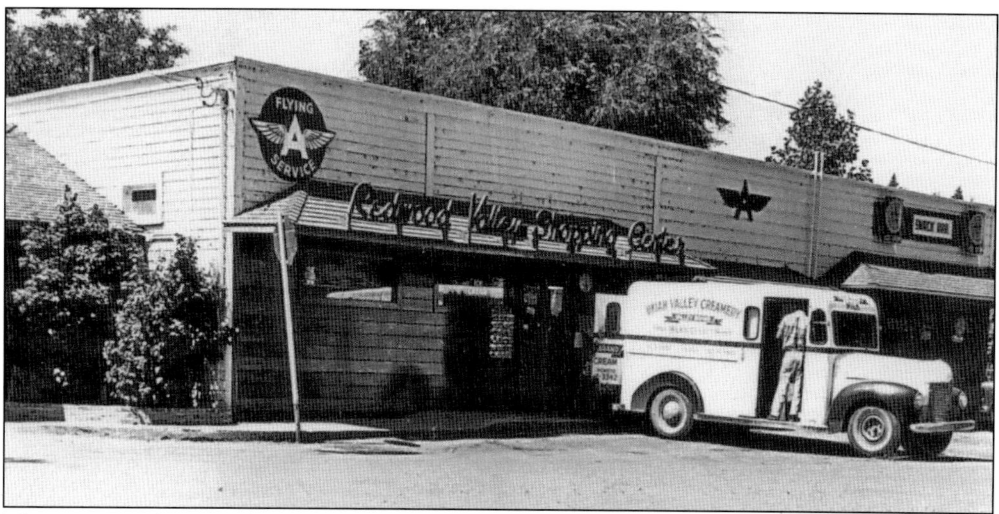

This is a rare photograph of Ukiah Valley Creamery making a delivery at the renamed Redwood Valley Shopping Center. Flying A is still the service station dealer, and a new snack bar sign is to the right. Notice the stop sign under Flying A. The store used to sit right at the intersection of School Way and East Road. (Courtesy of Janet Marsh.)

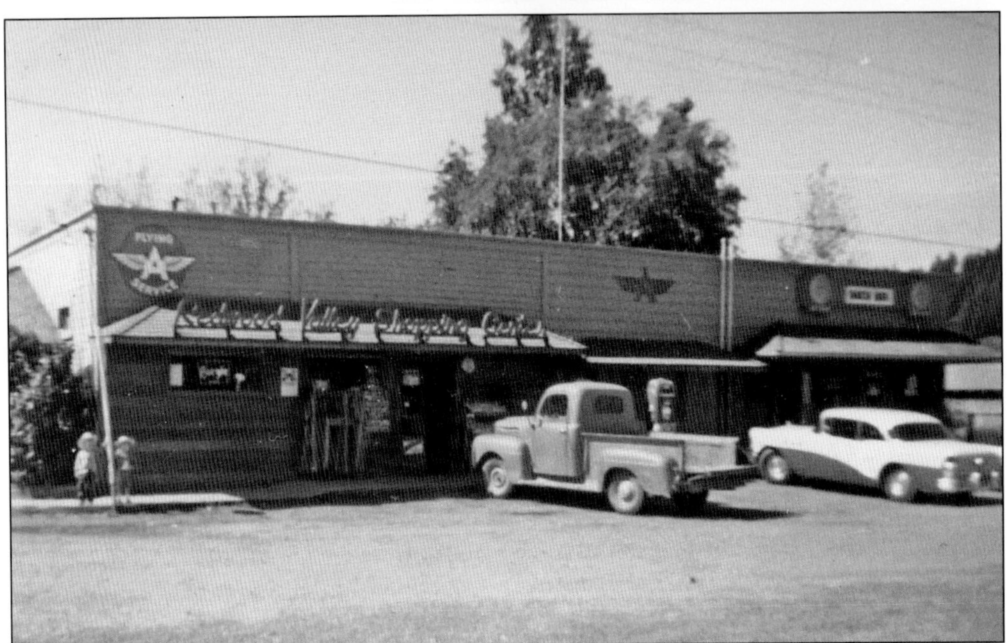

In this view, one can see the sign for the café, which was a popular local hangout. Under the stop sign at far left of the building are Jan and Robert Muir. This was when the store sat where the parking lot is now, and the camellia bushes are still there. (Courtesy of Janet Marsh.)

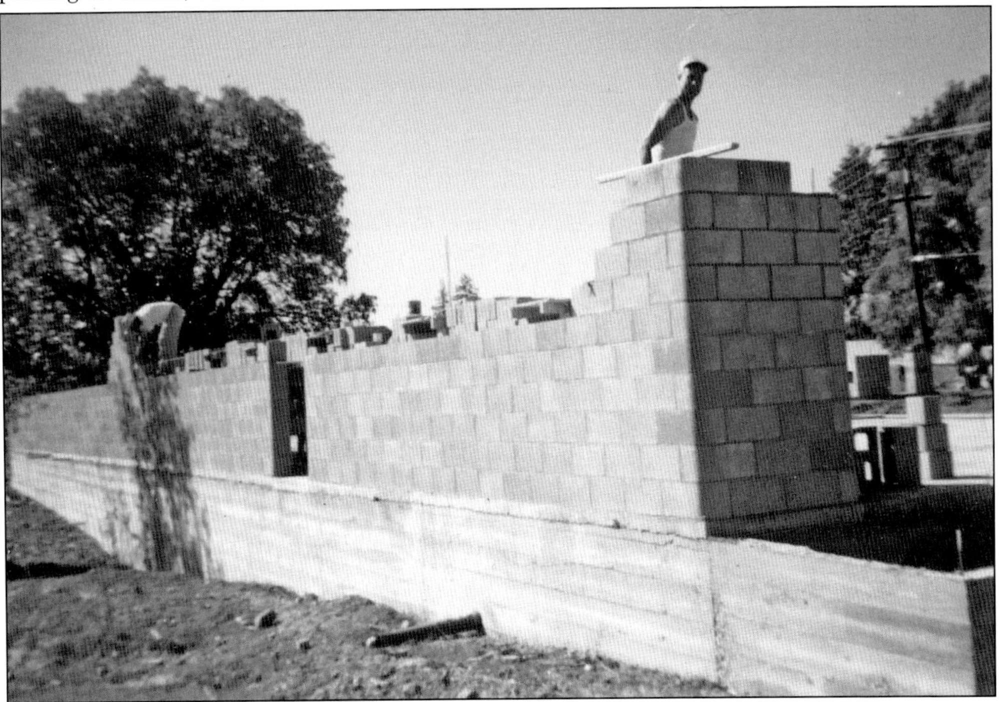

Here, a couple of builders work on the new Redwood Valley Store in the late 1950s. The old store was demolished, and the new store was built farther back from School Way to allow for gas pumps and additional off-street parking. Leo Bleier Sr. was the proprietor and owner of this new store. (Courtesy of Janet Marsh.)

In this early photograph, Harry Williams is on the far left. Harry was responsible for convincing Roy and Gladys Williams to move to Redwood Valley. He was from the Bay Area and encouraged Roy to establish a full-service garage and then, in 1940, to purchase the Redwood Valley General Merchandise Store from the Howlands. (Courtesy of Janet Marsh.)

Shown here is Charles Cliburn in his store, Redwood Valley Hardware, which was located on the east side of East Road, across from the main shopping center. It was later expanded to include apartments on the second story and shops on the first floor. At one time, the Peoples Temple parked their fleet of buses in the secure lot behind the building. (Courtesy of Janet Marsh.)

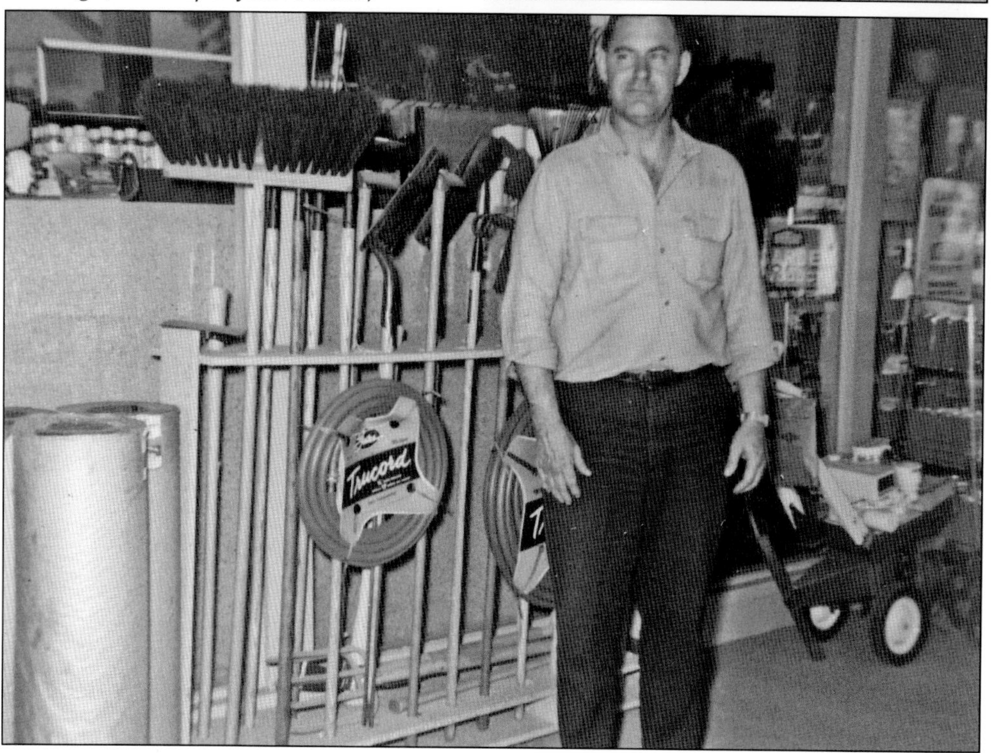

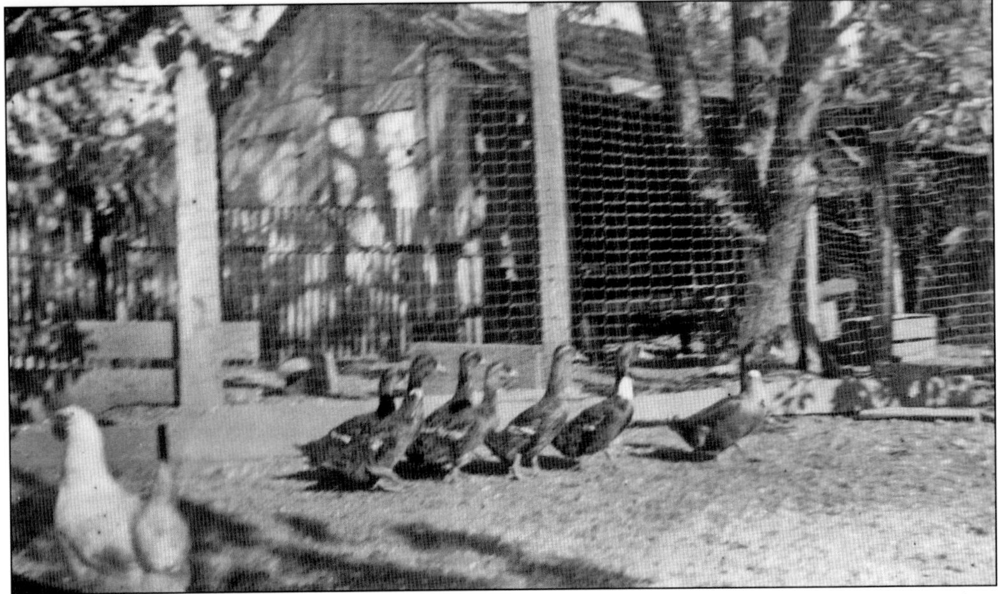

While the Roy Williams family owned the Redwood Valley General Merchandise Store, they also lived in a home behind the store. Behind the house was a pen for chickens and ducks; like most families of the era, they raised their own poultry and collected the eggs. This shed was later converted into a small apartment and is still in use today. (Courtesy of Janet Marsh.)

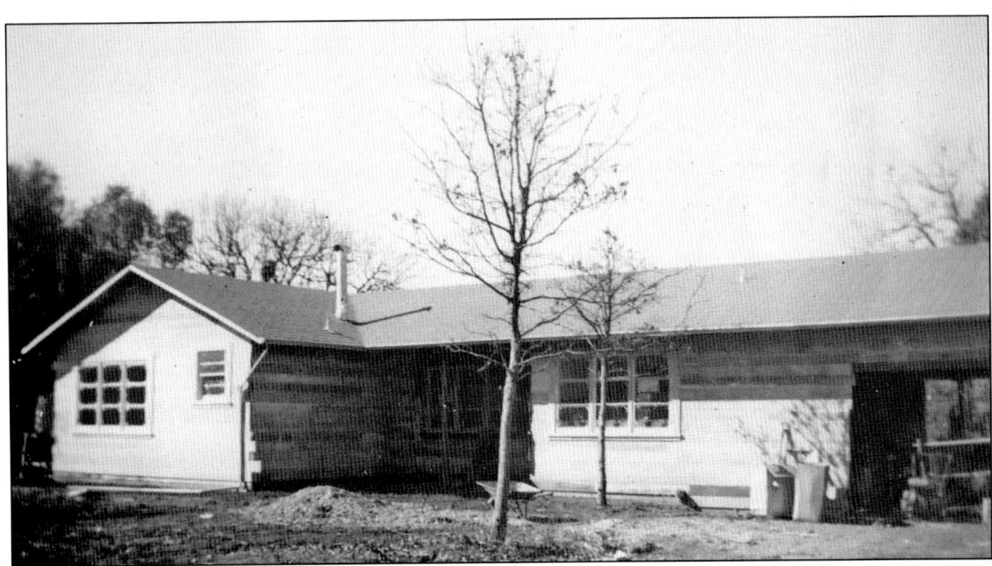

The Williams family had the convenience of living in a home located directly behind the store. When the new store was built, this home was cut in half and moved to the end of Road K. Over the years, it served as a care home for the elderly and a group home that was owned for a time by the Peoples Temple. (Courtesy of Janet Marsh.)

Elbert Lane, the local barber, is pictured inside the Redwood Valley Store. Lane gave many of the valley's boys their first haircut. He was also a school bus driver for the local Redwood Valley Union Elementary School. A real community-minded citizen, he was also a volunteer fireman and grand master of Grange 382. He was honored by being asked to portray Black Bart, California's infamous stage robber. (Courtesy of Janet Marsh.)

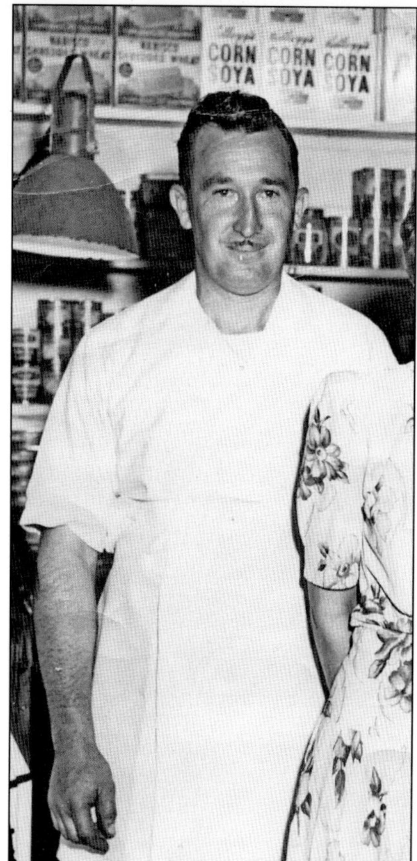

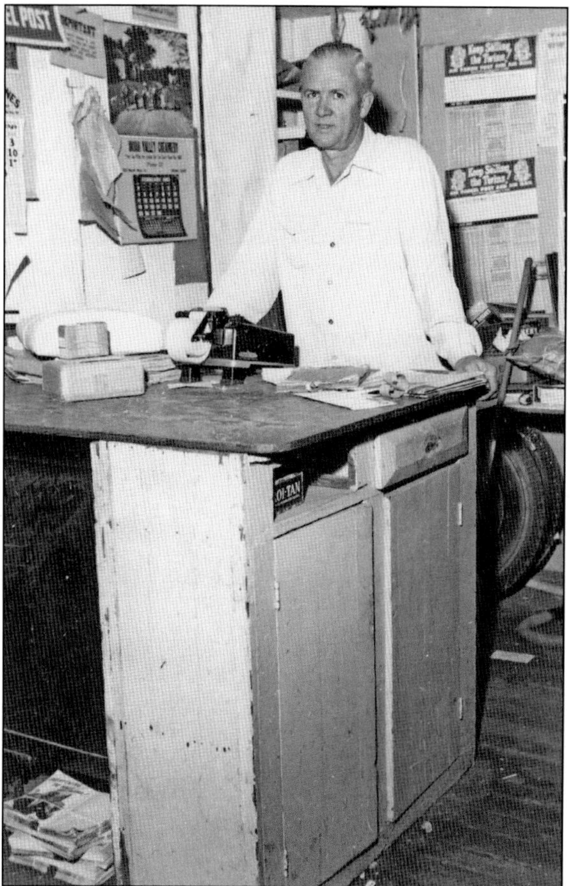

Roy Williams is pictured here in his role as postmaster inside of the Redwood Valley Store. The post office was established as the Redwood Valley Post Office in 1920, although the rural routes were still delivered out of Calpella by Tom M. Jameson. Members of the Redwood Valley Improvement Club wanted to name the Redwood Valley Post Office in honor of World War I hero Gen. John Pershing. (Courtesy of Janet Marsh.)

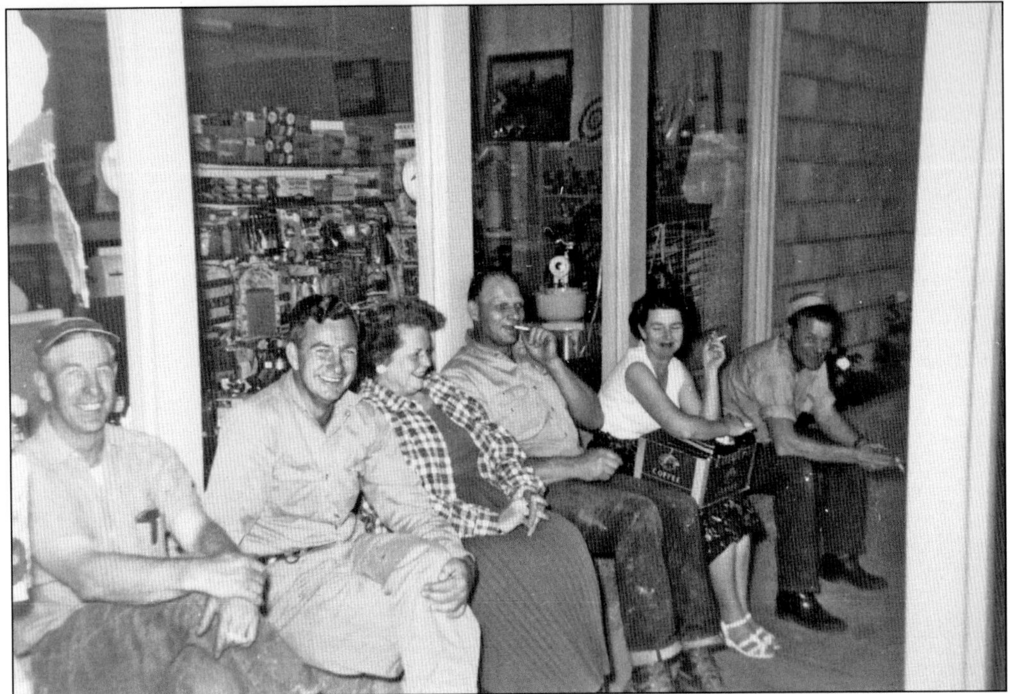

It was common to see people taking a smoke break in front of the store. The gang seen here are, from left to right, Everett Witter, Ed Hosheit, Gladys Williams, Tom Jameson (RVCVFD fire chief), unidentified, and Cecil Hughes. The shopping center served as the downtown for the valley and became a meeting place for locals to catch up on the latest valley news. (Courtesy of Janet Marsh.)

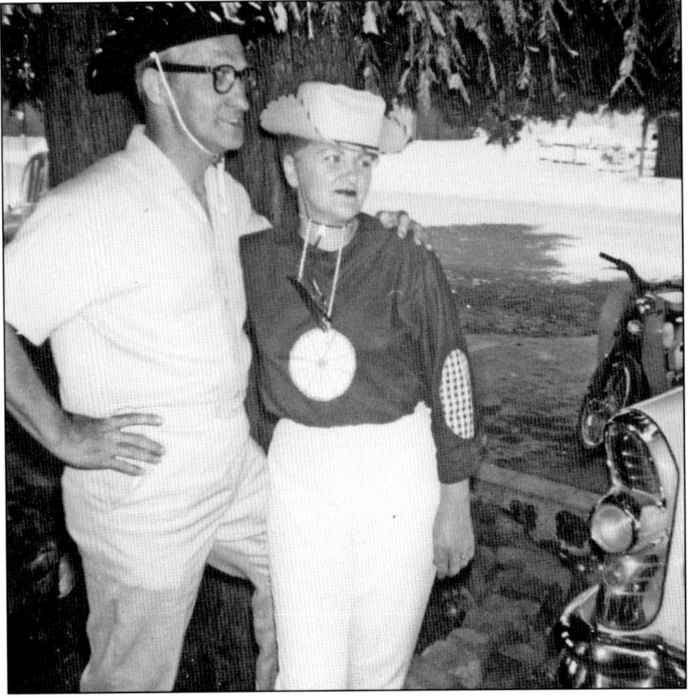

Doris and Rick Spencer are pictured getting ready for the Black Bart Day parade. Doris had a realty office on the east side of the shopping center, and Rick had a beauty shop right next door. (Courtesy of Janet Marsh.)

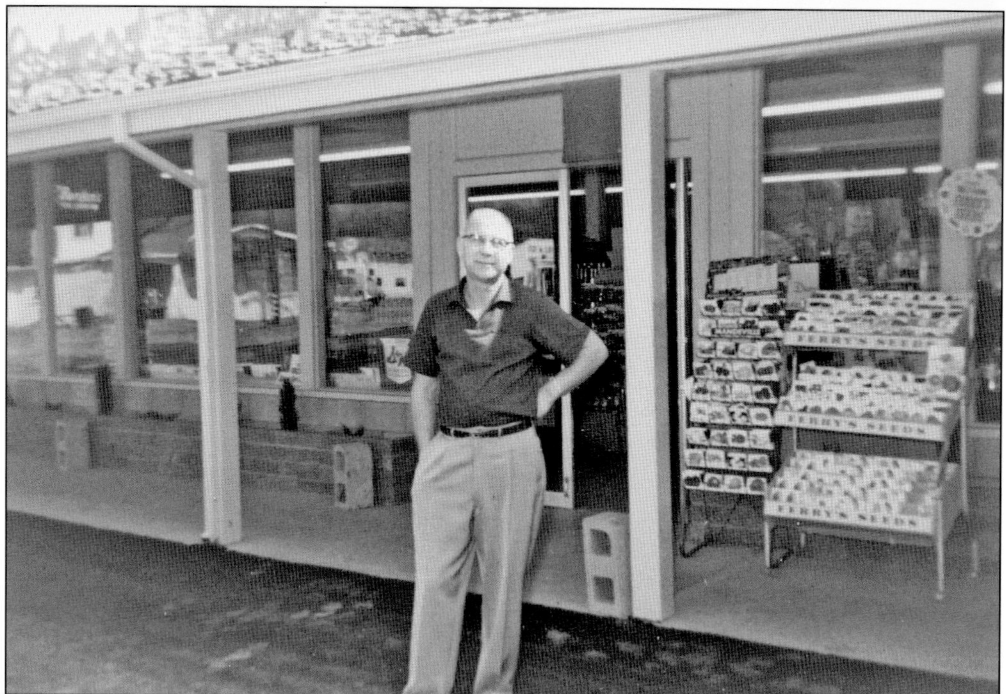

Leo Bleier Sr. is pictured here standing at the entrance to the Redwood Valley Store. Bleier Sr. was a greatly admired citizen. The kids of the valley knew they were welcome at the store; getting free candy was always a treat. At Christmastime, there was caroling in front of the store, and the employees dressed in costumes for Halloween. (Courtesy of Janet Marsh.)

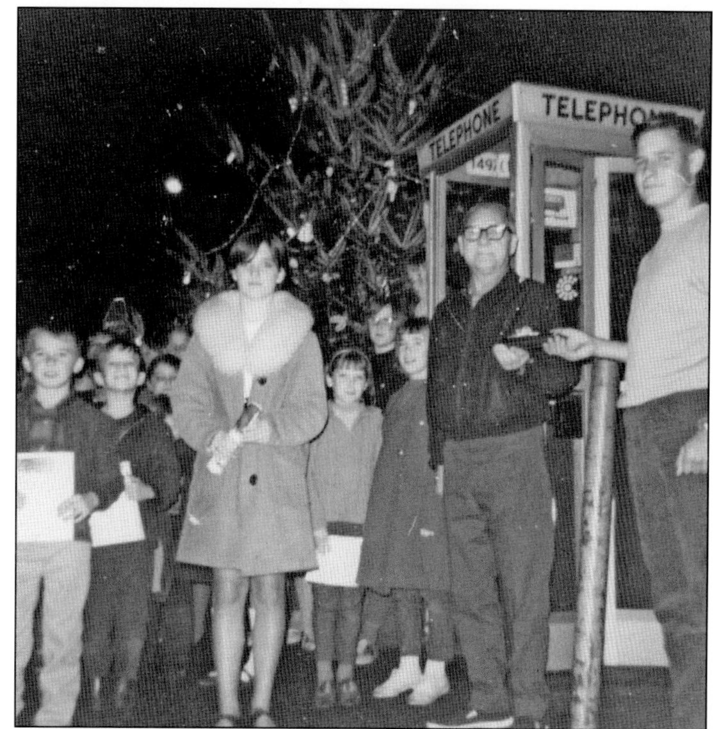

Each year, a Christmas tree was placed by the telephone booth at the corner of School Way and East Road. Kids from the local community church would sing carols in front of the store and have a gift exchange. Here, Leo Bleier Sr. joins in the singing and gifting. (Courtesy of Janet Marsh.)

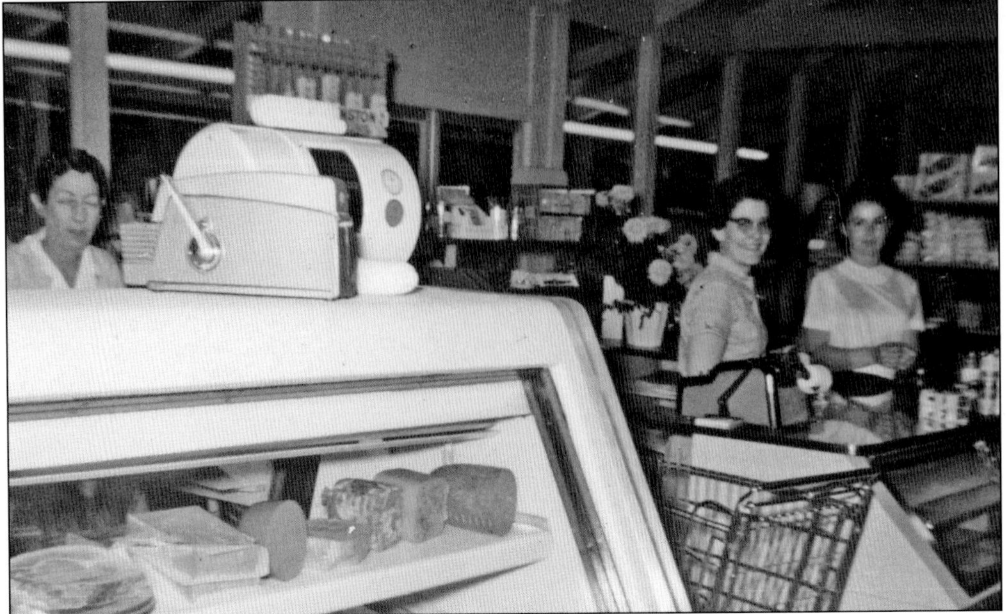

This is a rare view of the inside of the Redwood Valley Store, showing employees at the meat counter and the checkout area. The person at the meat counter cut and wrapped each customer's order the old-fashioned way. Customers received green stamps or blue chip stamps when they paid for their groceries. Later, one could redeem them for a number of useful household items. (Courtesy of Janet Marsh.)

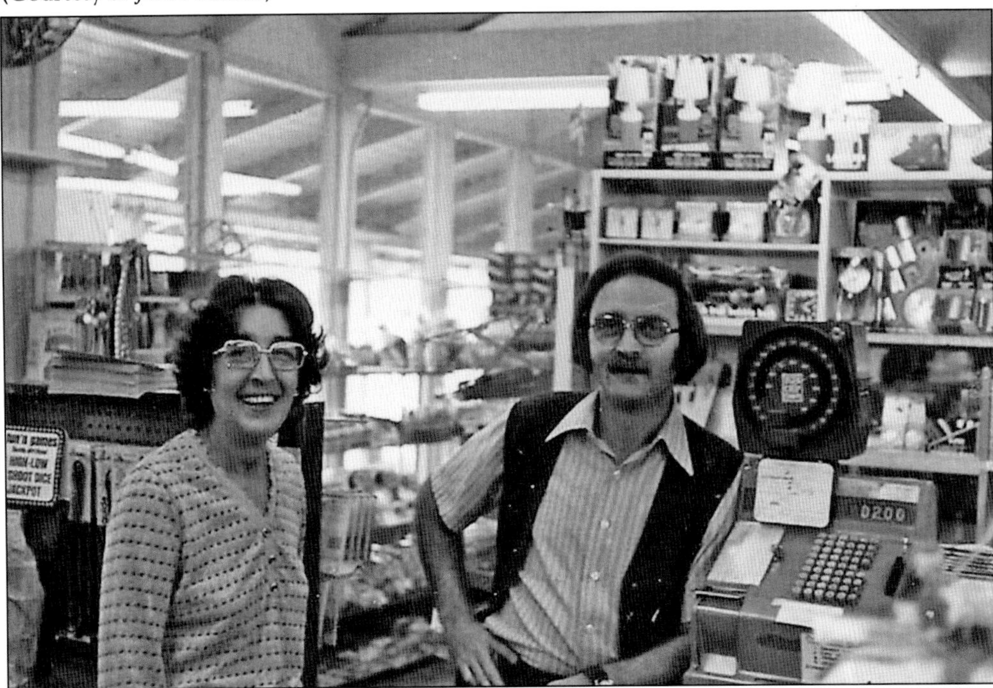

Evelyn Cliburn stands at the meat counter with owner Leo Bleier Jr. As one can see on the shelves in the rear of the photograph, the store was still carrying a great deal of general merchandise. It has moved more toward a grocery focus as the years have gone by. (Courtesy of Janet Marsh.)

Veikko "Vic" Soinila (left) and Cecil Hughes are pictured tending bar at Vic's Place in downtown Redwood Valley. Vic's Place was established in 1950, and the bar is still in his family. Vic was raised in the Finnish colony. A small farmers' market occupied the same building for a period of in the 1950s. Since then, several restaurants have been doing business in the south portion of the property. (Courtesy of Julie Soinila.)

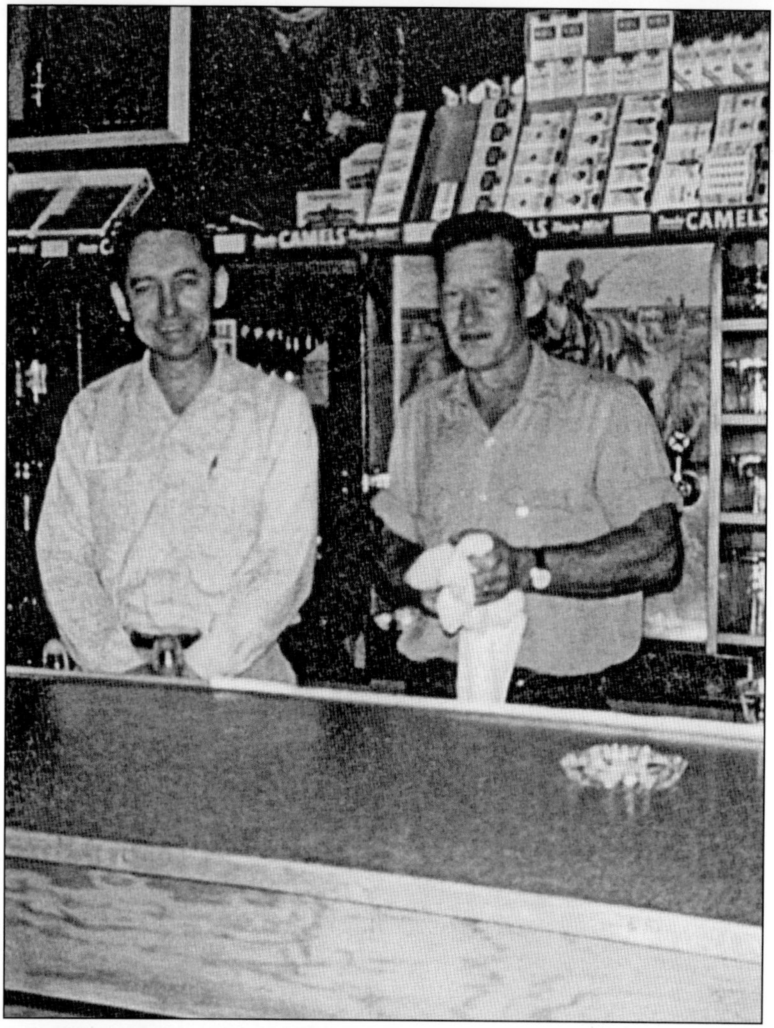

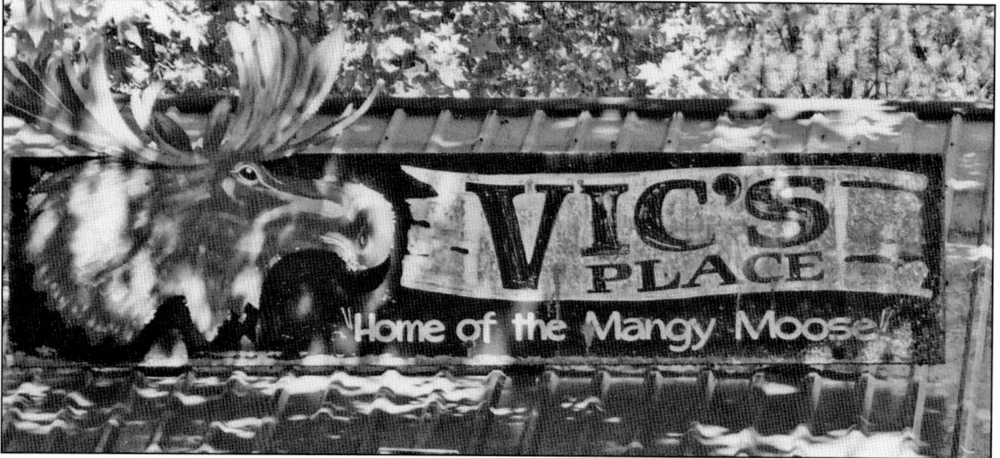

This is Vic's Place's sign today: "Home of the Mangy Moose." Over 65 years after its opening, it is still a popular local gathering spot. (Authors' collection.)

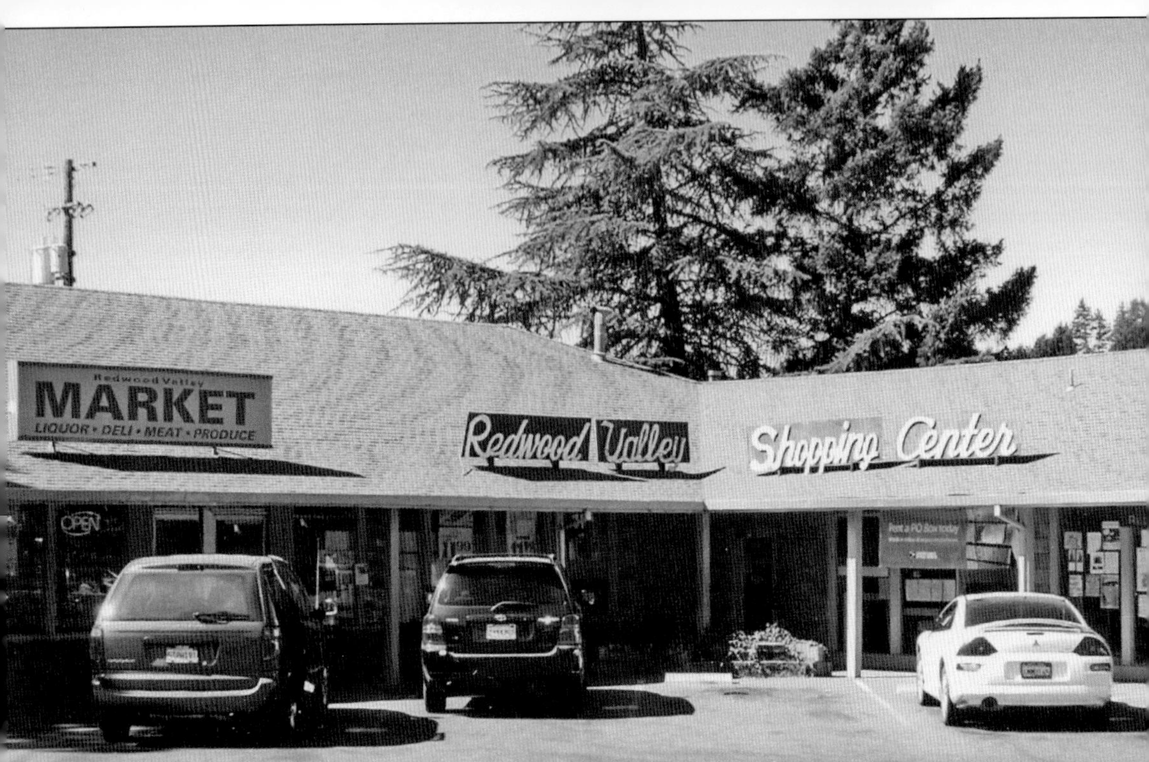

Under new management since January 2005, the shopping center was renamed the Redwood Valley Market, though the old sign has remained. It remains the hub of downtown Redwood Valley. (Authors' collection.)

Four

Schools and Churches

Now that the wilderness was under control, it was time for bringing in civilization. Schools were set up at several locations around the valley, as it was difficult for the children to travel far. A typical school year was only six months out of the year. The valley schools were one-room structures at first, with kindergarten through eighth grade. The students who went on to high school did so by traveling to Ukiah by horse, horse and buggy, bicycles, and then automobiles. Some were boarded out to families in Ukiah during the week. As of this writing, Redwood Valley has never had a high school.

In 1900, there were four schools: Occidental, near the present-day Calpella School site; Calpella, later changed to Forsythe; Redwood; and Mineral Springs, which was located at the head of the valley. A union school district was formed in 1920. Bonds were voted in 1921 (103-yes to 48-no), and the building was completed in 1922. This building burned in 1931. While it was being rebuilt with the insurance money, school was held at the Grange hall. This new building was torn down in 1956 and the present school constructed.

Churches in the valley sometimes used schoolhouses to conduct services. In 1918, the Redwood Valley Community Church was established and used the Redwood Valley Improvement Clubhouse for its meeting place. Also, the community Sunday school aid (CSSA) began as the result of a group of Christian ladies wanting to help the needy in the valley. The Improvement Club deeded the clubhouse and land over to the church in 1952. Calpella Community Church, which had been meeting in the local schoolhouse, purchased the building for $125 and moved the building to its present location in 1925. They did this by rolling the building on logs. The Baptist Church on West Road was established in the 1960s. During the mid-1960s, the Peoples Temple moved into the valley and set up a church on East Road. This congregation ended in a mass suicide in the jungles of Guyana at Jonestown in November 1978.

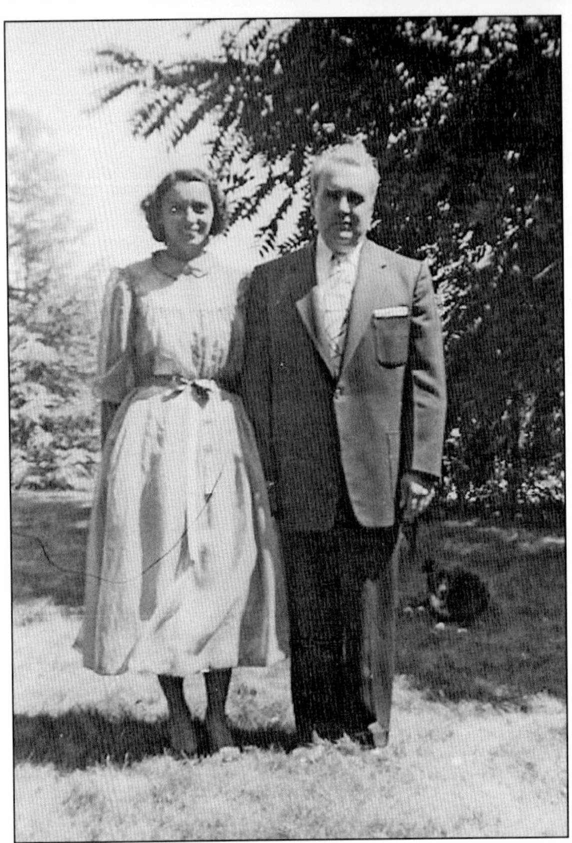

This is a photograph of Reverend Ezra (right) and Nels Kile. Ezra was the first pastor of the Redwood Valley Community Church; however, it was not a full-time paid position. He was the pastor from the late 1940s to 1952, when the church was incorporated. Interestingly, he conducted baptismal services in the Russian River below the School Way Bridge. (Authors' collection.)

A group of Christian-minded ladies seen here formed an early organization to help the needy of the valley. This meeting took place in the Watson home in 1920. Some of the attendees include Valeska Howland, Rachael Jameson, Florence Woolley, Emma Page, Lee Riggs, and LuVern Kistler. (Authors' collection.)

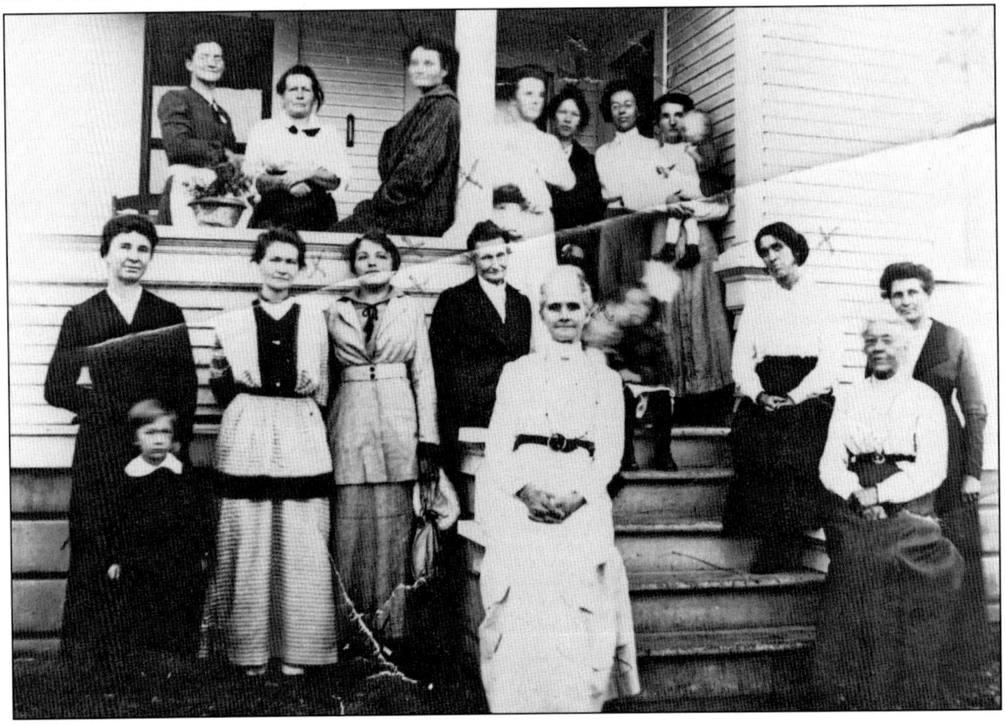

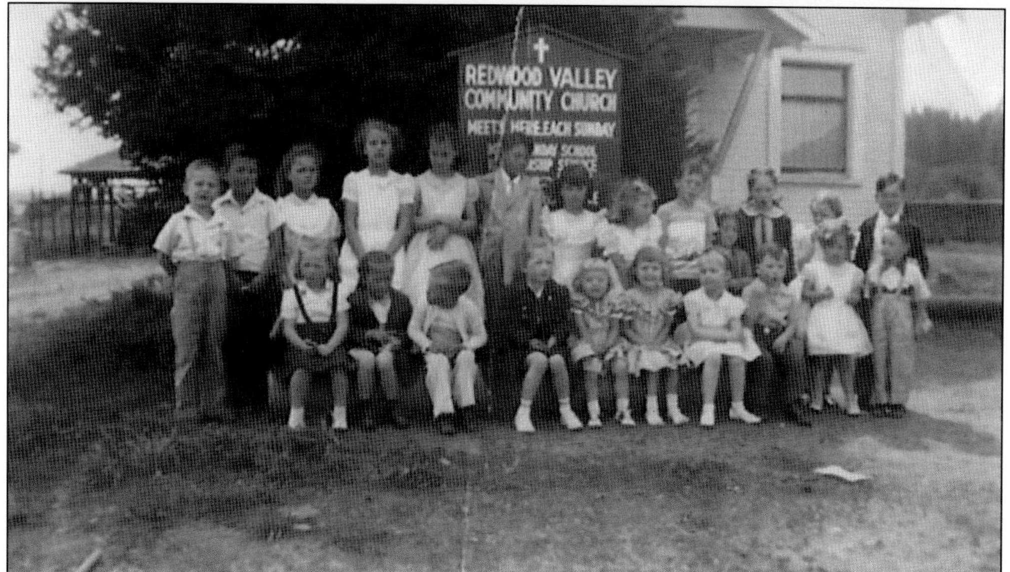

In this late 1940s photograph, a group of Sunday school students pose in front of the Redwood Valley Improvement Clubhouse. As the sign indicates, it was used by the Redwood Valley Community Church on Sundays for services. To the right is a boxcar sitting on the railroad tracks just south of the Redwood Valley Station. The redwood tree behind the sign is still in front of the church campus. (Authors' collection.)

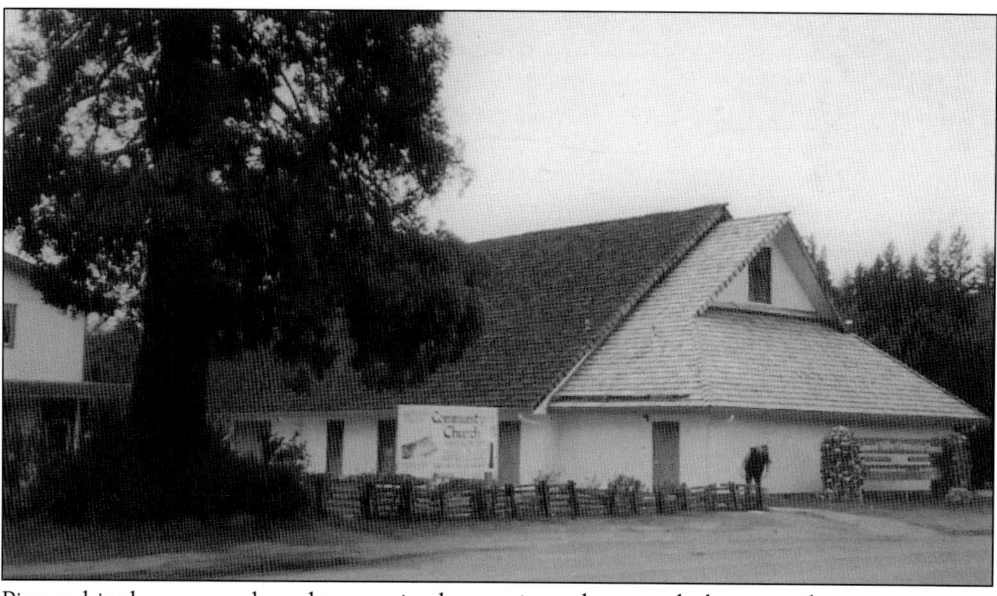

Pictured is the same redwood tree as in the previous photograph, but now the new sanctuary that has taken the place of the old clubhouse is in the background. At the time this image was captured, the sanctuary had just undergone a remodeling; the "thermometer" in the front gauges the funds that have been raised. (Authors' collection.)

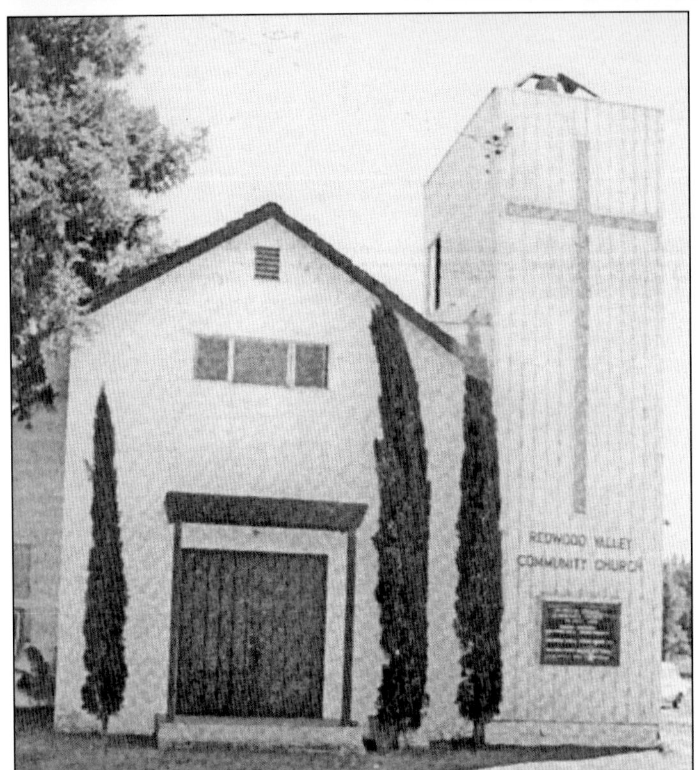

The Redwood Valley Community Church is pictured here as it appeared throughout the 1960s. The bell tower was added to the side, and a Sunday school classroom was included in the tower. During this time and into the 1970s, the church stood firmly in the shadow of the Peoples Temple, located only half a mile away. The bell at the top of the tower is still in use today, on the church campus. (Authors' collection.)

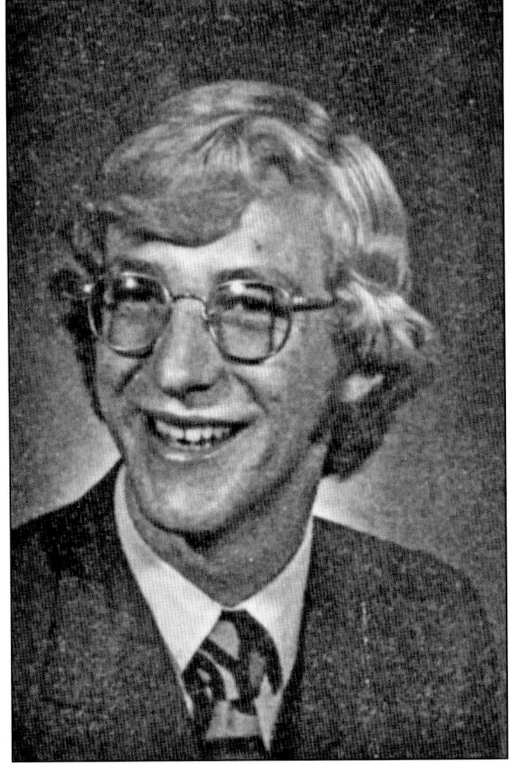

Richard "Rick" Warren, a former Redwood Valley resident, was a 1973 graduate of Ukiah High School. He was the fall-semester student-body president and helped start an on-campus Christian club called the Fishers of Men. He started a megachurch, Saddleback, and is the national bestselling author of A *Purpose Driven Life*. Warren led the prayer at Pres. Barack Obama's first inauguration. (Courtesy of the Ukiah High School Yearbook.)

This photograph was taken in 1972 at Rev. Jim Jones home on East Road in Redwood Valley. It was published in the *Ukiah Daily Journal* on November 20, 1978. The date of publication of this photograph was tied to the mass suicide that had occurred in Jonestown, Guyana. The boys with Jones are two of his adopted sons. (Courtesy of the *Ukiah Daily Journal.*)

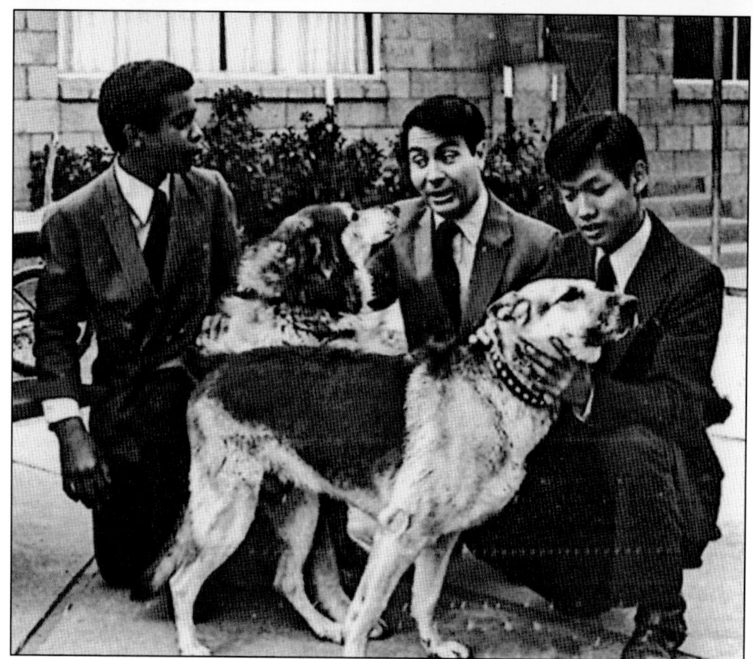

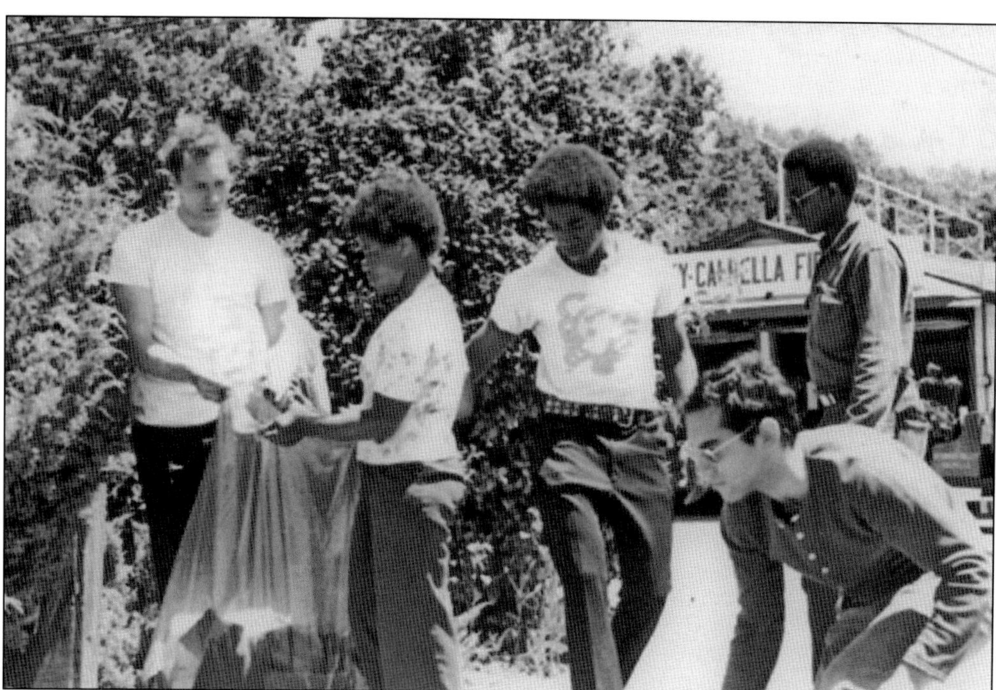

During their time in Redwood Valley, Peoples Temple members tried to show the citizens that they would be a productive part of the community. Here, young people from the Peoples Temple help gather litter in the field across from the firehouse in downtown. (Courtesy of Charlotte Wilson Campbell.)

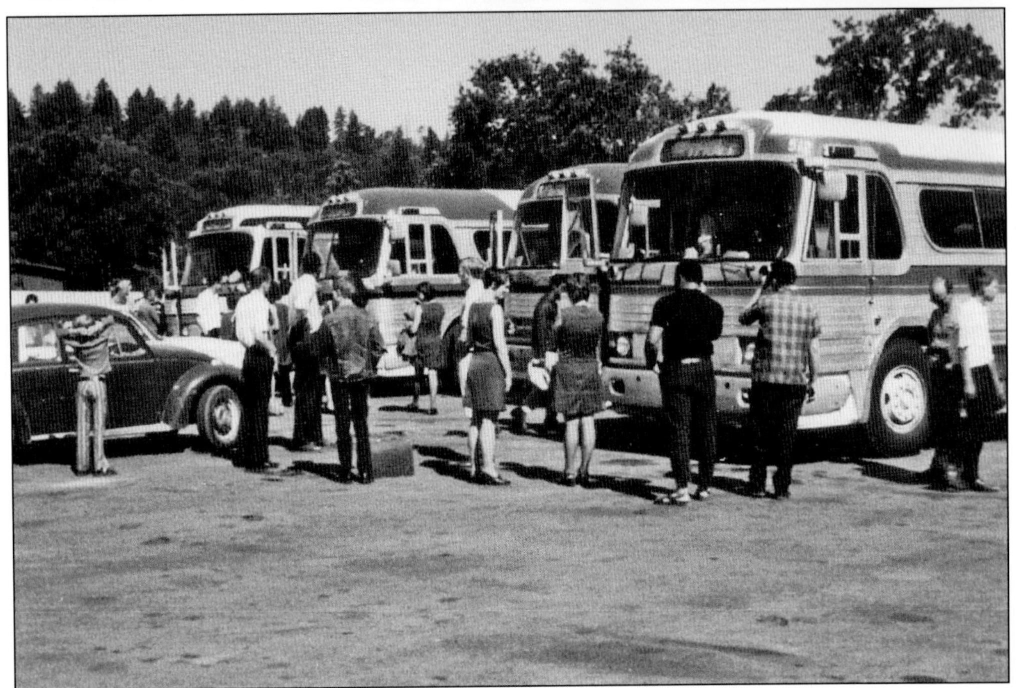

Jones's congregation was so large that it took several buses to transport them to various events. Here, they board buses to head south to the Bay Area and then to Los Angeles for the weekend. These trips included children, who were expected to be in school on Monday and not fall asleep during class. (Courtesy of Charlotte Wilson Campbell.)

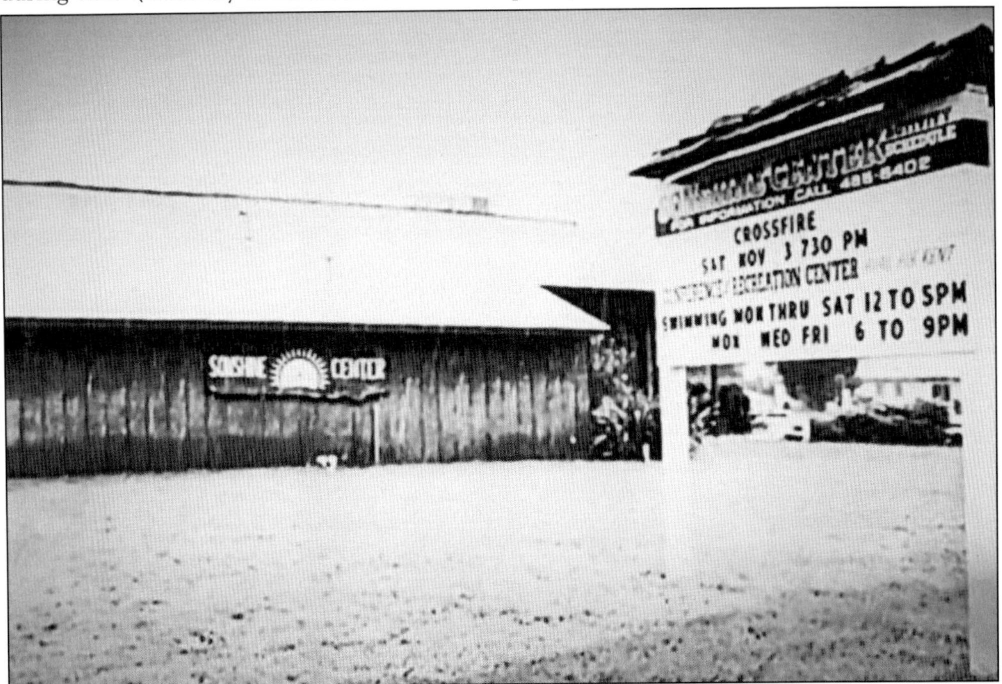

After the tragedy in South America, the home of the Peoples Temple became a health and recreation center called Sunshine Center. (Authors' collection.)

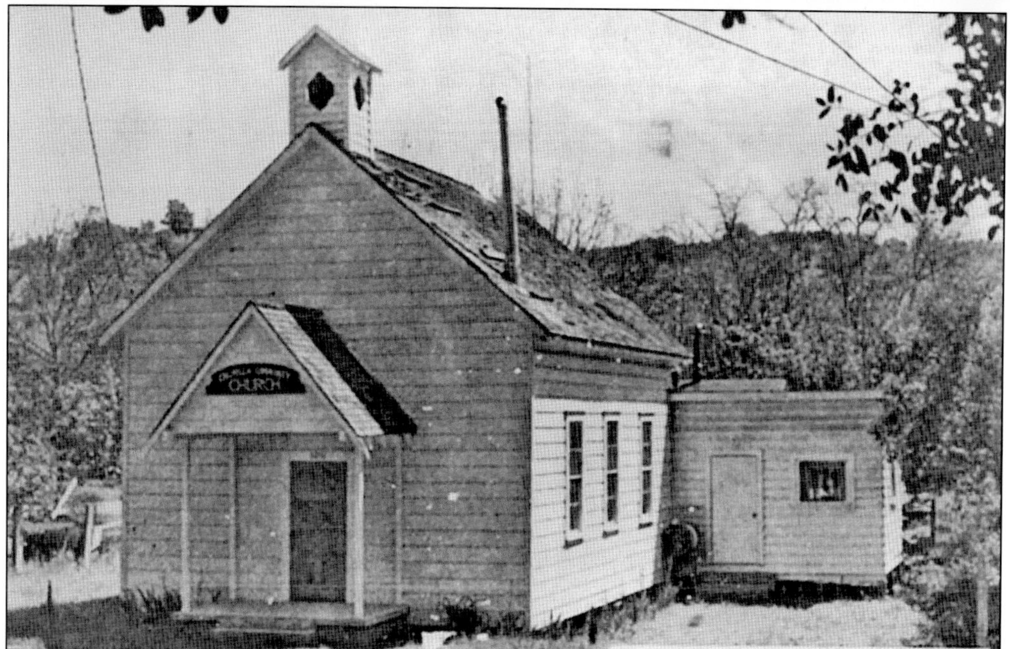

The Calpella Community Church on Third Street in Calpella is shown here in 1925. The church congregation had met for many years in this building when it housed the local one-room school. In 1925, the congregation purchased the building from the school for $125 and moved it to its present location by rolling it on logs. (Courtesy of the Testa family.)

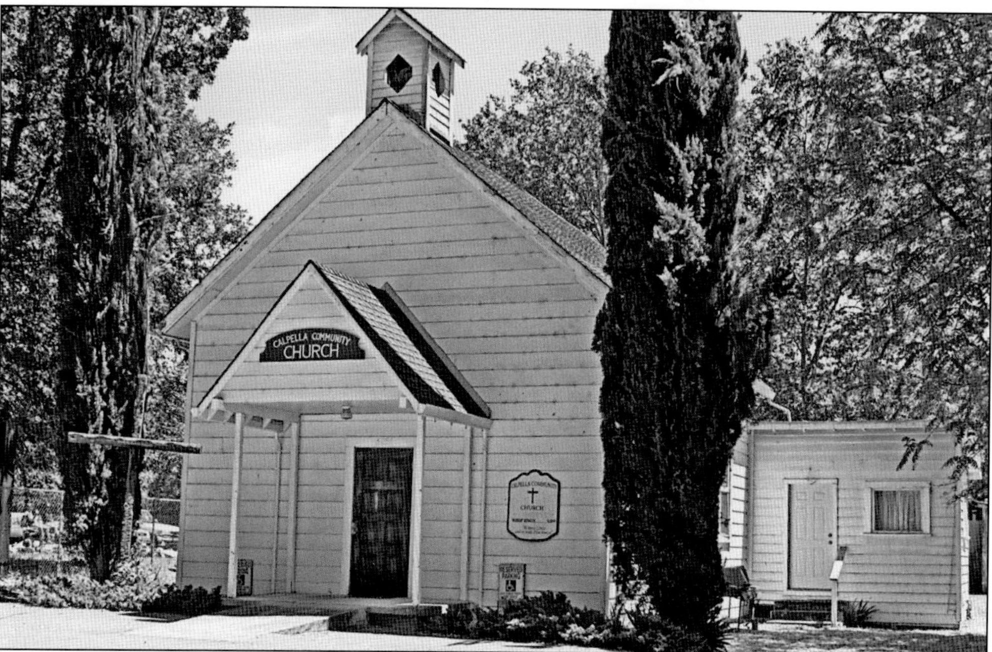

Here is the Calpella Community Church as it appears today. The Italian cypresses are now over 75 feet tall and can be seen in the previous photograph as small one-foot-tall seedlings. They are now 90 years old. Compare this photograph with the cover image; they are the same building. (Courtesy of Jim McCleary.)

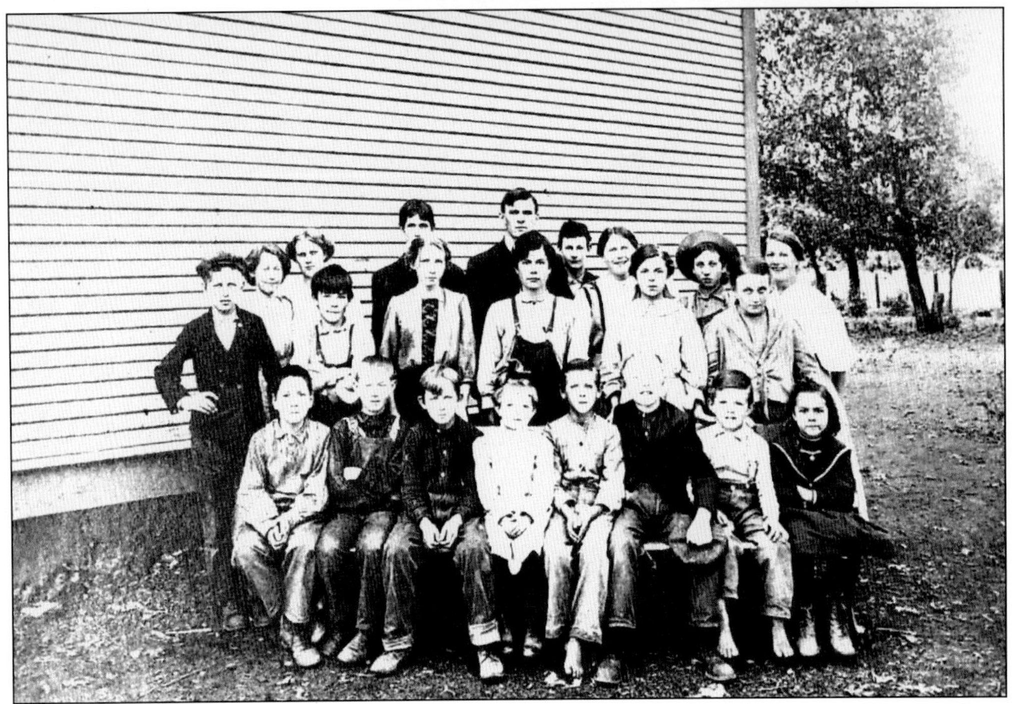

This is the Forsythe School in 1910. From left to right are (first row) John Lorenz, Harvey Klein, Walter Carter, Lydia Banek, Eugene Schamber, Walter Bean, Teddy Banek, and Caroline Lorenz; (second row) Solomon Luffelbean, Gloss Van Arsdale, Minnie Tolman, Roy Van Arsdale, Minnie Keller, and Bessie Banks; (third row) May Keim, Bernice Silsbee, Hugh Seward, Tom Jameson (teacher), Ernest Banks, Anna Schamber, Russell Tolman, and Alice Carter.

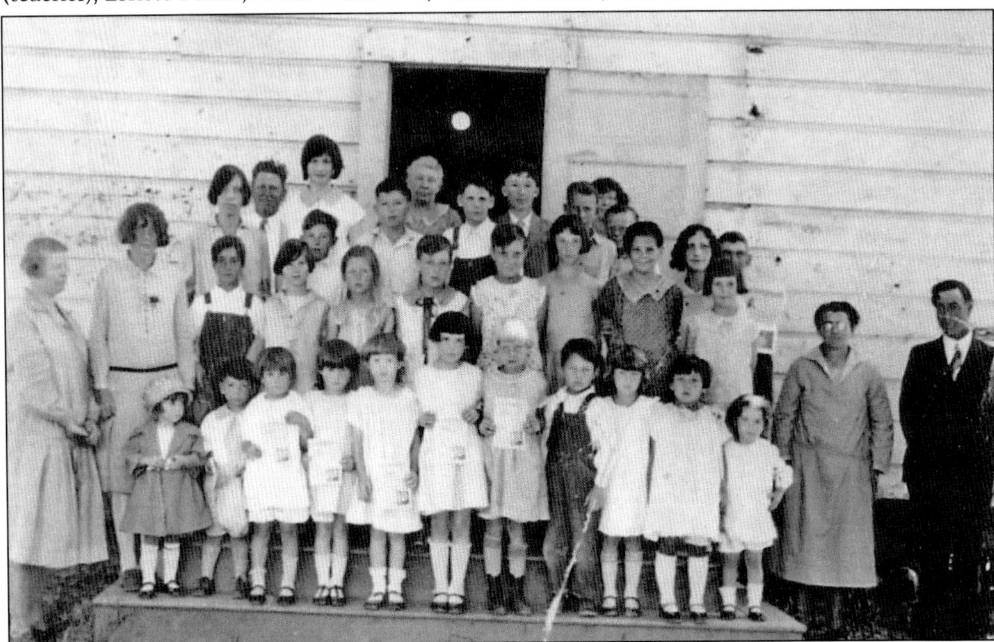

Pictured here is the Calpella School class of 1916. Later, this building became a church, and a new school was built across the road. (Courtesy of the Testa family.)

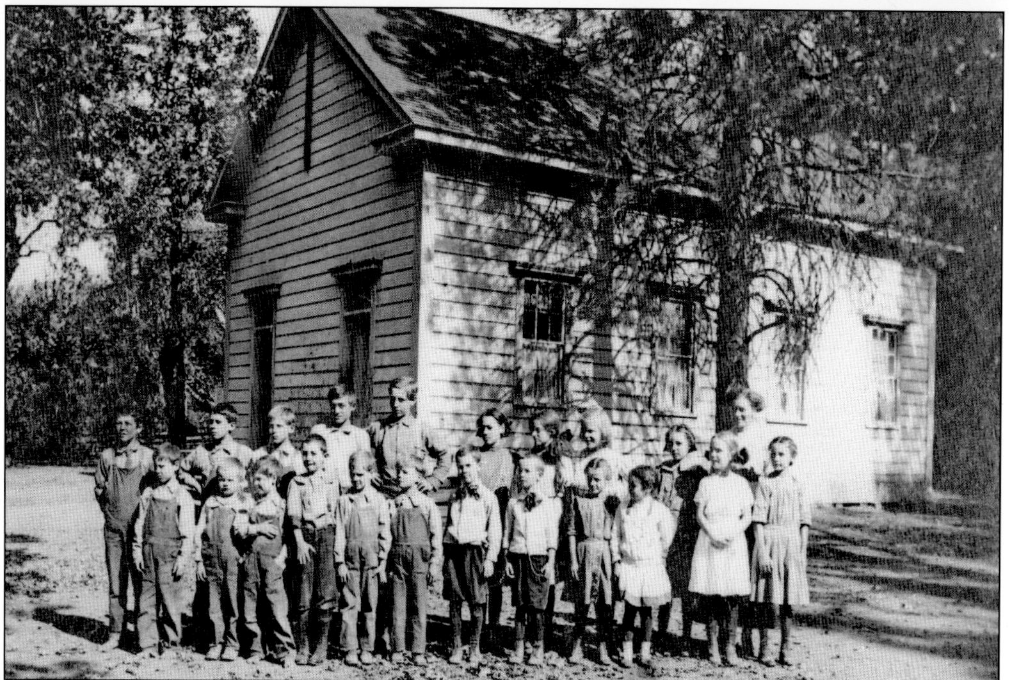

A Redwood Valley school, perhaps Mineral Springs School, is shown here. Students pictured include Emil Poma, Ida Poma Bricarelli, and Gene Schamber with teacher Marguerite Higgins (later Gowan).

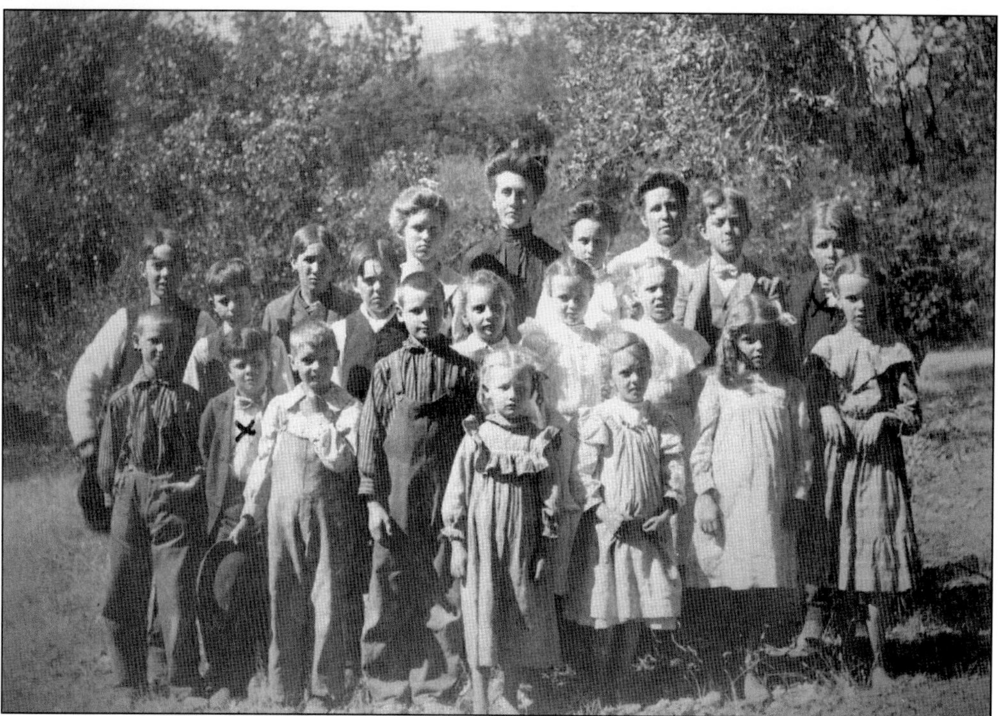

Seen here is a Redwood Valley school class; The boy identified with an X is Edgar Winsby, and the boy at the end of the back row is Frank Winsby.

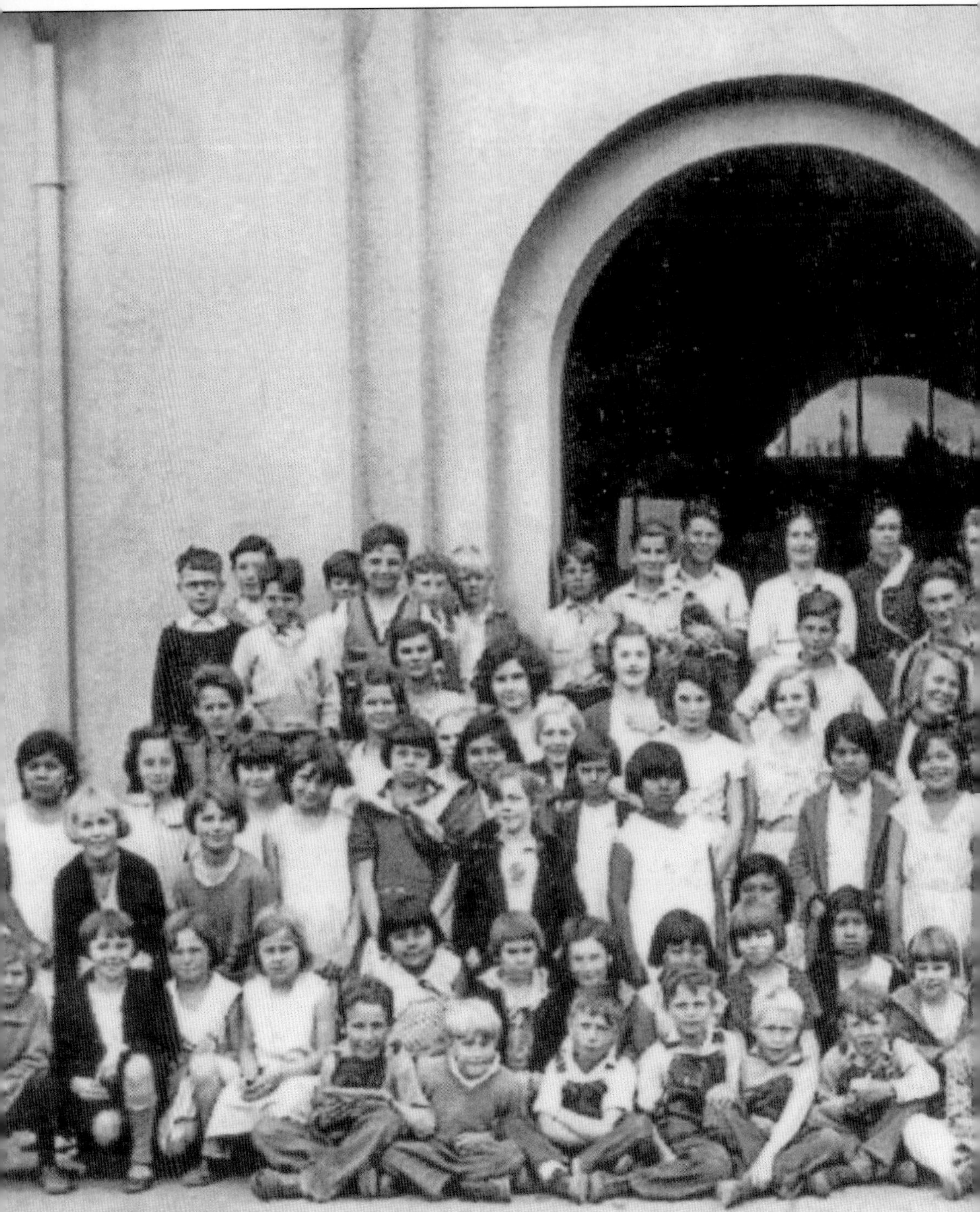

The classes of the 1932–1933 school year are in front of the Redwood Valley School. Notice the diversity of the student body. There are Native American, the blond Finns from the Finnish colony, and other ethnic backgrounds represented here. Shortly after this photograph was taken, a portion of this school burned, and classes were conducted at the Grange hall. A new school was

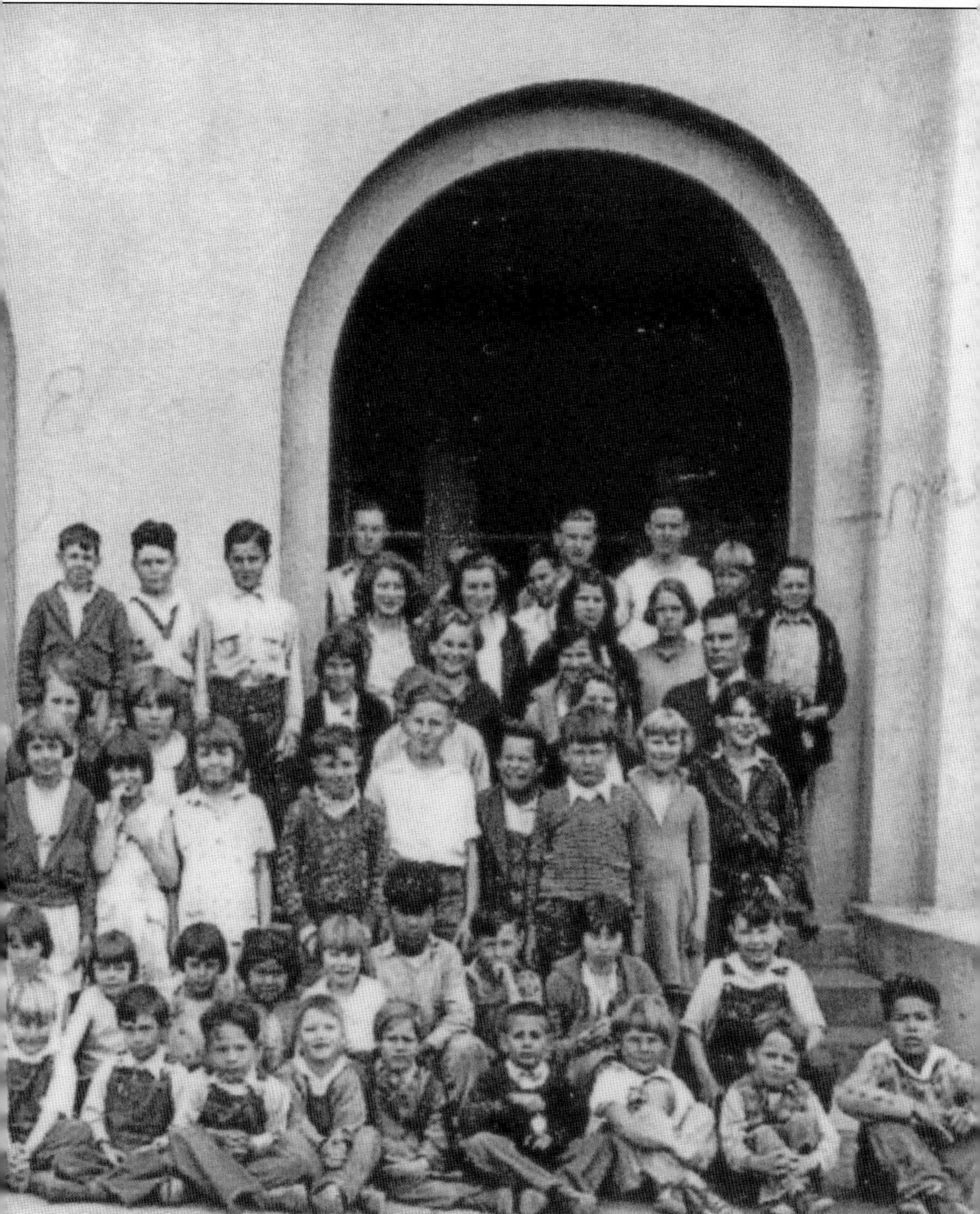

constructed in 1956 on this site. On June 3, 2010, the Redwood Valley Elementary School was closed due to low enrollment. A nearly complete listing of the students shown here is available at the Held-Poage Memorial Home and Research Library, located at 603 West Perkins Street in Ukiah. (Courtesy of Barbara Hooper Brown.)

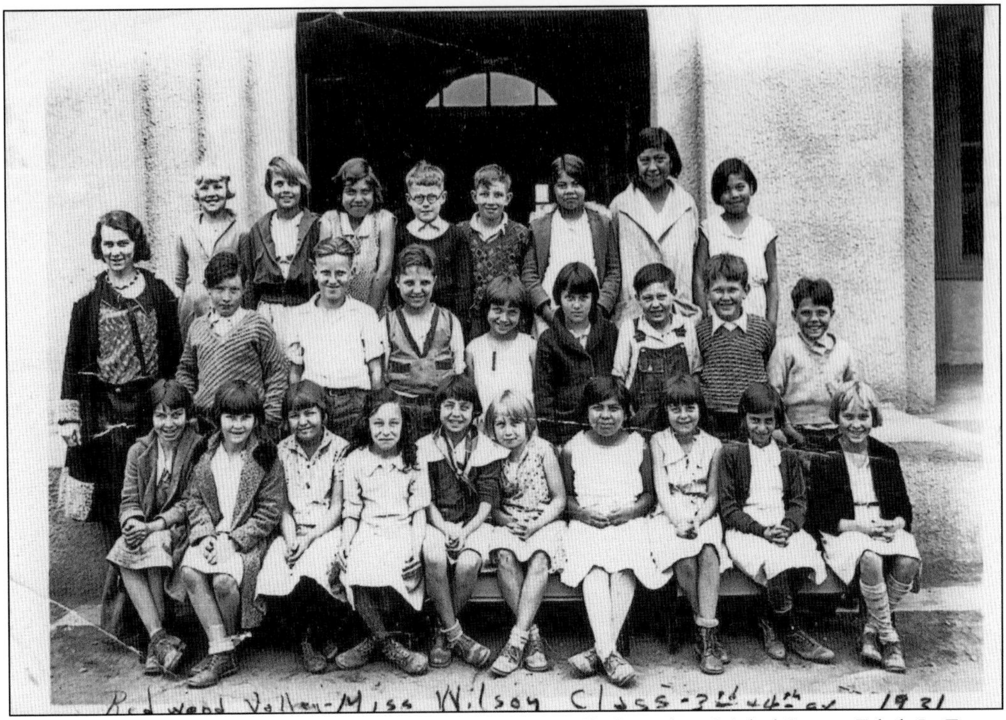

From left to right are (first row) Bernice Thompson, Lucille Reordon, Mabel Stone, Edith LaFaret, Grace DeCarla, Frances Thompson, Jane Jackson, Doris Dance, Letta Lolonis, and Rosalind Gullickson; (second row) Robert Jackson, Bob Kartes, Bill Wooly, Tanis White, Virginia Hull, Bobby Travers, Ted Torngren, and John Woolly; (third row) Artis Ford, Ruth Dyers, Leora Jackson, John Howland, Aldo Tollini, Dorene Scott, Ella Fred, and Geraldine Palmer. (Courtesy of Marsha Johnson Isbester.)

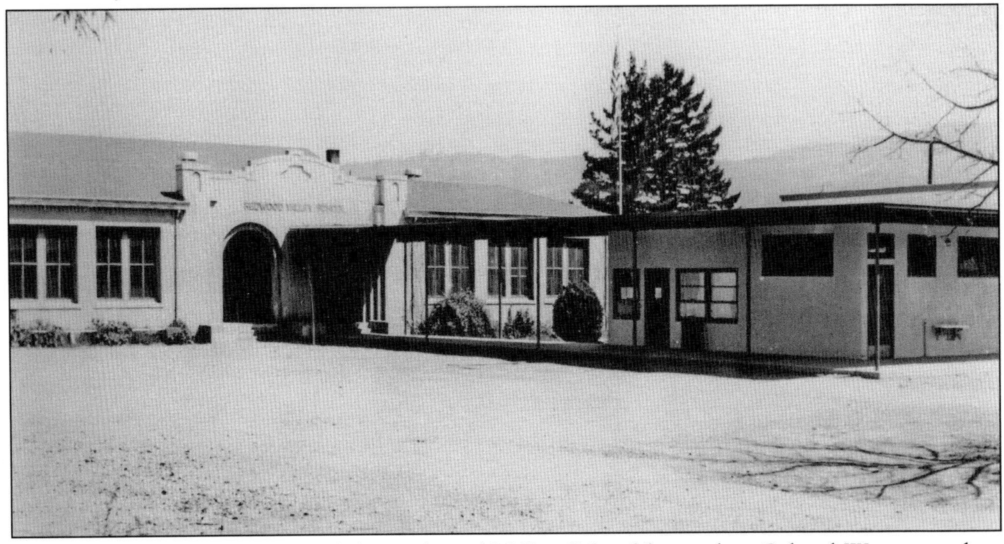

This photograph of the front of the Redwood Valley School located on School Way was taken at the end of the 1955–1956 school year. The following year, the new school was constructed on this site. The citizens of the valley had passed a school bond for completion of a new and more modern school. The trees in photograph are still there. (Authors' collection.)

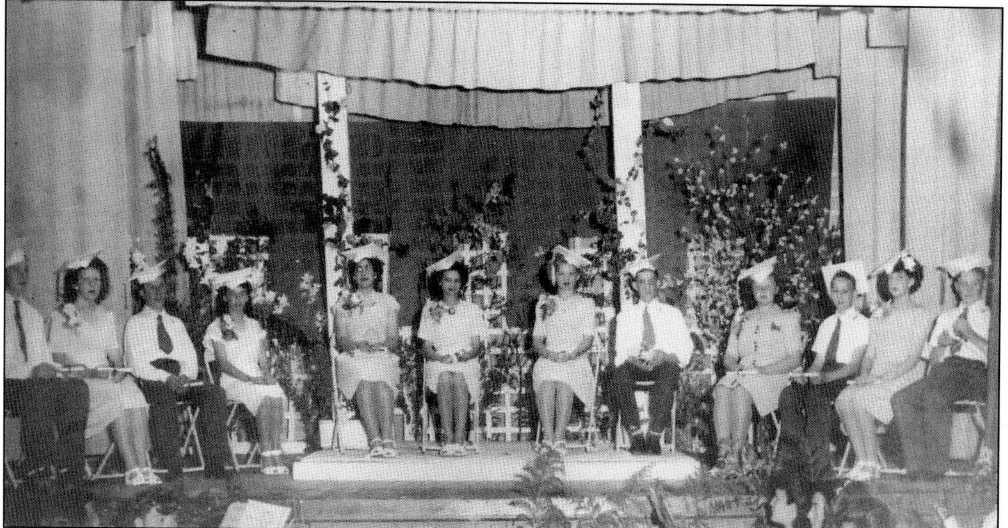

Pictured here is the Redwood Valley School graduating class of 1943–1944; from left to right are Jimmie Goudge, Donna Brown, Pete Sozzoni, Josie Fornasero, Wanda Hohn, Sophie Lolonis, Beth Banks-Guntley, George Sanapietros, Barbara Basket, Harold Dockins, Barbara Rawles-McCulloch, and Seymore Bruch; absent that day were Charles Fredrickson and Tempalou Terry.

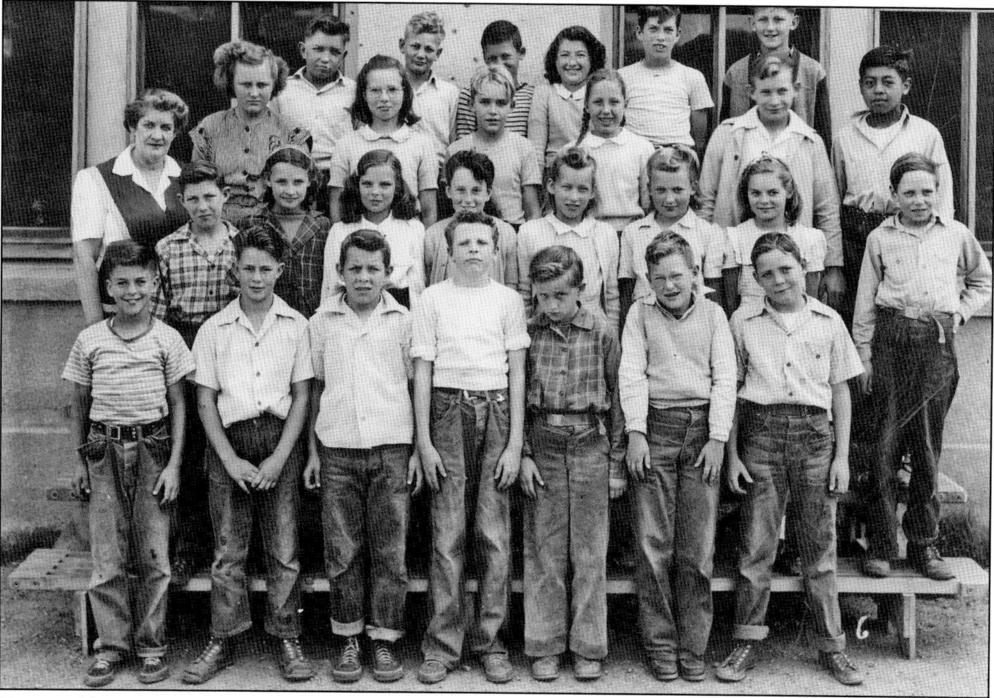

Pictured here in 1947 are Mrs. Clark's sixth-grade Redwood Valley students; from left to right are (first row) Floyd Rovera, Don Buck, Jim Brown, Dick Ford, Don Butow, John Hamon, and Tom Rawles; (second row) Harold Buddy, Lucy Riley, Bonnie Mares, Florence LaFaret, Shelma Banks, Jean Banks, Mary Beckurt, and Arthur Loukes; (third row) Lodey Joice, Betty Gray, Elwood Hays, Patricia Sibbets, Robert Farley, and Jim Ratter; (fourth row) Eddy Jackson, Roy Stone, Ralph Beson, Shirley Kipper, Marvin Kipper, and Steve Sires. (Courtesy of Lucille Rovera Neese.)

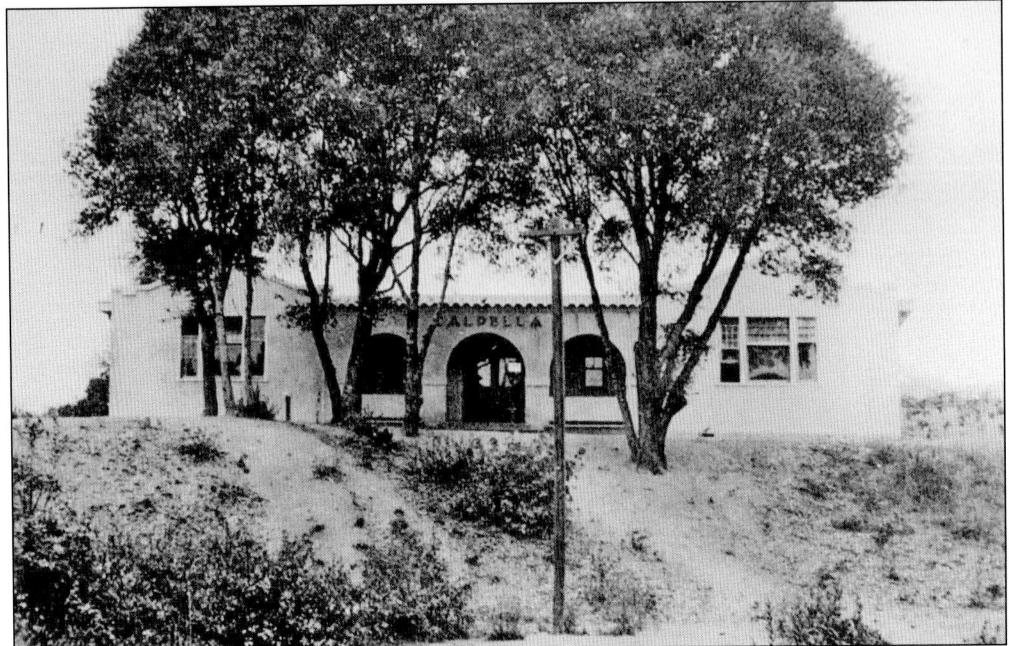

The main building of the Calpella School is pictured here soon after its construction. It was built on land donated by the Gaetano Testa family; it was adjacent to their vineyard in Calpella. Presently, it is used as a private school. It sits on the hill directly above the Calpella Community Church, which was the original Calpella School. (Courtesy of the Testa family.)

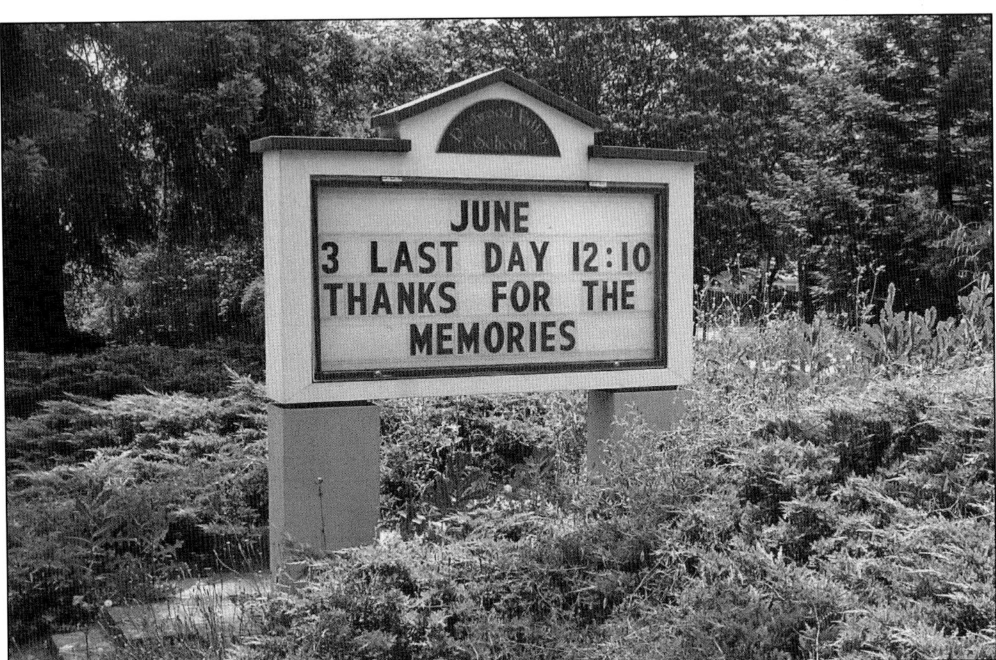

This sign was posted to announce the last day that Redwood Valley School would be open: June 3, 2010. It was closed by the Ukiah Unified School District due to low enrollment and budget shortages. "Thanks for the memories." (Authors' collection.)

Five

Colonies and Clubs

The Finnish colony, or *sointula*, was a community within a community. However, its members also participated in the events and social life with the rest of the valley. It contained a bungalow that was occupied by members of the Finnish community. The colony was officially incorporated on October 29, 1913. Stocks sold for $10 each with total sales of $12,000. They had a large barn and silo near the Bungalow (located near the intersection of Road E and East Road). The colony also owned the field across the road, which extended down to the river, where they put in a dam for irrigation, washing of clothes, picnicking, fishing, and summer swimming. They took their meals together, and as the years passed, moved out to their own plots.

On an early map of the valley, a Scotch colony, Bonnie Brae, is shown in the area of Road A and B below Salt Hollow. This group was not as organized as the Finns to the north but probably larger in number. They had many group events, such as baseball games and costume parties for Halloween.

The Redwood Valley Improvement Club was started in 1912, "to advance any interest that will benefit the farming community of Redwood Valley." It built its own clubhouse on School Way and led the way to achieving better roads and bridges as well as postal, fire, and electrical services for the valley.

The Redwood Valley Grange 382 was founded on May 10, 1917. Grange members first met at the Mechanics Hall in Calpella. In 1921, on land purchased from J.M. Wooley for $10, they completed their 30-by-60-foot meeting hall. The roster of Grange Masters includes George Magneson, A. LeRoy Ford, and John Finne. The Grange used its considerable influence to lobby for improvements for the valley. It attempted to have nearby Leonard Lake saved for public use but was unable to raise the needed $150,000. The hall on East Road was and is used for meetings such as the water district and other public events.

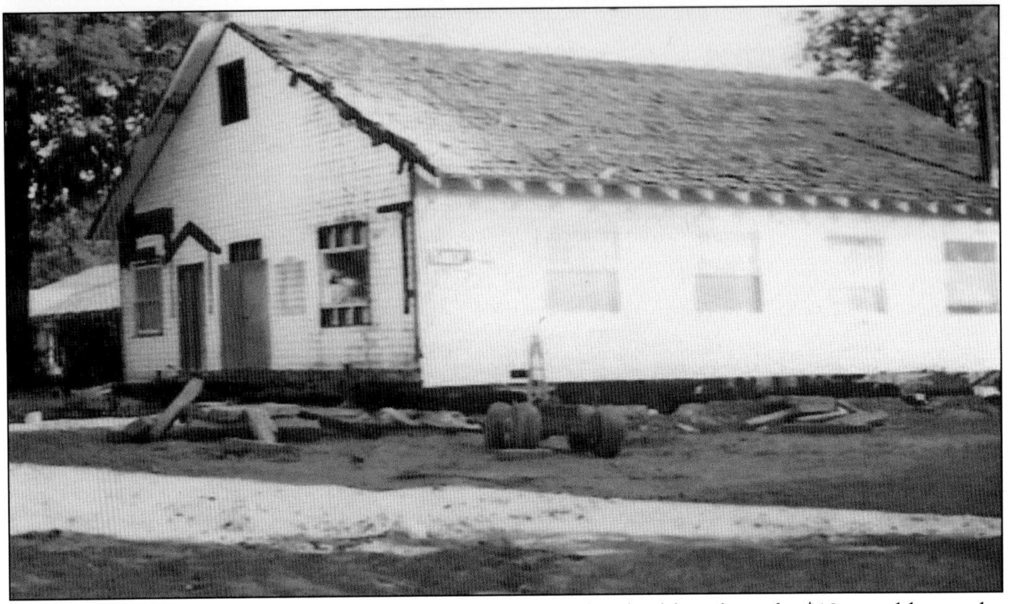

After six years, the club was able to build a clubhouse on land sold to them for $10 in gold coins by George Magnuson. He specified the deal would be completed when the clubhouse was begun. He also specified the width and length that the clubhouse should be. The members laid out logs to the specified size on the School Way property, and the deal was completed. (Authors' collection.)

Redwood Valley Feb, 14th, 1924.

"Redwood Valley Improvement Club,"

Greetings, By an action taken at the last meeting of the"Redwood Valley Farm Center" the Secretary was authorized to write to yourOrganization cordially inviting you to appoint one of your Members to act with one appointed from the"Grange" and our appointee Mr Yarbrough, to serve as a "Committee of Arrangements" to plan and call a Mass meeting of all the residents of Redwood Valley to meet at such time and place as you may designate, to receive and the District Manager of the P.G.& Electric Co. to discuss the Proposition of bringing in Electricity for the service of our Community.

You are invited to meet with Mr Yarbrough at his House (The Heilman Place) on the evening of Feb, 20th,

Yours very respectfully.

H.R. Bohna Sect.

The club, along with others such as the Grange were able to help make improvements in the valley. A planning meeting was called at the Yarbrough place to arrange for a mass meeting of valley residents for the purpose of discussing the proposition of bringing electricity to the valley. This invitation is dated February 14, 1924. A year later, rudimentary farmers' lines were laid. (Courtesy of Janet Marsh.)

This map is included to point out the main areas of Redwood Valley, starting at the top: Fort Weller (former site), Skull Mountain Ranch, Kirk Ford's Ranch, Rancho Yokayo, Finnish colony, Grange hall, Forsythe School, Charcoal Kilns, Howland's Store, post office, Salt Hollow, Scotch colony, Bonnie Brae, Calpella, and Lake Mendocino. (Courtesy of University of California publications in *American Archaeology and Ethnology*.)

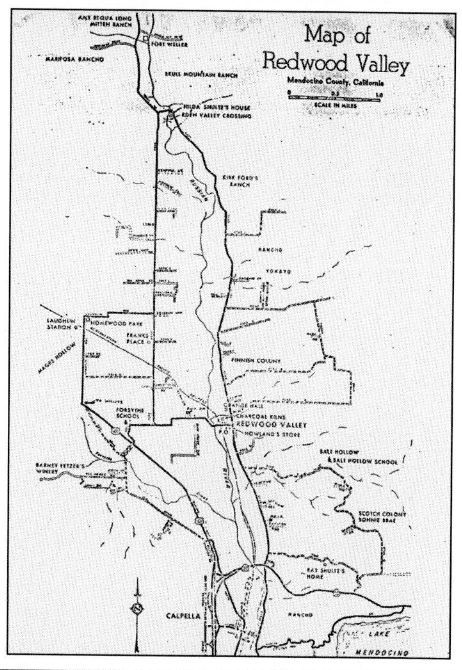

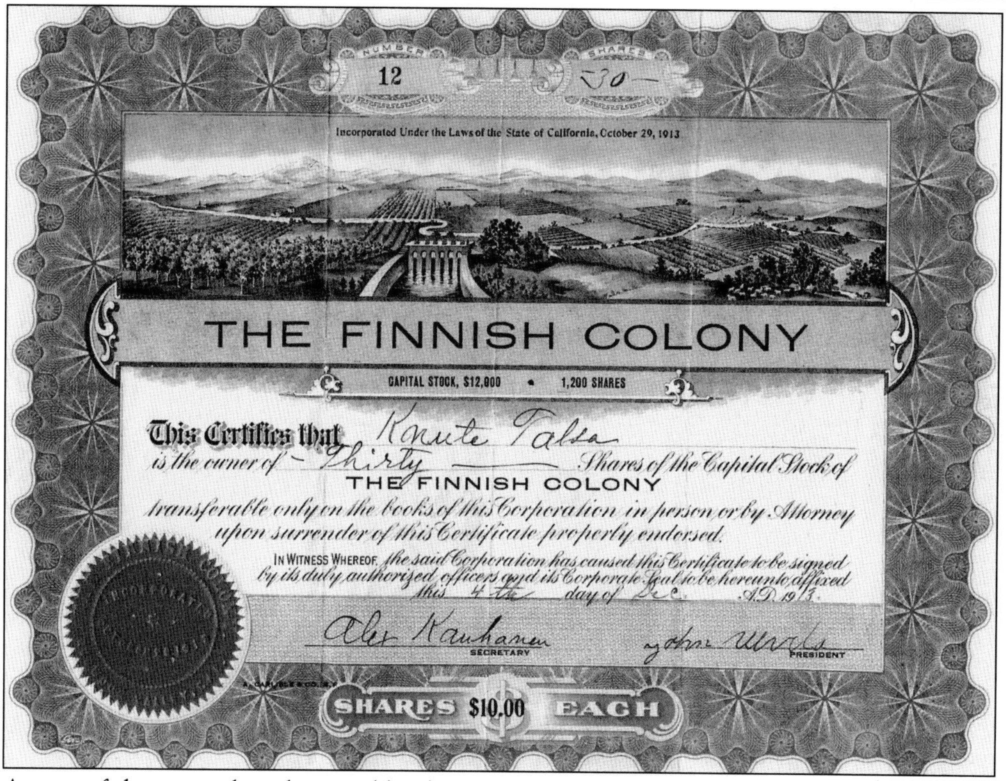

NUMBER 12 SHARES 30

Incorporated Under the Laws of the State of California, October 29, 1913

THE FINNISH COLONY

CAPITAL STOCK, $12,000 • 1,200 SHARES

This Certifies that Knute Talso is the owner of Thirty Shares of the Capital Stock of THE FINNISH COLONY transferable only on the books of this Corporation in person or by Attorney upon surrender of this Certificate properly endorsed.

In Witness Whereof, the said Corporation has caused this Certificate to be signed by its duly authorized officers and its Corporate Seal to be hereunto affixed this 4th day of Dec A.D. 1913.

Alex Kauhanen SECRETARY John Ulvila PRESIDENT

SHARES $10.00 EACH

A copy of the original stocks issued by the Finnish colony of Redwood Valley on December 4, 1913, is shown here. It is issued to Knute Talso and signed by secretary Alex Kauhanen and Pres. John Ulvila. The colony was incorporated on October 29, 1913. The idealized view of Redwood Valley at the top of the stock was never to be. (Authors' collection.)

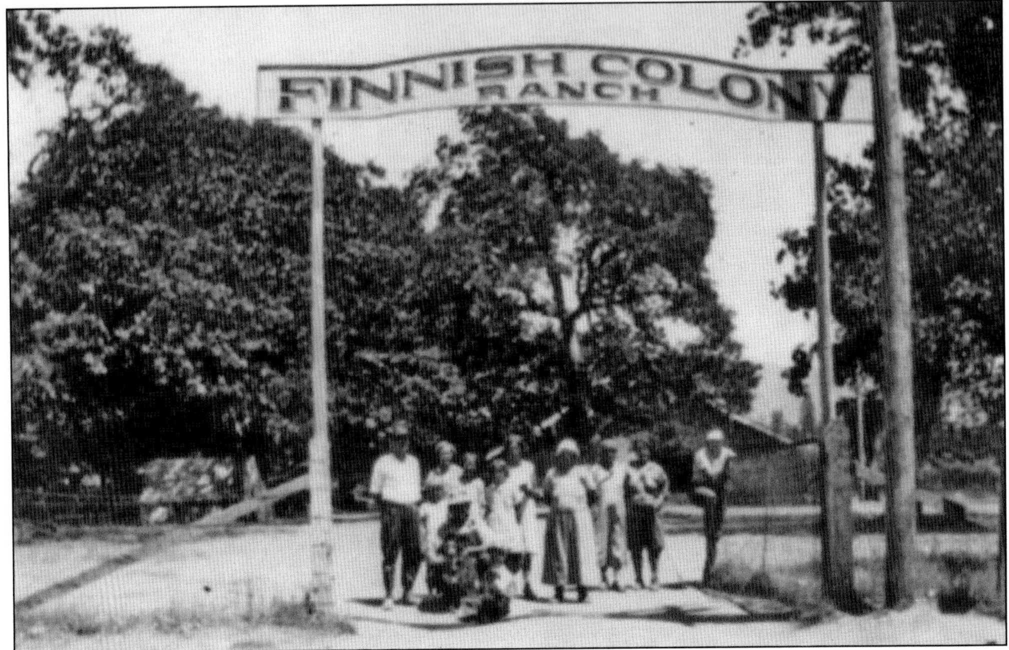

This is a very rare view of a group Finnish colonists standing under the sign that they had constructed and proudly erected, indicating the Finnish Colony Ranch. In the background is the roofline of the substantial bungalow that was constructed after W. English's ranch house had burned down. (Courtesy of Carol Soinila.)

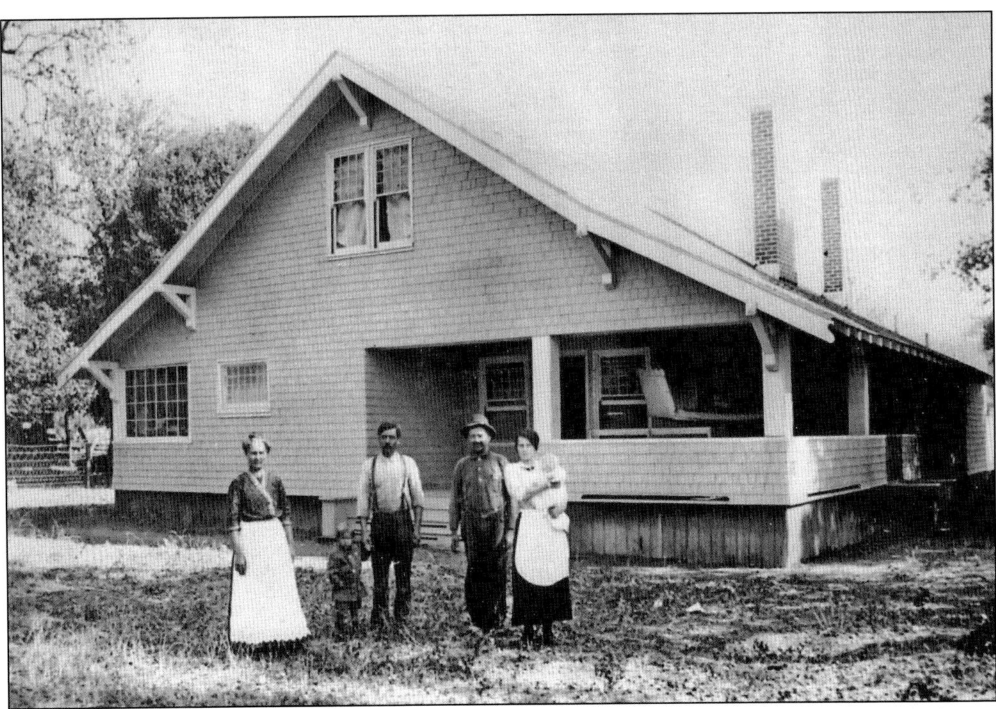

The Finnish Bungalow is pictured here in the 1920s. This building still survives and is being renovated by its present owner

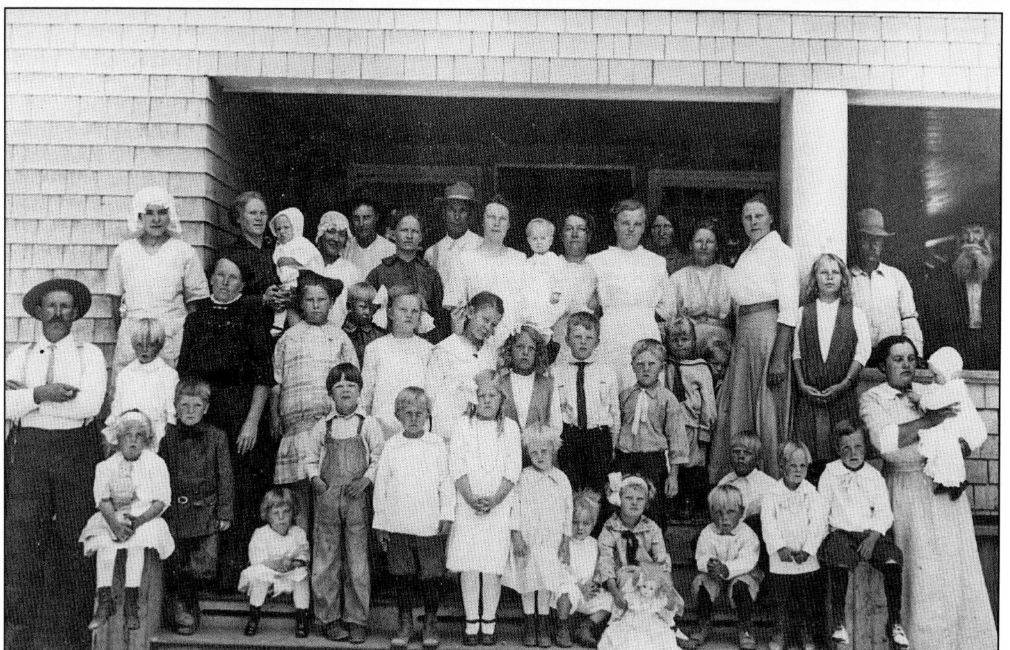

Shown here is a gathering of Finns in August 1915 at their new communal house. Here, they held celebrations of Finnish and American holidays, dances, and Christmas. Alex Kauhanen played Santa Claus. When the residents stayed here, they took their meals and saunas together until they moved out to plots of their own, on the 1,400 acres of the colony land. It was a socialist setting. (Courtesy of Julie Soinila.)

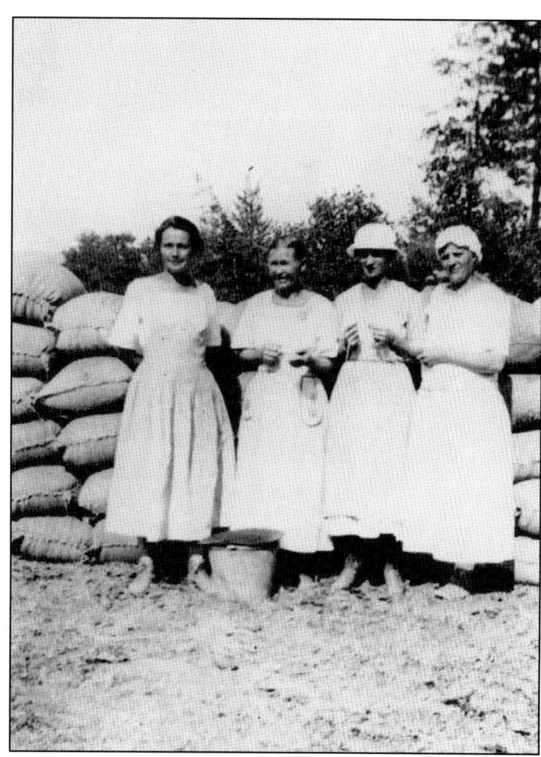

These Finnish ladies pause from sewing wheat sacks closed. Pictured from left to right are Annie Hietala, Fiina Soinila, Mary Wainio, and Ida Rinta.

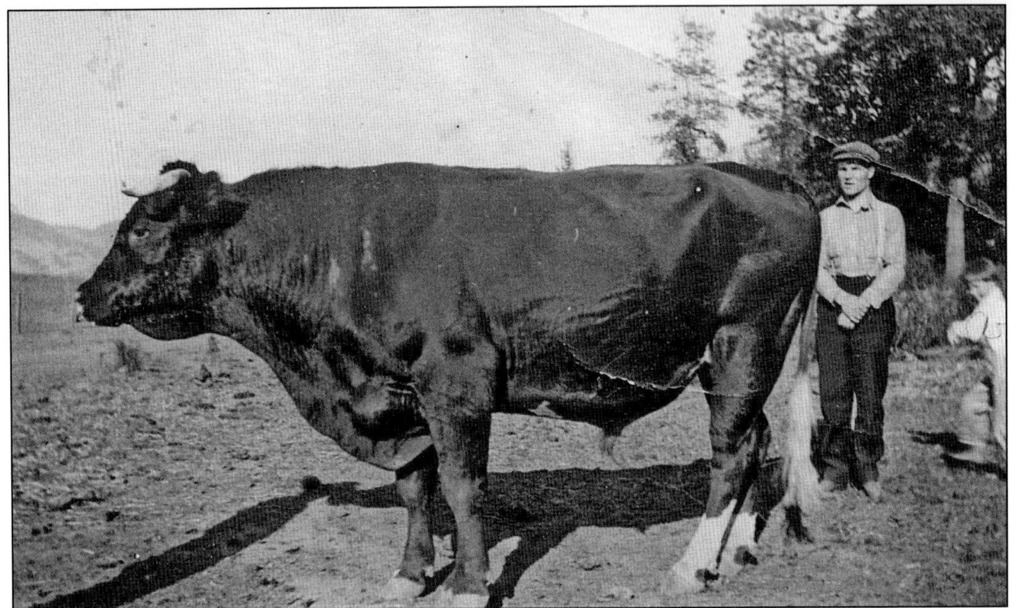

Another enterprise that the Finns undertook was purchasing a bull for use in cattle breeding around the valley. It was quite a specimen. Standing next to the bull is Knute Talso and his son Arne. Tom Jameson related a funny story about when this bull escaped and knocked down several fences as it made its way westward across the valley. (Courtesy of Julie Soinila.)

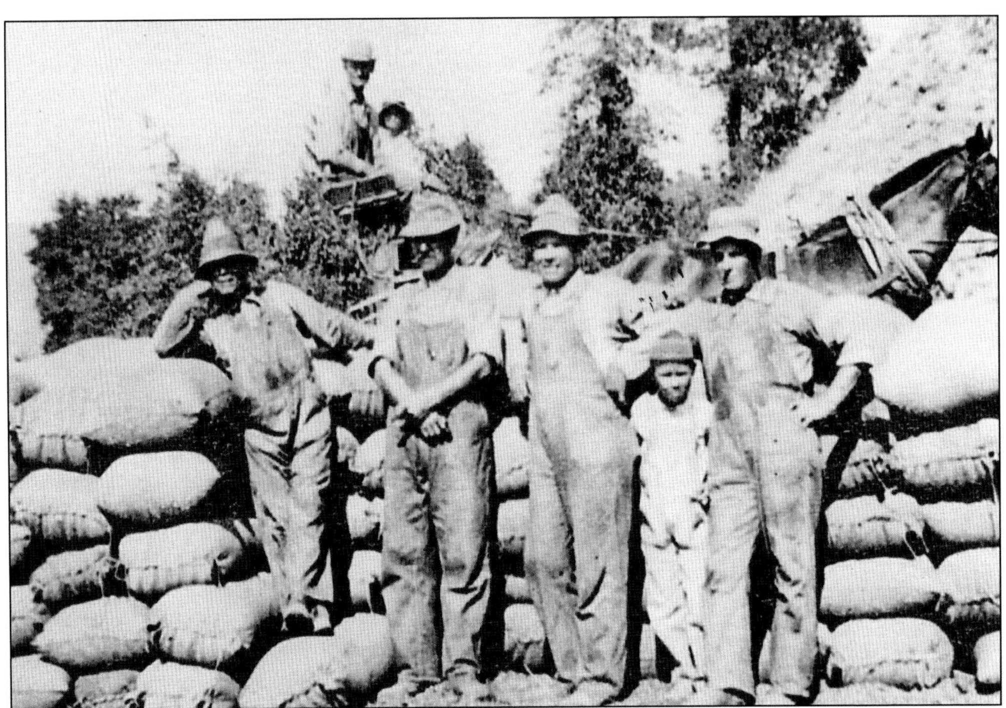

A group of unidentified Finns stack wheat for transport in the wagon at the rear of the photograph. It was to be sold for income for the colony. Notice that the young children also assisted in this work.

It is difficult to imagine laundry day down by the river. The Finnish ladies hold their pots for washing clothes. The fire for heating the wash water is seen in the foreground of the photograph. The ladies are, from left to right, unidentified, Hanna Niemi, Mary Wainio, unidentified, and Annie Hietala.

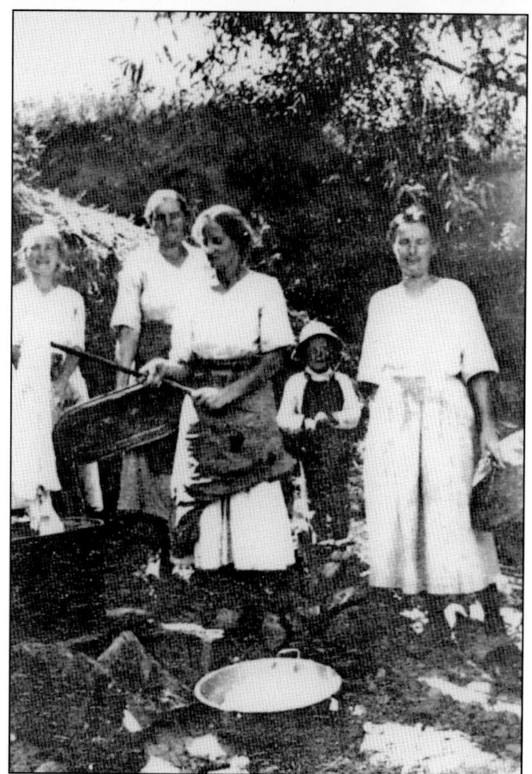

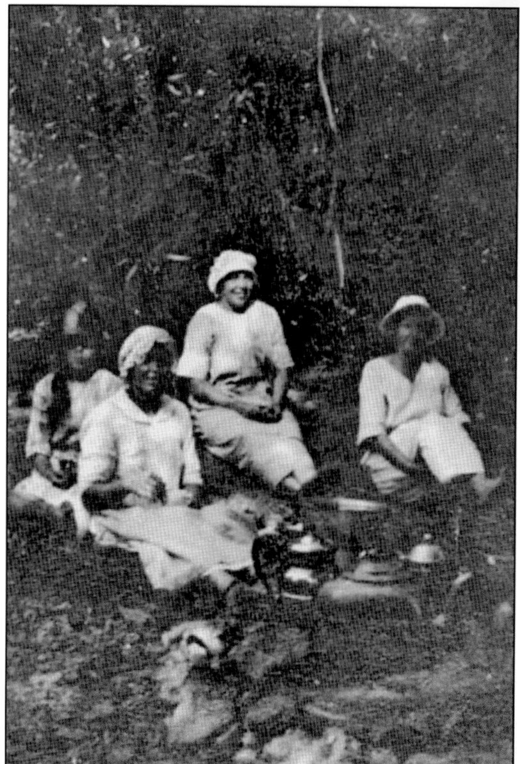

It was not all work and no play on laundry day; from left to right, two unidentified females, Fiina Soinila, and Annie Heitala take their mid-morning coffee break. This was an important ritual and never overlooked. Marguerite Gowan related that one could set a watch by when the Finns take their coffee break.

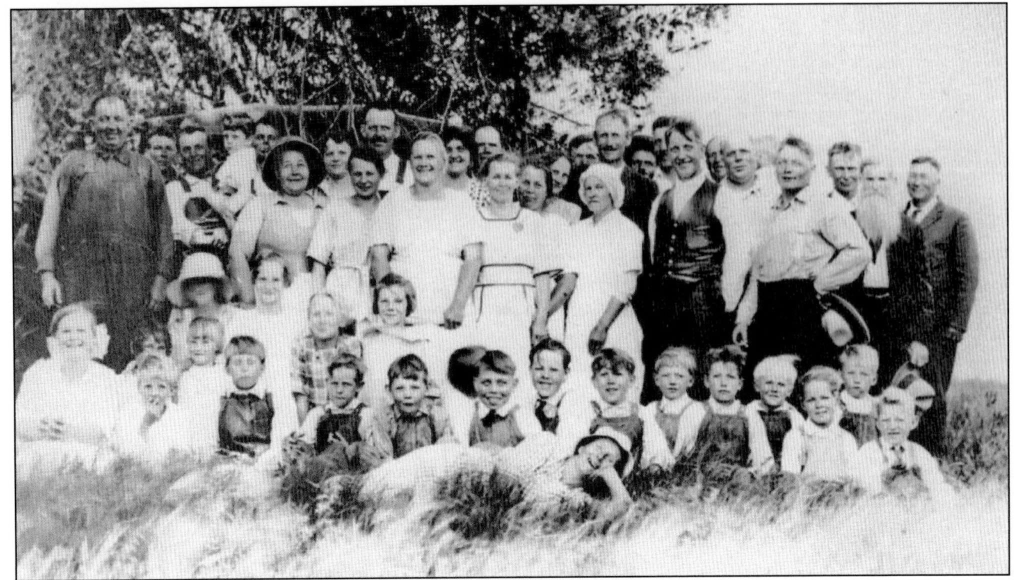

This 1920s Mother's Day gathering was held at the Finnish colony. The mothers are all decked out in their ever-present white outfits. Easily recognized are Alex Kauhanen on the far left and Matt Jacobson second from the right.

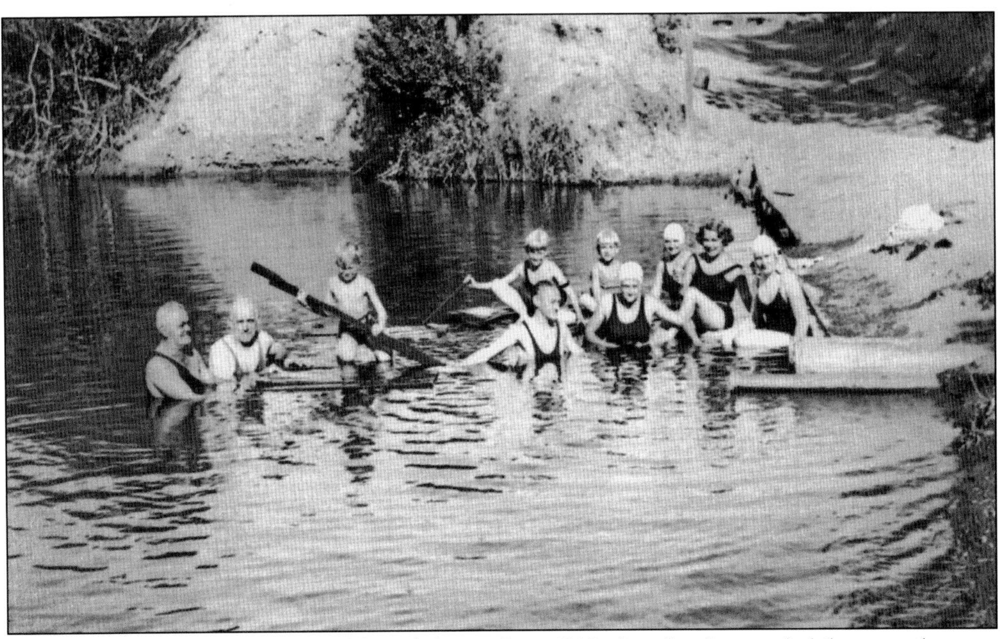

When the Finns purchased the old English ranch in 1912, their land extended down to the west fork of the Russian River. They installed a dam for irrigation, fishing, and swimming. Notice the full-body swimming suits. Amazingly, there are remnants of this dam still visible today. This photograph was taken in 1933.

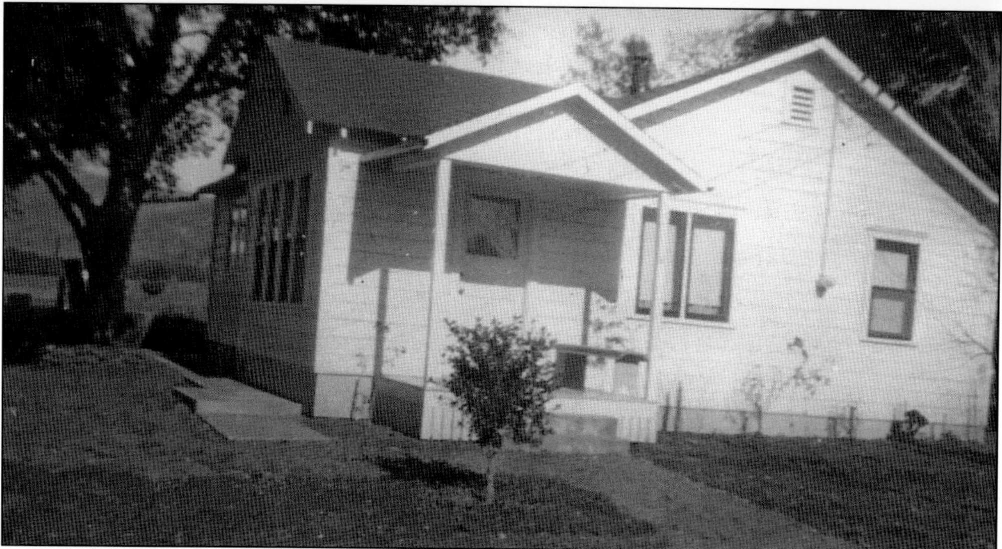

Pictured here in early 1952 is a typical colony house, located at the corner of Road E and Colony Dive. They were often small but well maintained. To the left in the photograph are the eastern hills, to which the colony land extended to the top. (Authors' collection.)

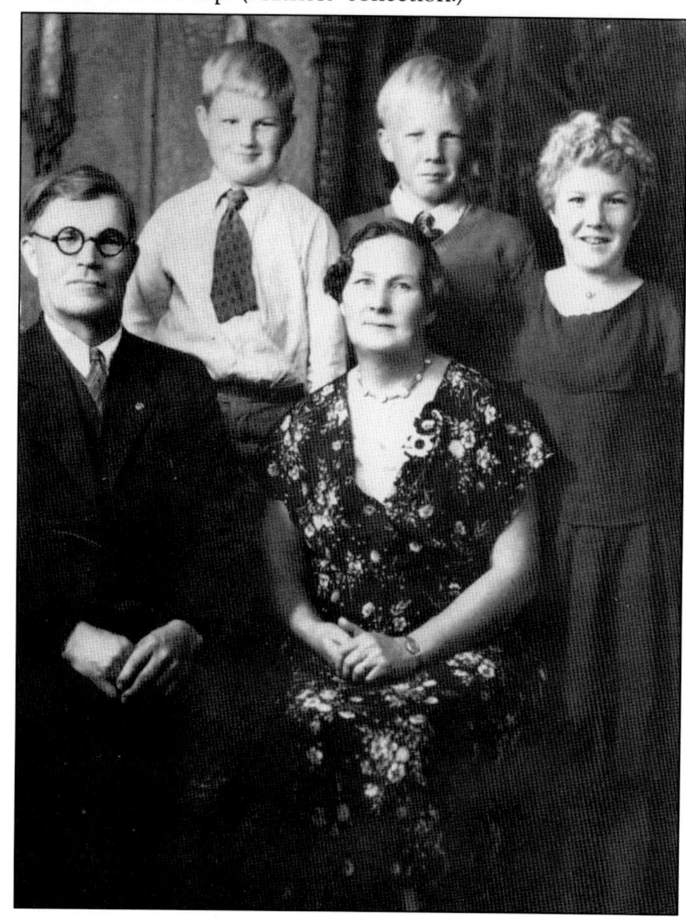

Knute Talso's second family is pictured here in the mid-1930s. He married Lena Nyrhila, a widow. Knute became the president of a reconstituted colony after the initial group voted to dissolve the colony in the mid-1920s. The couple is pictured here with their children, from left to right, Walter "Harold," E. Leonard "Mike," and Verna, who were all born on the colony. (Authors' collection.)

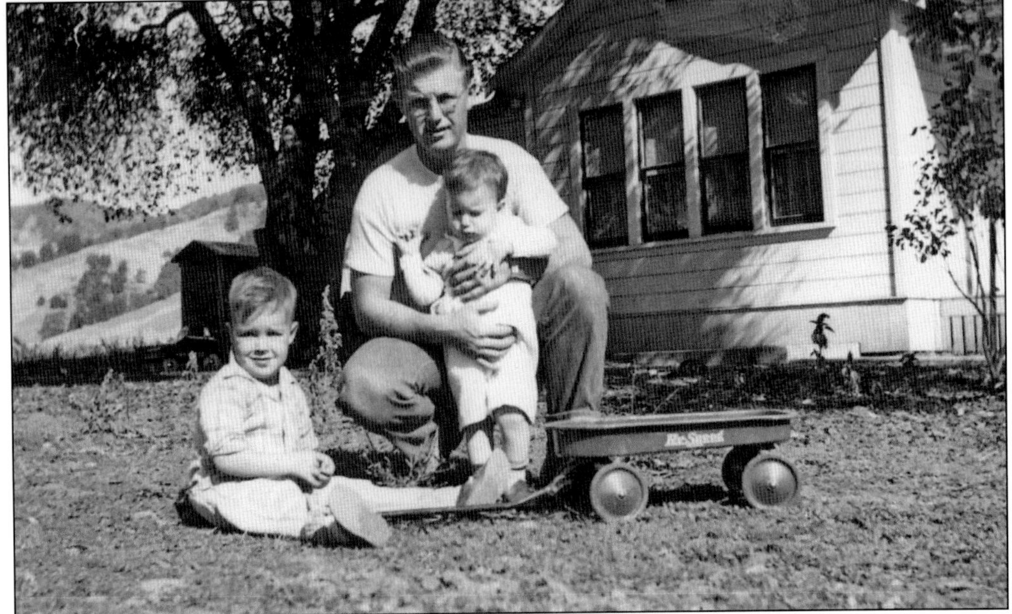

Subsequent generations of Finns continue to live in Redwood Valley. Pictured here is Walter Harold Talso holding son Marvin, with his eldest son, Michael, in the foreground. Marvin now has a son and grandchildren living in Redwood Valley; they are the fifth generation to do so. (Courtesy of Palma Sozzoni Talso.)

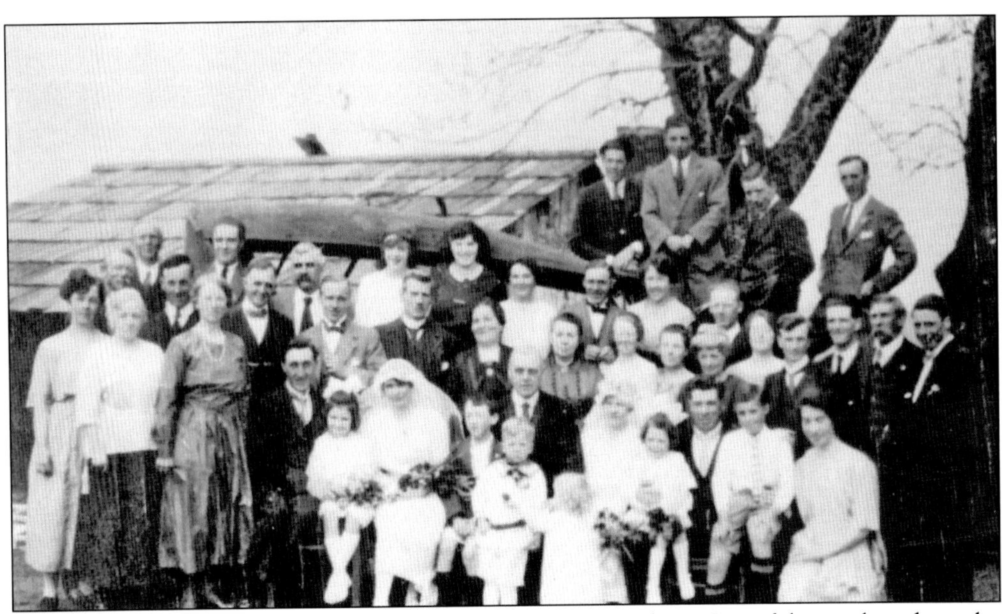

This is a rare photograph of a double wedding on the Scotch colony. One of the newlywed couples is identified on the left foreground as Jock and Mary Wilson. Photographed in the mid-1930s, notice the rustic home in the background and the early automobile behind the wedding party.

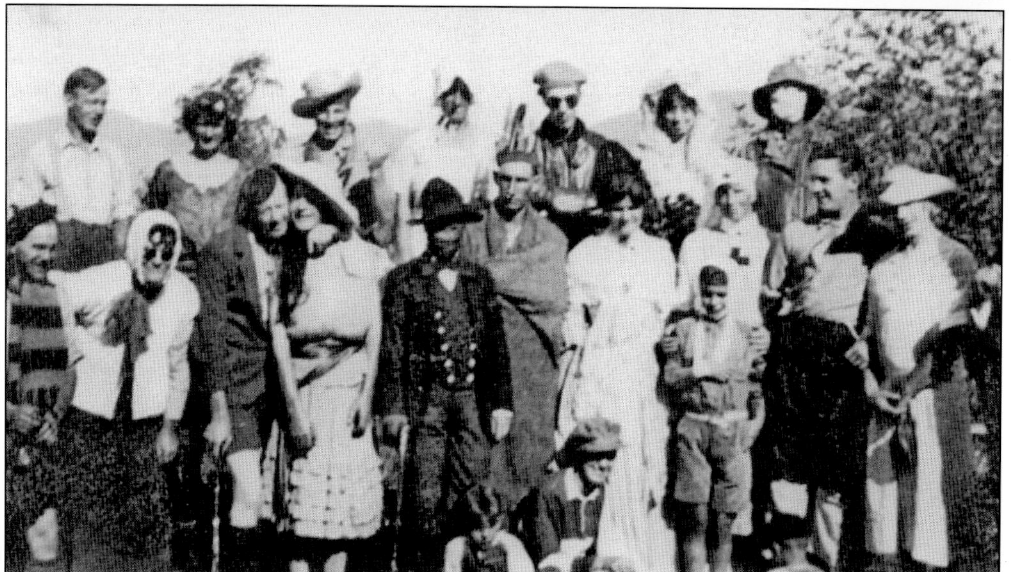

This is a wonderful photograph of a Halloween party on the Scotch colony, with everyone dressed in costume. One can identify people dressed as a cowboy, a pioneer, artists, a scarecrow, General Grant, Native Americans, a nurse and patient, a sailor, an old person, and a couple.

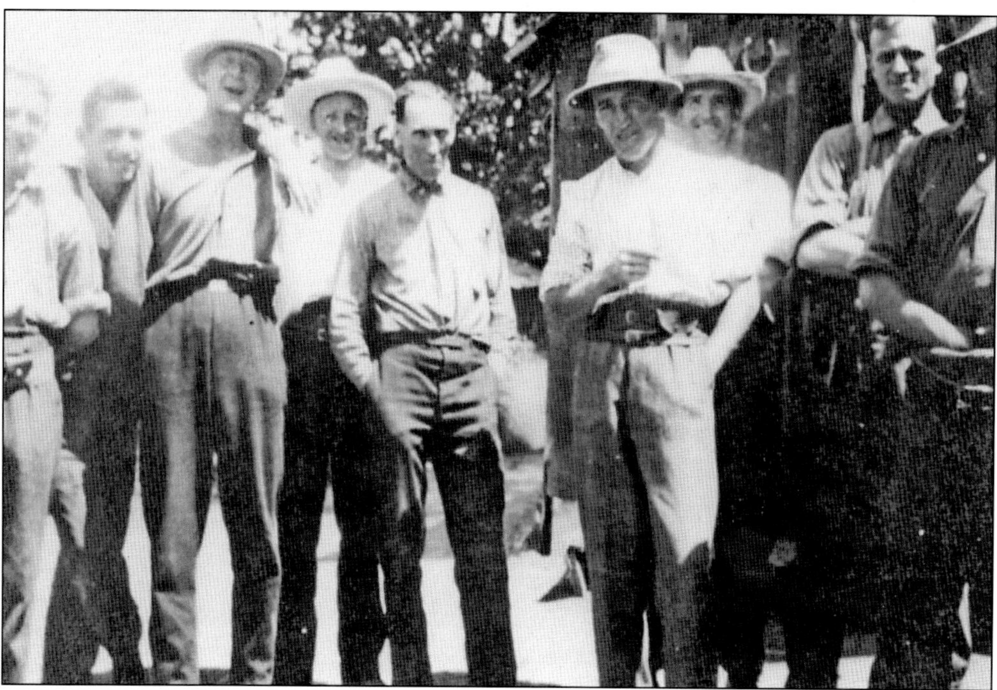

This is a Scotch colony group photograph. Shown fifth from the left is David Anderson, who was the originator of the colony; he bought an 1,800-acre ranch from Tom Orr and divided it into 10- and 20-acre plots.

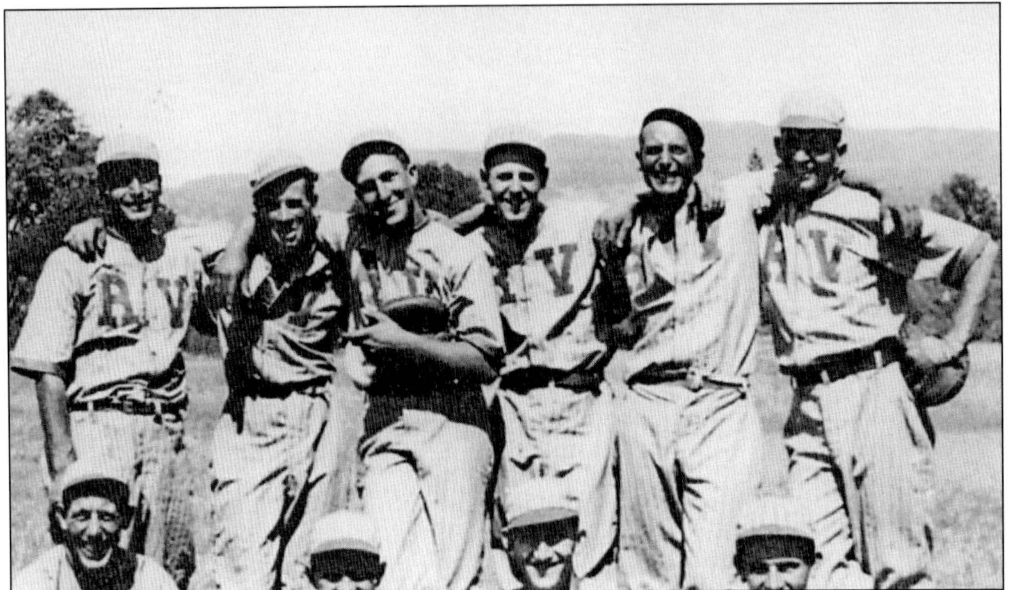

Proudly displaying "RV" on their striped baseball uniforms is a group of men who comprised the baseball team representing the Scotch colony.

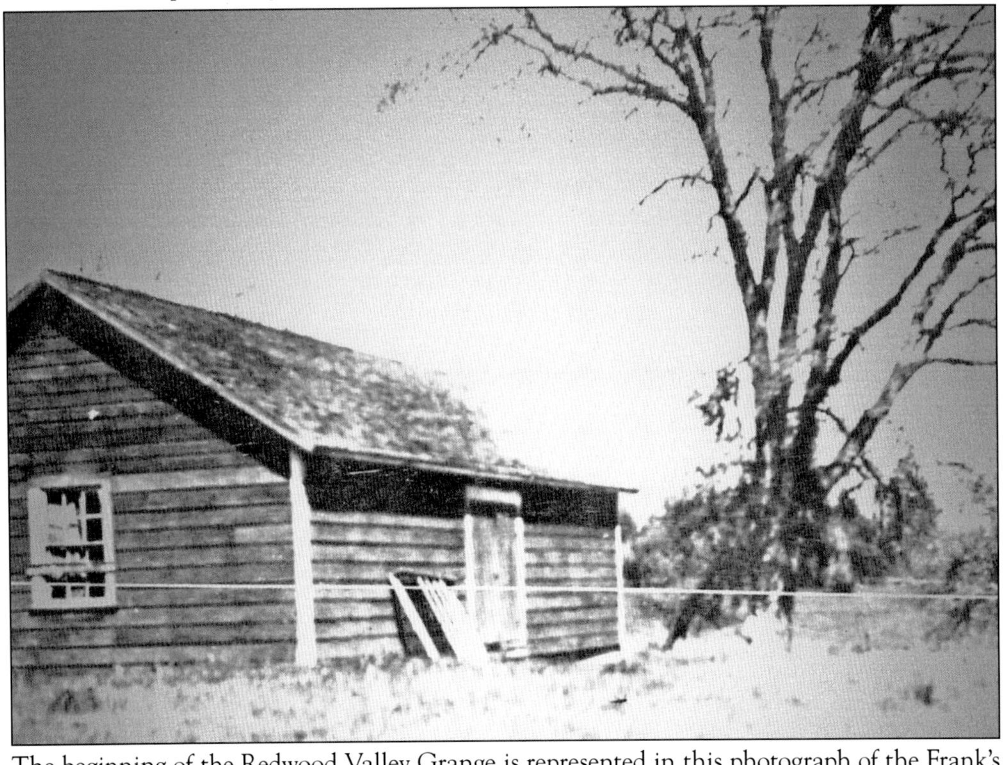

The beginning of the Redwood Valley Grange is represented in this photograph of the Frank's winery, originally part of the Brown ranch, which was used for dances and Grange meetings. The first master was George Magneson, the same gentleman who sold the land for the Redwood Valley Improvement Club. The land for the Grange was later purchased from the Woolleys for the same sum as the clubhouse in downtown: $10.

LEASE.

THIS LEASE MADE THIS 11 th· day of April 1921, by and between the REDWOOD VALLEY IMPROVEMENT CLUB, of Redwood Valley, Mendocino County, California, party of first part, and the REDWOOD VALLEY GRANGE of same County, and State, party of second part.

Witnesseth: That the party of first part agrees to lease to party of second part a certain building s[illegible]uadet in Redwood Valley, Mendocino County Cali. known as IMPROVEMENT CLUB HALL, for the purpose of holding their meetings therein, on the second and fourth Friday ni[illegible]hs of each month, for aterm of one year, from the date of this lease [illegible]r and consideration one dollar per month, payable monthly.

The second part agrees to funish their own ligths and fuel and repair any damage to building or furniture caused by them. It is also agreed that second part may use above said Hall any other time, than above specified by consend of the board of trustees of the REDWOOD VALLEY IMPROVEMENT CLUB.

WITNESS: Our hand and seal and the day above writtin:

Trustees of the Redwood Valley Improvement Club.

Trustees of the Redwood Valley Grange.

This document is a lease between the Redwood Valley Improvement Club and the Redwood Valley Grange. It allows the Grange to rent the clubhouse for $1 a month while the grange building was being constructed. This arrangement only lasted for four months, as the Grange hall was finished and the first meeting was held on August 21, 1921, in the new building. (Courtesy of Janet Marsh.)

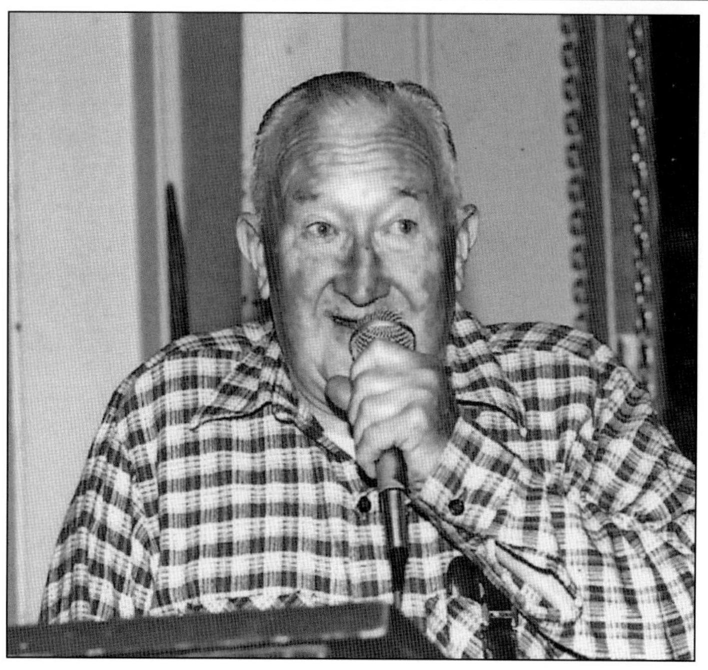

Here, Elbert Lane addresses the crowd at a birthday celebration in his honor. Lane was the town barber as well as a bus driver for the local school district. Remarkably, he served as the Grange 382 Grange Master in three different decades: the 1930s, 1940s, and 1950s. (Courtesy of Linda Phelps-Wilson.)

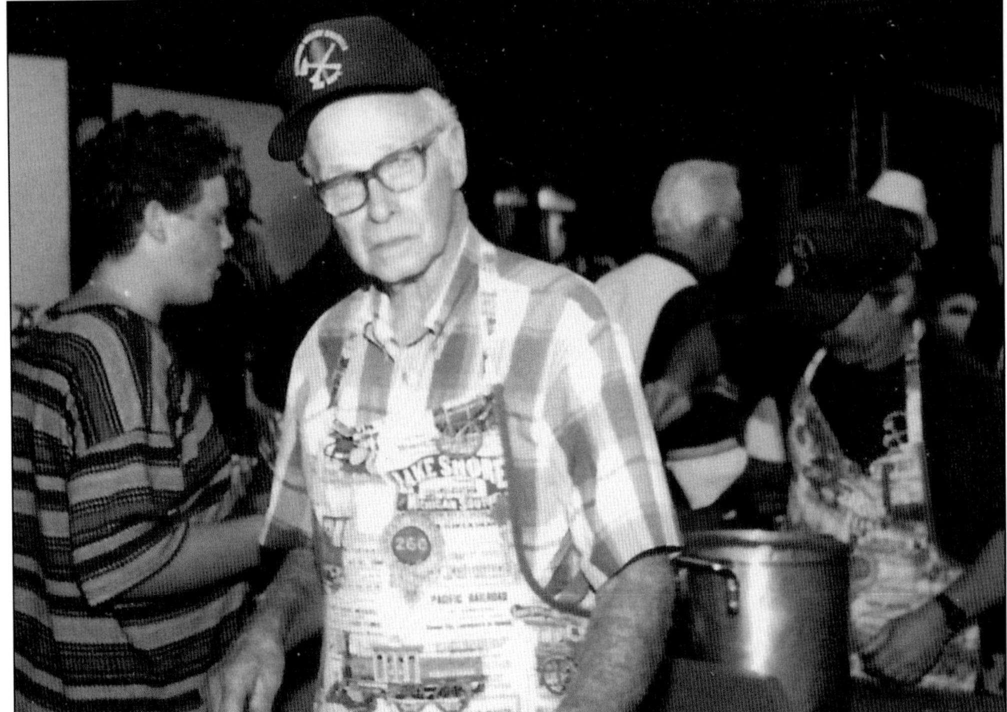

Here is a photo of John Pringle as he served salad at the Redwood Valley Calpella Volunteer Fire Department's annual barbeque. Pringle was very active in the affairs of Redwood Valley Community Church as well as the Grange 382 master during the war years of 1943–1944. (Courtesy of the Redwood Valley Calpella Volunteer Fire Department.)

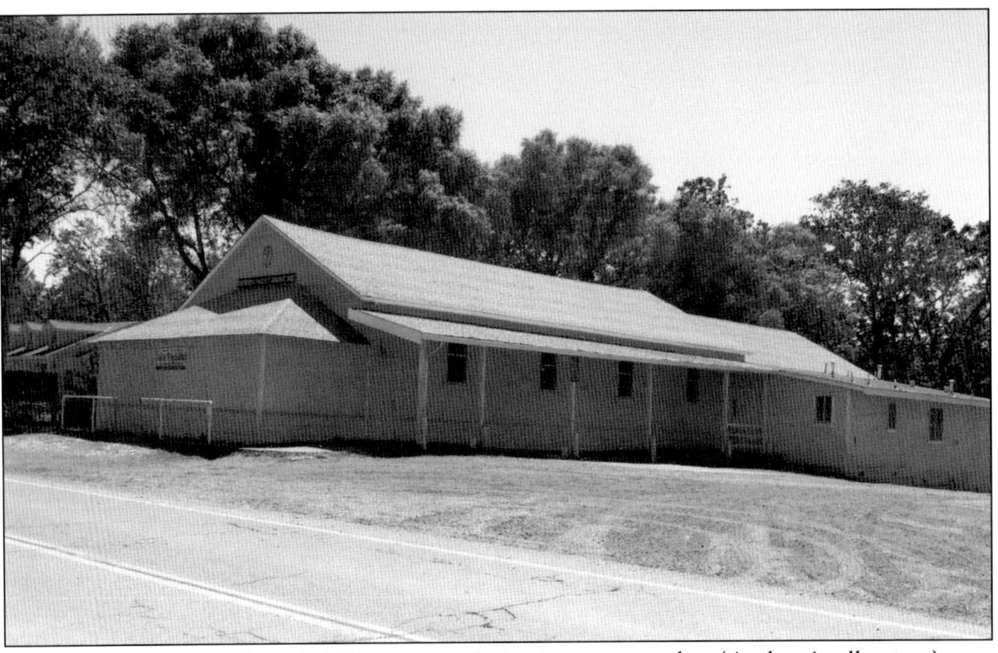

Pictured here is the Redwood Valley Grange 382 as it appears today. (Authors' collection.)

Six

Agriculture, Industry, and the Railroad

The agriculture products of the valley have evolved over the years; presently, grape growing is the main industry. Previously, many different crops were raised: pears, hops, grains, plums, and so forth. Raising livestock in the early years for sale or family use was widespread. The first bonded winery was established by Louis Finne, and the wines of Redwood Valley have earned their own appellation and are world-renowned.

Past and present industries and businesses include the charcoal kilns, Redwood Valley Supply Co., realty offices, beauty shops, bakeries, Lake County Fruit Exchange, a manganese mine, Calpella Plywood Plant, North Sonoma Wines, Redwood Valley Shopping Center, Vic's Place, Barra's fruit-drying yard, Taylor's Tavern, Coyote Valley Casino, Little Bakers Market, the industrial park, a cheese-making plant, a pallet mill, a Savings Bank of Mendocino County branch, organic soil operation, Redwood Valley Gravel, Pizza Etc., cafés and restaurants, a health clinic, service stations, and garages, as well as many wineries and tasting rooms.

There were several mills in and near Redwood Valley: E.M. Hansen Jr. Lumber Company (1960–1995), Burgess Lumber Company, Nelson Mill (1910–?), Plywood Fabricators (1960–1985), Redwood Valley Hardwood (1950–1960), Isaac C. Reed Mill (October, 1865–?), St. John Mill (1940–1950), Staley Shingle Mill (1920s–?) in Reeves Canyon, and T and K Sawmill Corporation. As timber was depleted, most mills closed.

After surveys for the railroad were made in 1899, construction started, with freight and passenger services beginning on May 5, 1902. This made a significant change to Redwood Valley residents. Employment increased to maintain the tracks and supply wood for the first wood-burning engines. Residents enjoyed receiving daily newspapers and faster mail service. The train also transported their crops, wood, charcoal, tan oak bark, and manganese to the Bay Area. The flag station at Redwood Valley was named Basil for over 30 years in order to eliminate any confusion with northern stations such as Sherwood Valley and Ridgewood. This was very unpopular; at the request of the Redwood Valley Improvement Club, it was changed back to Redwood Valley. Presently, there is no railway service.

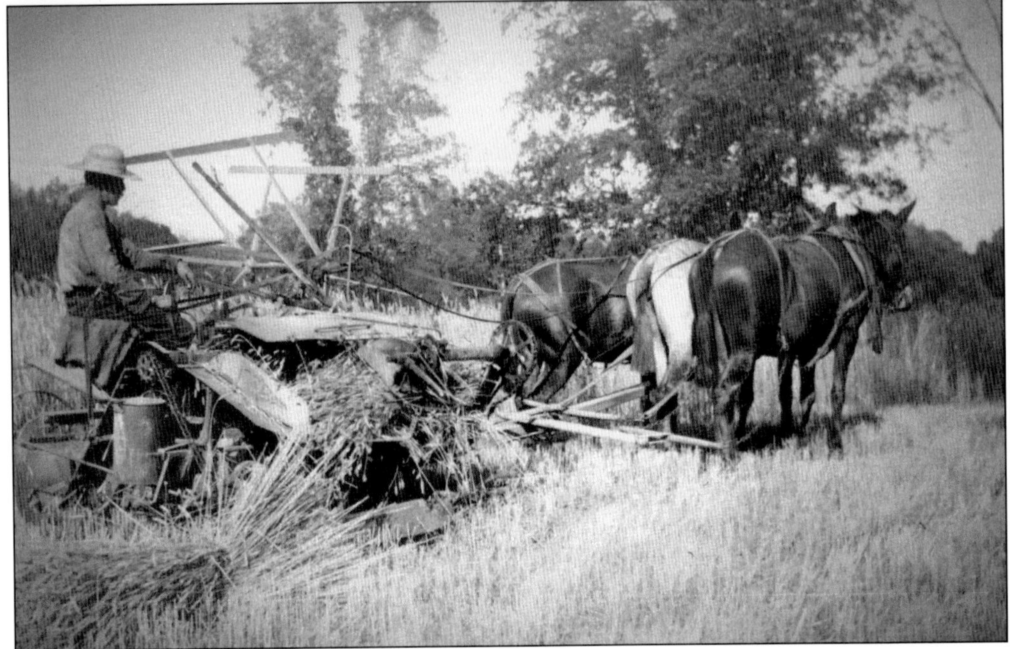

One of the early agricultural pursuits in the valley was food for livestock. Pictured here is a straw binder at work. As the machine was drawn through the field, it bound the straw into bundles to be transported and sold or put into storage for livestock. This photograph is believed to have been taken on the Finne Ranch.

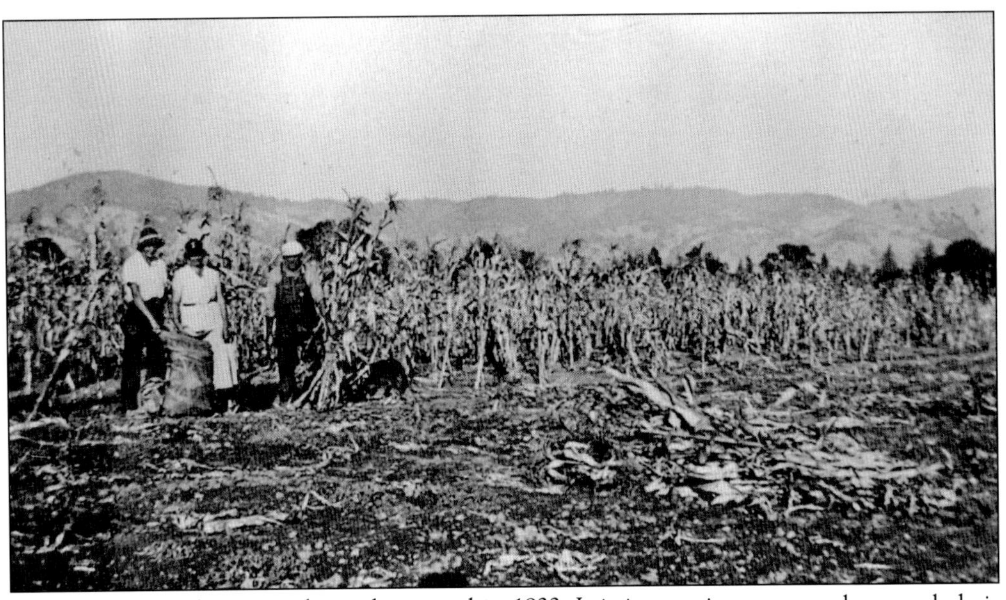

In this photograph, corn is being harvested in 1933. It is interesting to note that one lady is wearing jeans, and the other, a dress.

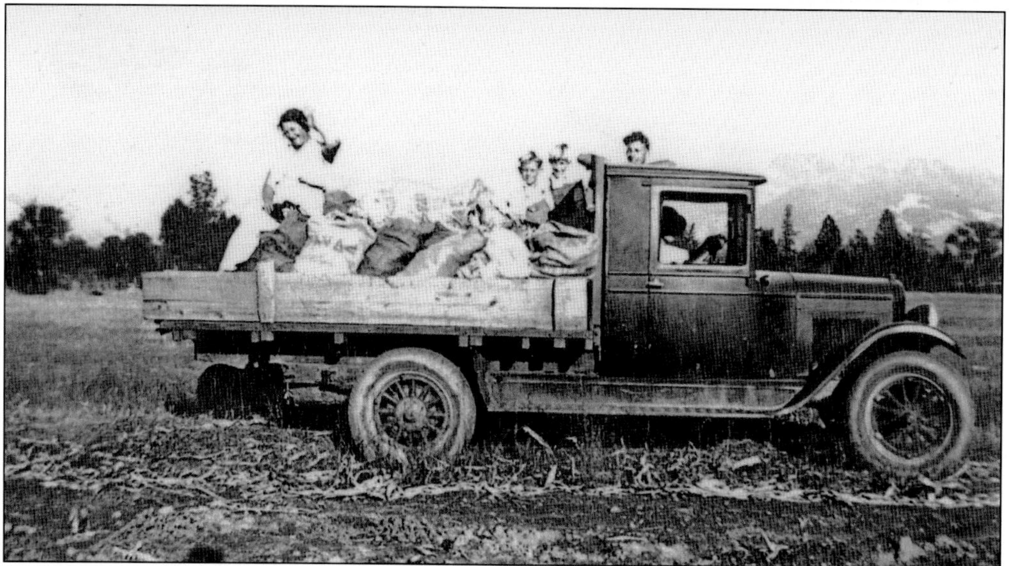

Hauling the corn harvest was a whole family undertaking, as can be seen in this photograph.

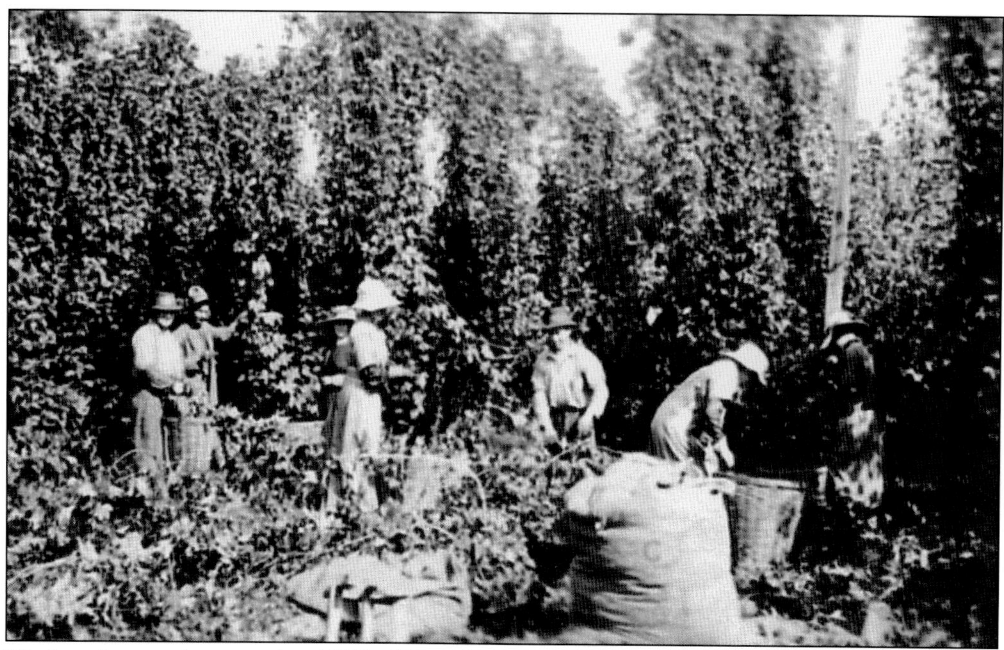

Workers harvest hops at the Alf Ford Ranch in 1914. This was a tedious and time-consuming process, but pickers could make $2.50 to $3 per day, as the farmer paid $1 per hundred pounds harvested, according to a *Mendocino Dispatch Democrat* article of 1906. The Ford Ranch had 25 acres in hops. In 1906, hops could be raised and make a profit at 7¢ or 8¢ per pound.

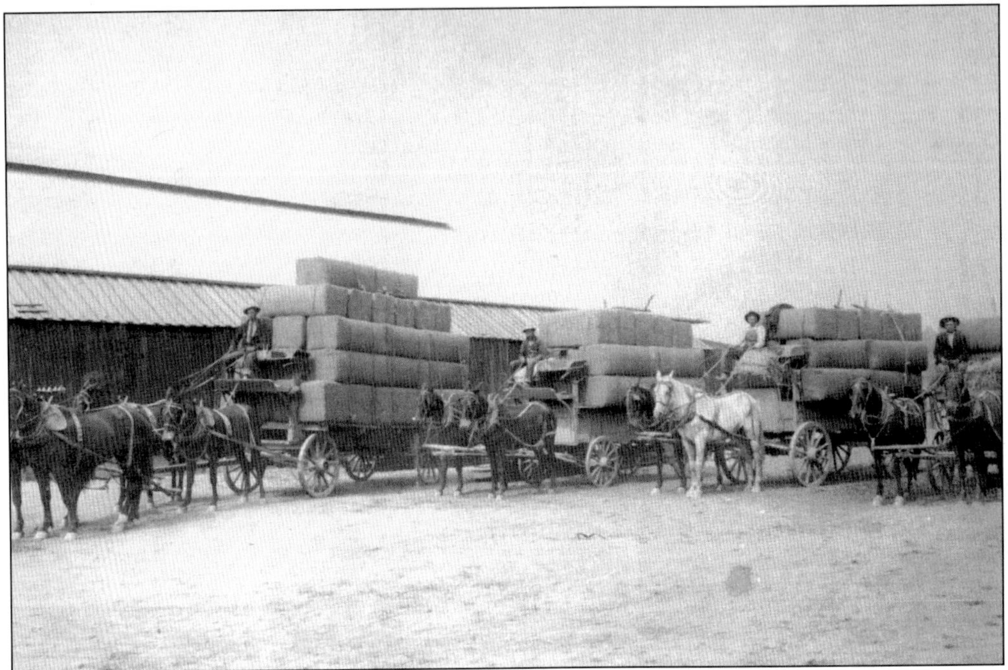

These hops are being transported for sale after being bundled into the large burlap bales. In 1916, Redwood Valley had 90 acres under hops, and the output was 750 bales. The season for harvesting usually lasted a little over three weeks. Among the hop growers in the valley were Wooley, Banker, Ford brothers, J.A. Ford, and E.M. Nuckolls. (Courtesy of the Testa family.)

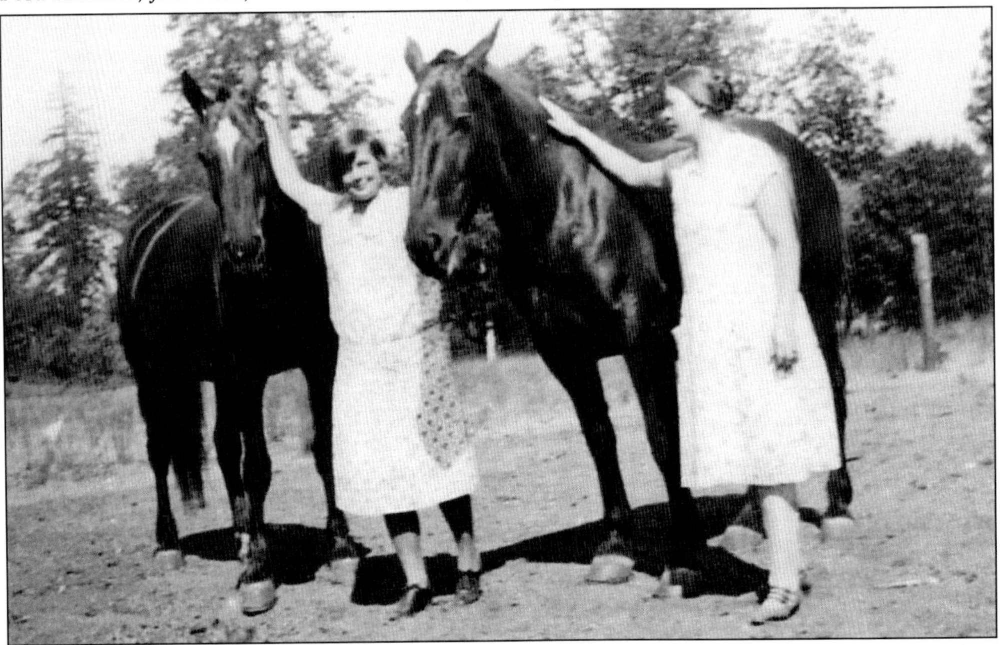

Raising horses for sale and pleasure was also undertaken in the valley and continues to this day. Annie Hietala (left) and another woman are pictured here with their horses. None of the horses in Redwood Valley achieved the fame of their neighbor to the north at the Howard's Ridgewood Ranch—Seabiscuit.

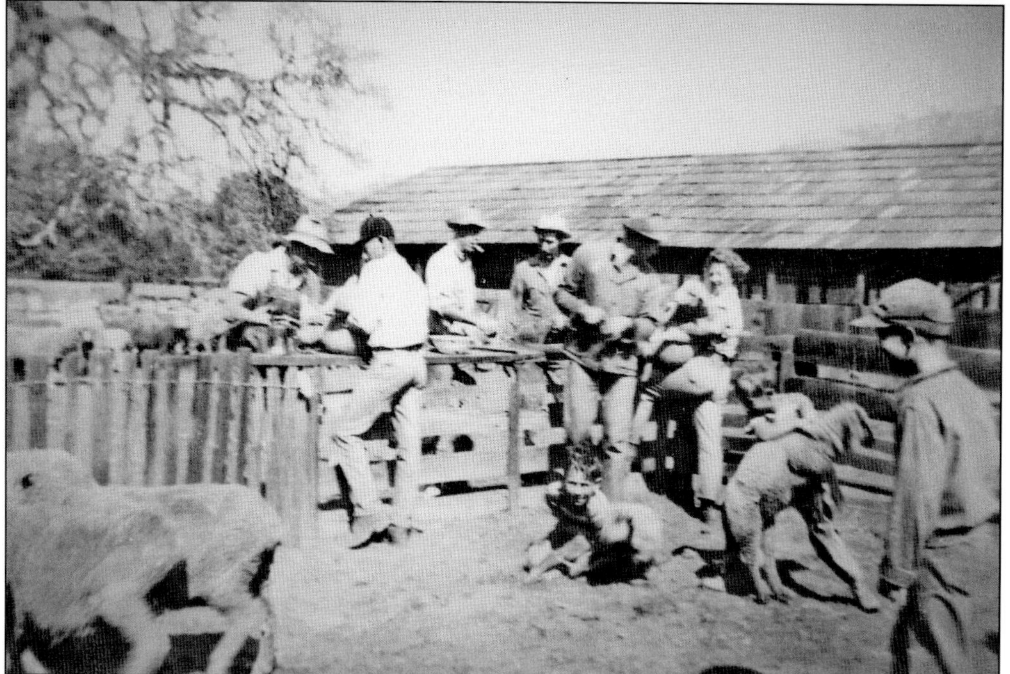

This photograph was taken during sheep shearing at the Schultz Ranch in 1953. From left to right are John Ricetti, Ray Schultz, Bob Johnson, Hilda Schultz, Marvin Ford, Johnnie Ricetti, Thomas Ricetti, Johnnie Ford, and Jimmy Ford.

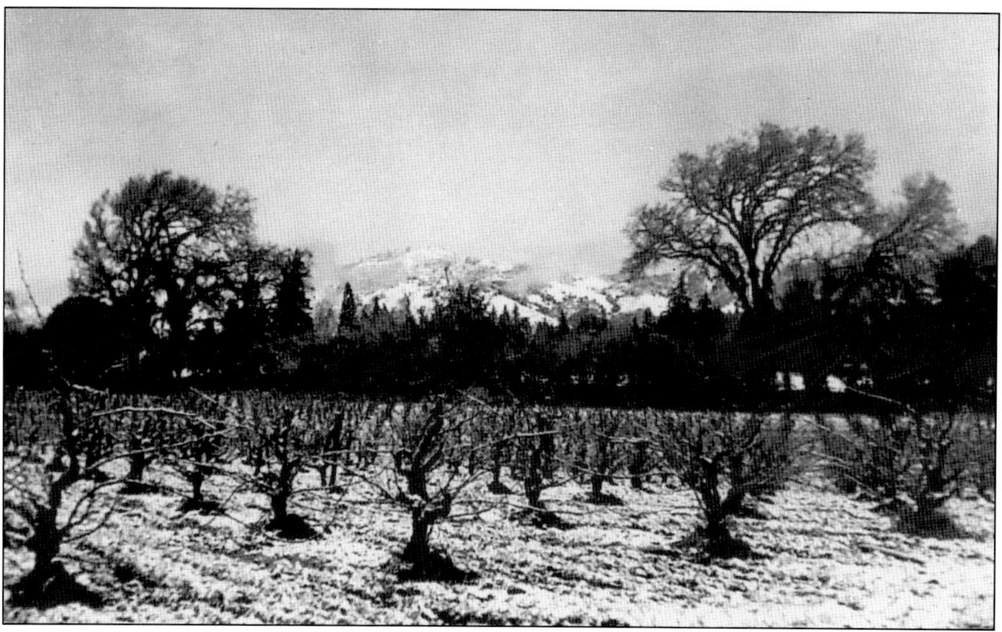

As the years passed, grapes became the crop of choice. The vineyards reminded many of the Tuscany region in Italy, and the soil seemed to allow the grapes to thrive. Eventually, they became the biggest legal cash crop in the valley and achieved their own geographic designation (appellation). This photograph was taken to show the newly fallen snow in the valley and the far hills, an infrequent occurrence.

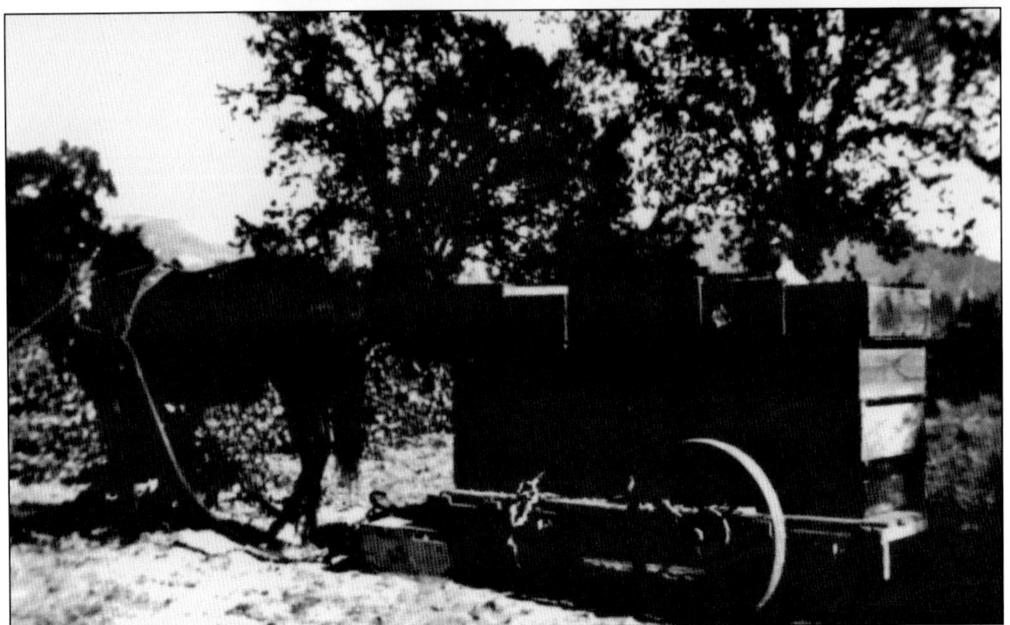

Pictured here in 1928 is a sled with skids on the front, in place of wheels, hauling grapes from the vineyard. At this time, wooden boxes were used for harvesting, as pickers were paid by the box. The boxes can be seen toward the back of the wagon. The crop would next be sent to the railroad station for transport south.

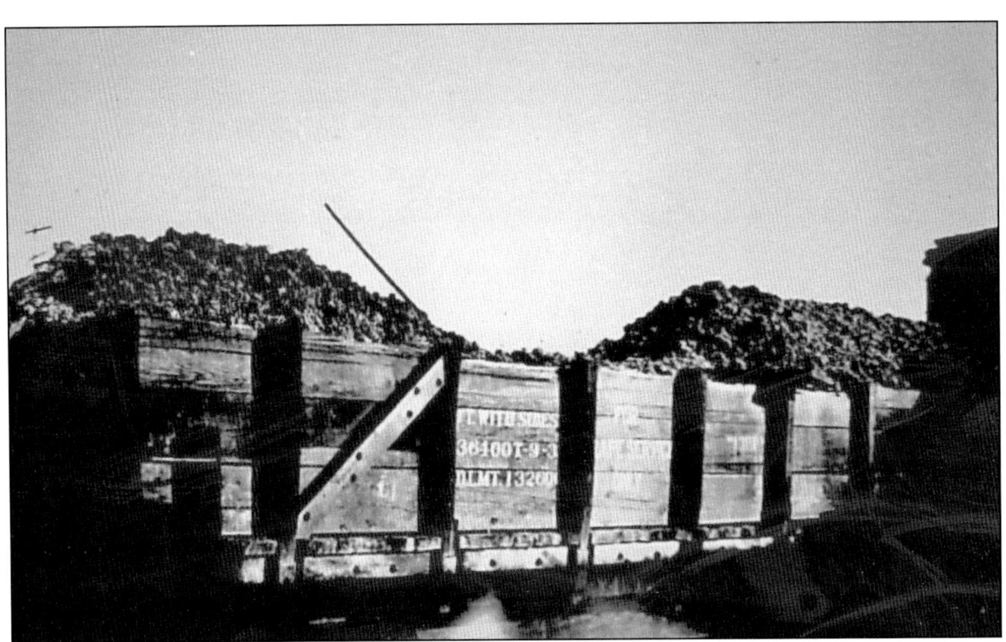

At the railroad station, the grape crop was loaded into wood containers on the train labeled "For Grape Service Only" and sent south for processing at wineries such as Asti in Sonoma County. This photograph was taken in 1930s.

This is a relatively unique photograph, as the workers rarely took time out for taking photographs. This group picks grapes around 1930. Many times, it was a family affair, with children taking part and helping to earn money.

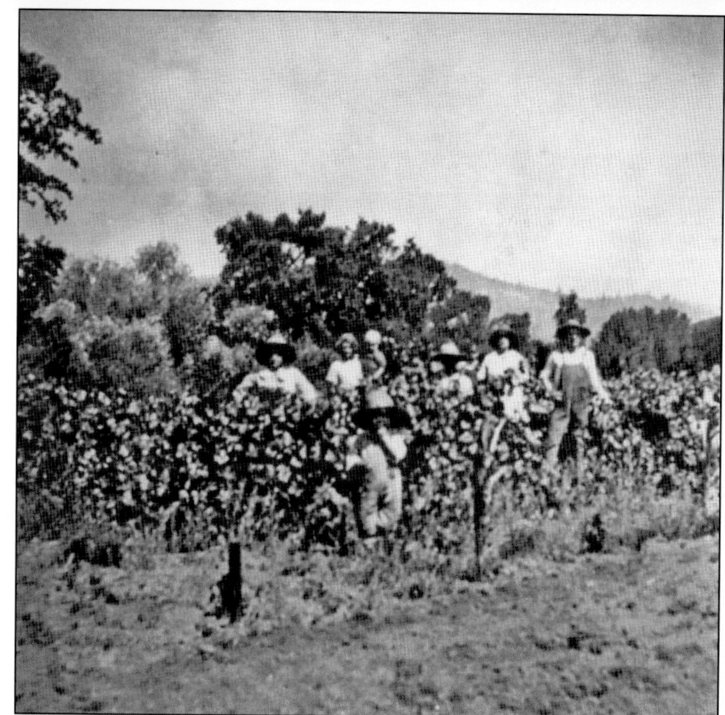

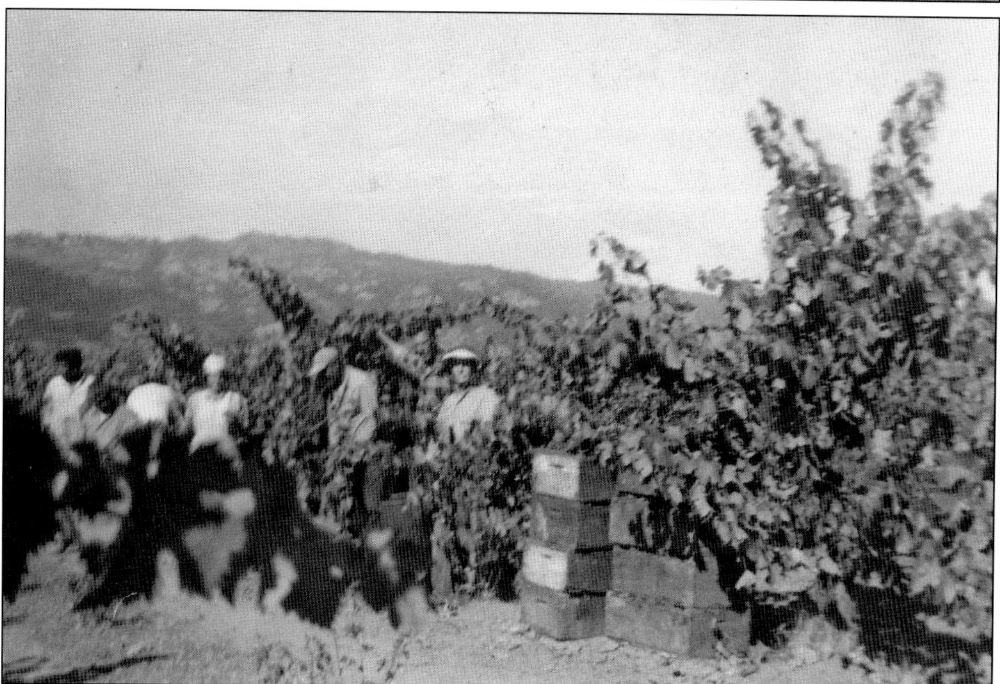

As seen in this photograph from October 1959, little has changed in the harvesting of grapes since the 1930s. This photograph shows the boxes used out in the field. A chalk mark was made on the end to give each worker credit for that box. Also, the vineyard owner's name and location were often stenciled on the box end. Natalina Martinelli is pictured here facing the camera, wearing a white bandana. (Authors' collection.)

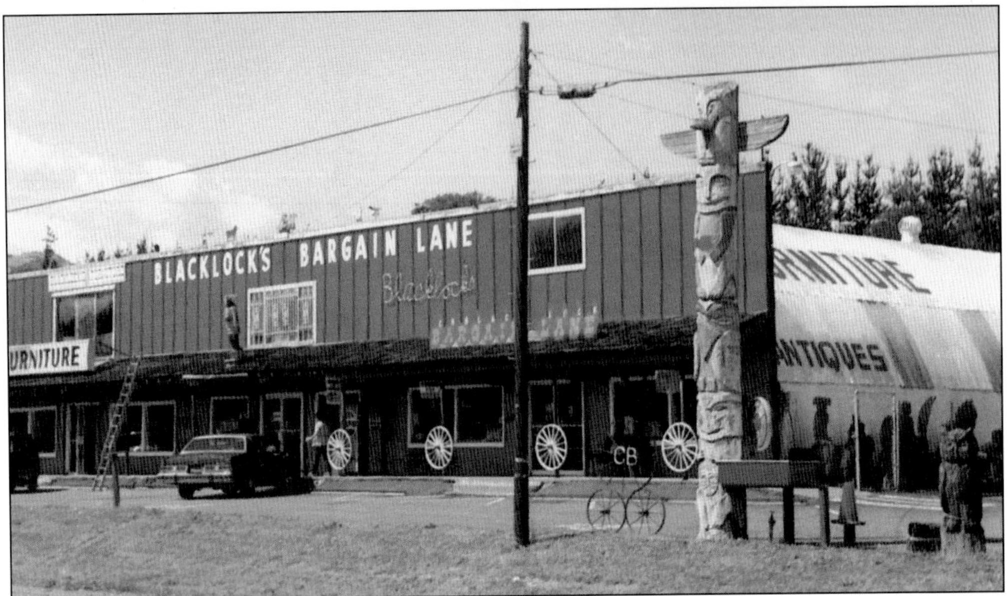

Blacklock's Bargain Lane was on the east side of Highway 101 in Redwood Valley. It was painted bright red with totem poles out front. Blacklock's carried antiques, Indian baskets, dolls, and guns, as well as old and new furniture. It referred to itself as "the browsing spot of the far west with the country store atmosphere." (Courtesy of the Crockett and Addelle Blacklock family.)

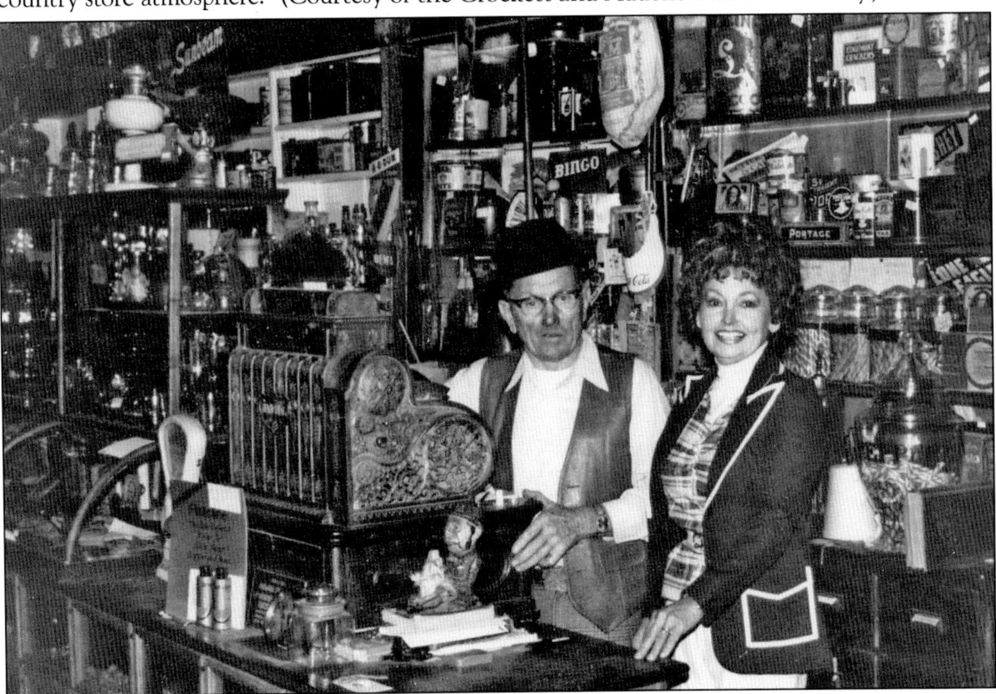

The proprietors and owners of Blacklock's, Crockett and Addelle Blacklock, are pictured here in their establishment. They had a wide variety of items, as evidenced by the shelving behind them. Both were community-minded citizens and donated needed items to worthy causes, such as the pews in the Calpella Community Church, which are still in use. (Courtesy of the Crockett and Addelle Blacklock family.)

This photograph shows the stenciling of the vineyard grower's name and location at the end of the wooden grape boxes. In this case, the name is "A. Garzini and Calpella, Cal." Andy Garzini stands to the left, and John Pasero sits on the right. (Courtesy of Lucille Rovera Neese and Susan Neese Mathis.)

Charlie and Martha Barra are pictured here at the Redwood Valley Vineyards. Charlie purchased 175 acres of vineyards in the upper valley in 1955. He was one of the first growers on the North Coast to plant chardonnay, Riesling, cabernet sauvignon, and pinot noir. Barra of Mendocino wines are made from 100 percent organic-certified vineyards. (Photograph by Tom Liden, courtesy of Redwood Valley Vineyards.)

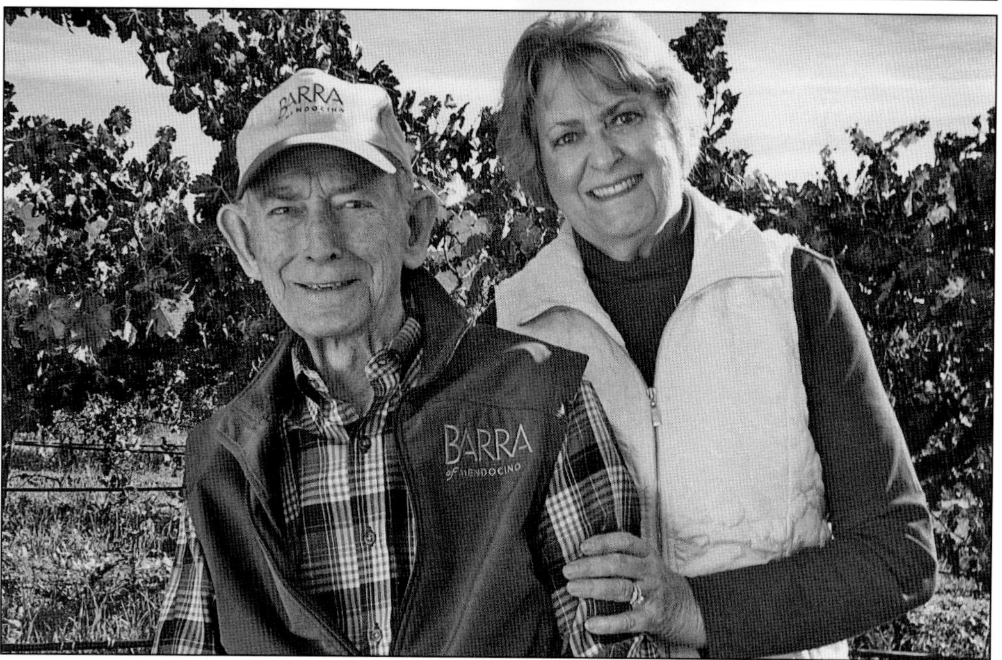

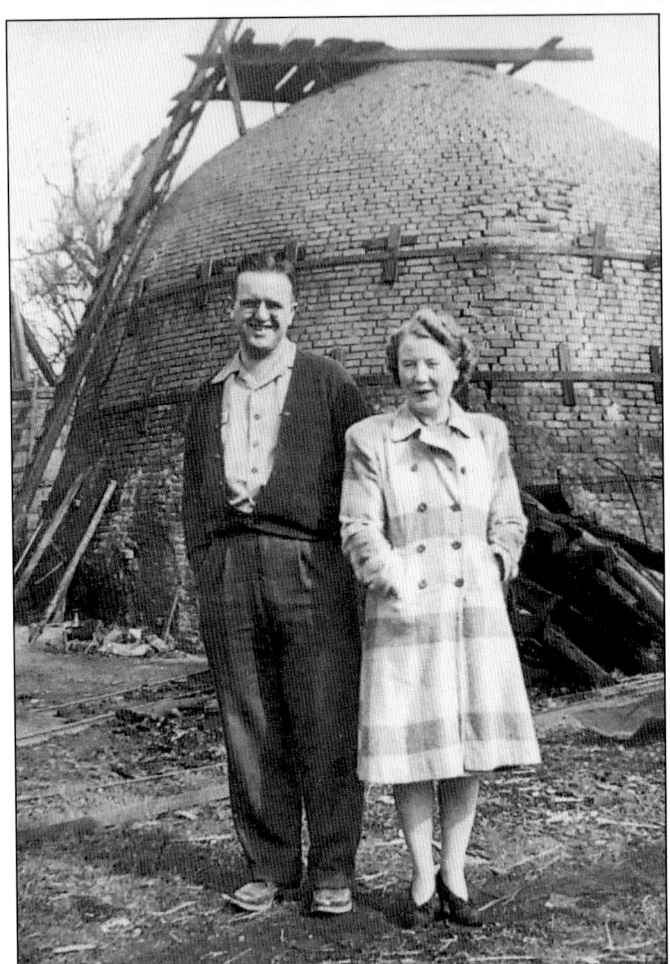

Seen here are Fred and Mary Goudge. Members of the Goudge family operated the Charcoal kilns from the close of World War I to the beginning of World War II. The Noble Electric Steele Company of San Francisco built and operated the charcoal kilns on the site north of School Way and adjacent to the railroad tracks. There were three kilns in which 40 to 50 cord of wood, having been precut into four-foot logs, were placed and baked to achieve the desired charcoal.

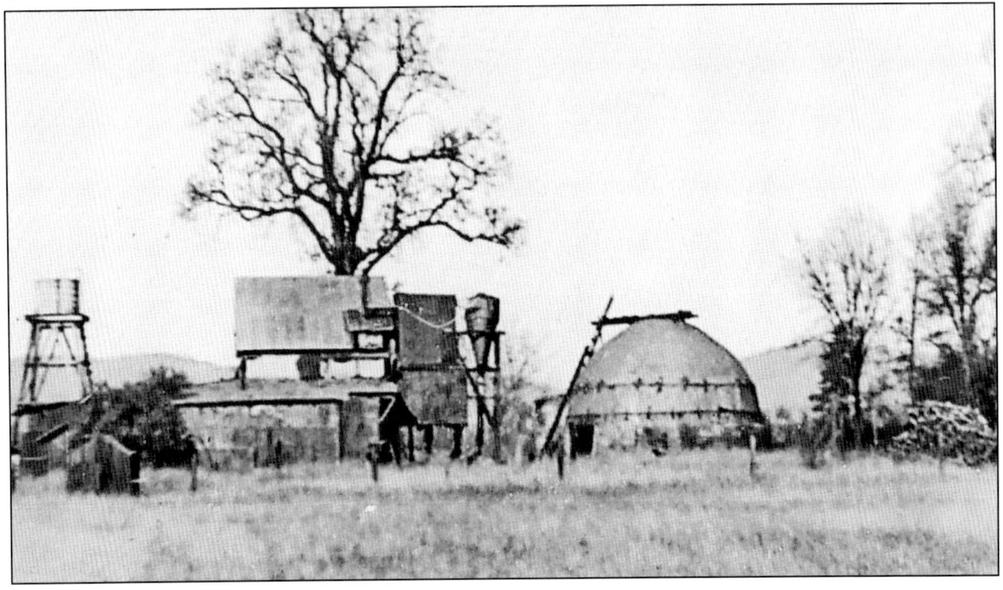

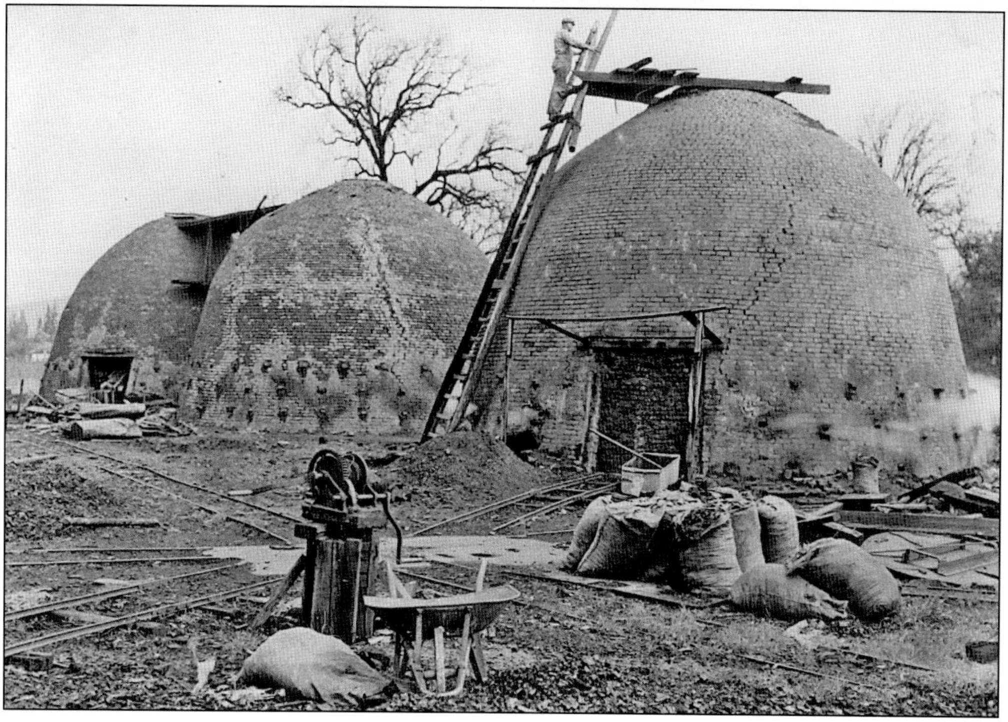

After the charcoal has baked for three to four weeks, it cools for an additional two weeks. The tracks shown took the charcoal out to the railroad cars just to the left of the photographs for hauling to the Bay Area. There were two spectacular fires at the kilns, one in 1920 and again in 1933. The community firefighting volunteers were able to save the kilns in both instances.

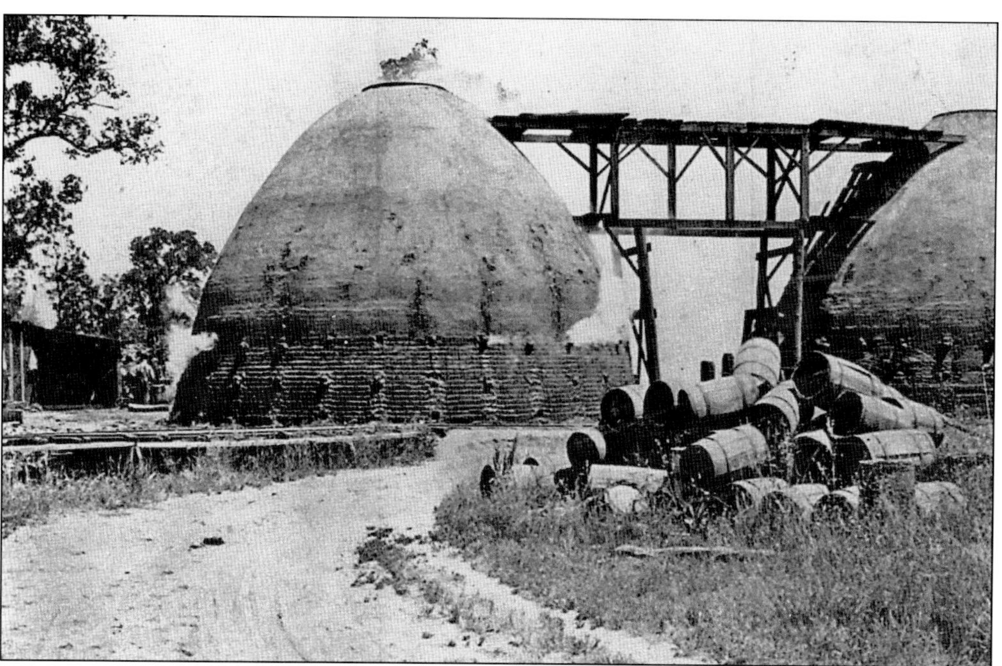

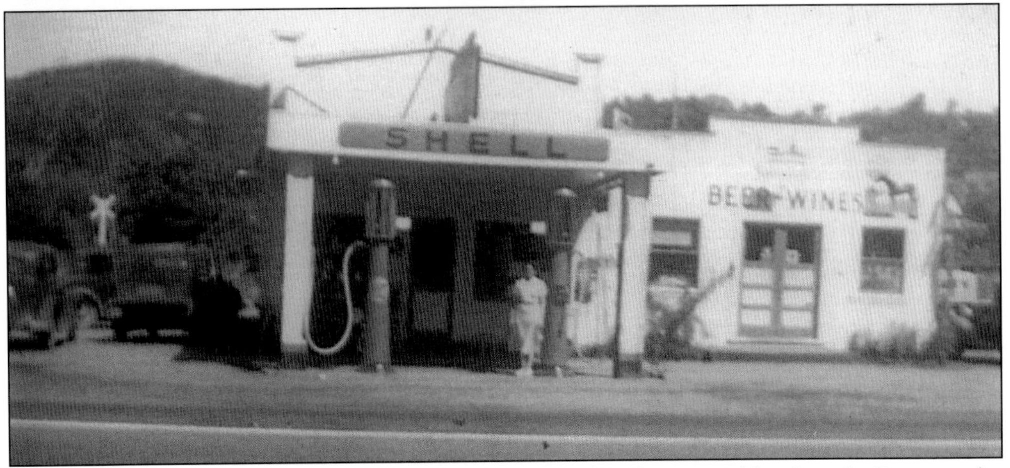

A Shell Service Station and grocery store were owned and operated by Angelo Poma at the southeast corner of Highway 101 and Moore Street in downtown Calpella. Notice the railroad sign to the left rear; it is still there. Photographed in the 1930s, this is where the Superette is now located. (Courtesy of the Testa family.)

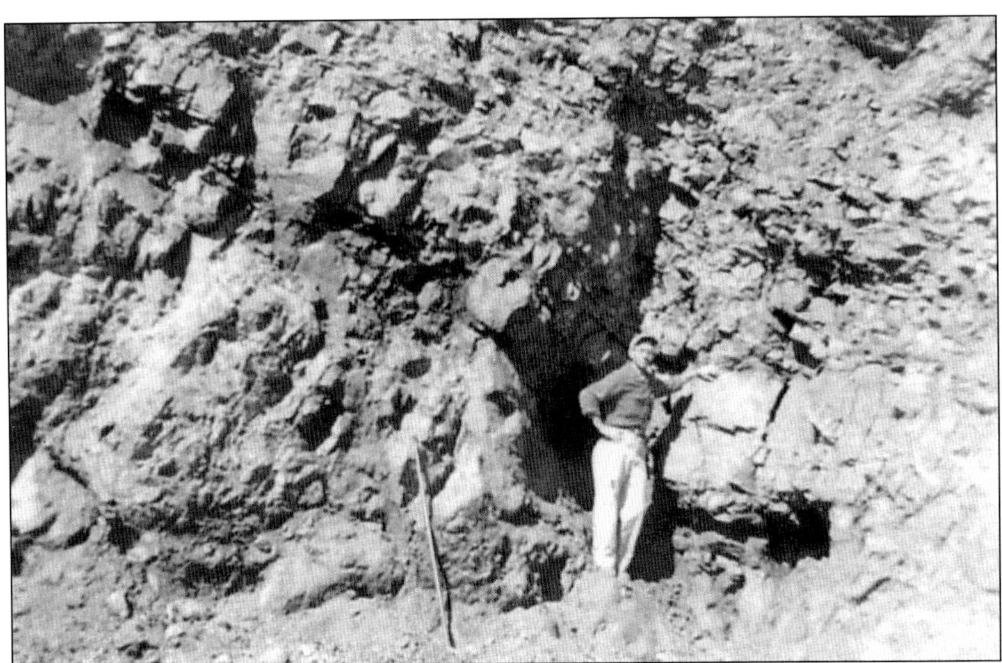

The manganese mines were operated by the Noble Electric Steele Company of San Francisco from 1914 to 1917. They were located on the Skull Mountain Ranch at the head of Redwood Valley. This photograph was taken in 1956.

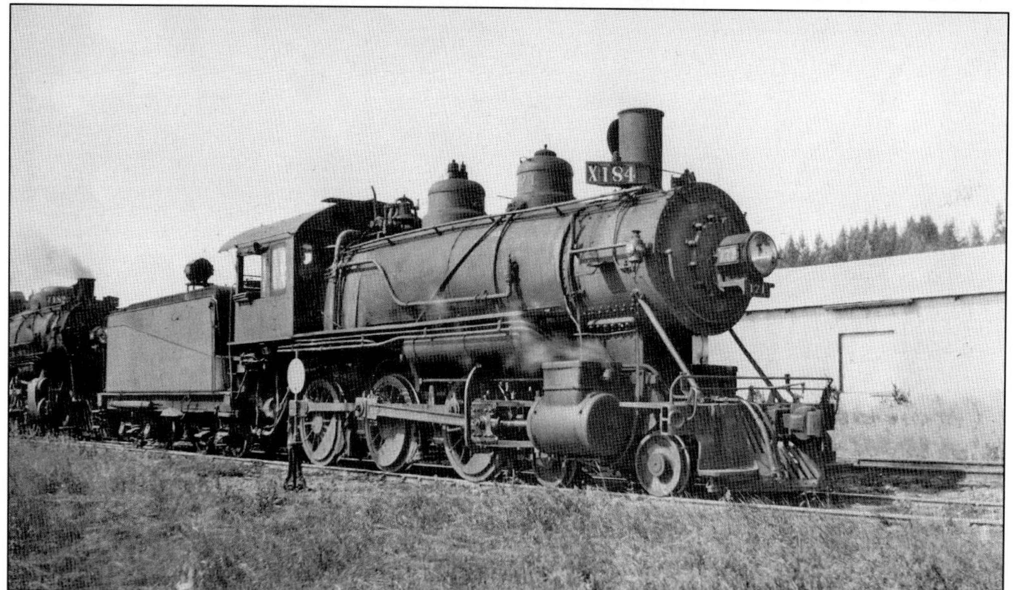

Engine No. 171 is pictured here double-heading with engine No. 184 toward the Laughlin grade and then onto Willits. A second helper engine, such as No. 171, was added at the Redwood Valley Station to assist in the steep climb over the hill. The building in the background served as warehouse for agricultural products to be shipped by rail. The railroad station greatly supported Redwood Valley's agriculture and other industries.

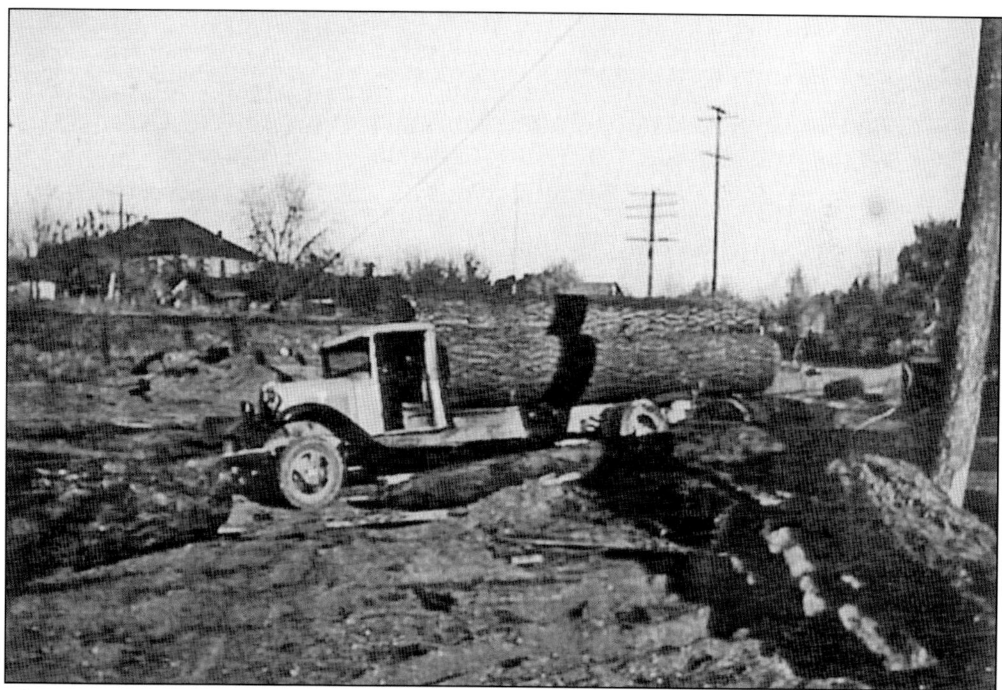

This is a 1930s photograph of two logs from Cave Creek already loaded at the Calpella logging operation. The logs were so huge, they had to be cut in half to order to be placed and transported on the early trucks. (Courtesy of Lucille Rovera Neese and Susan Neese Mathis.)

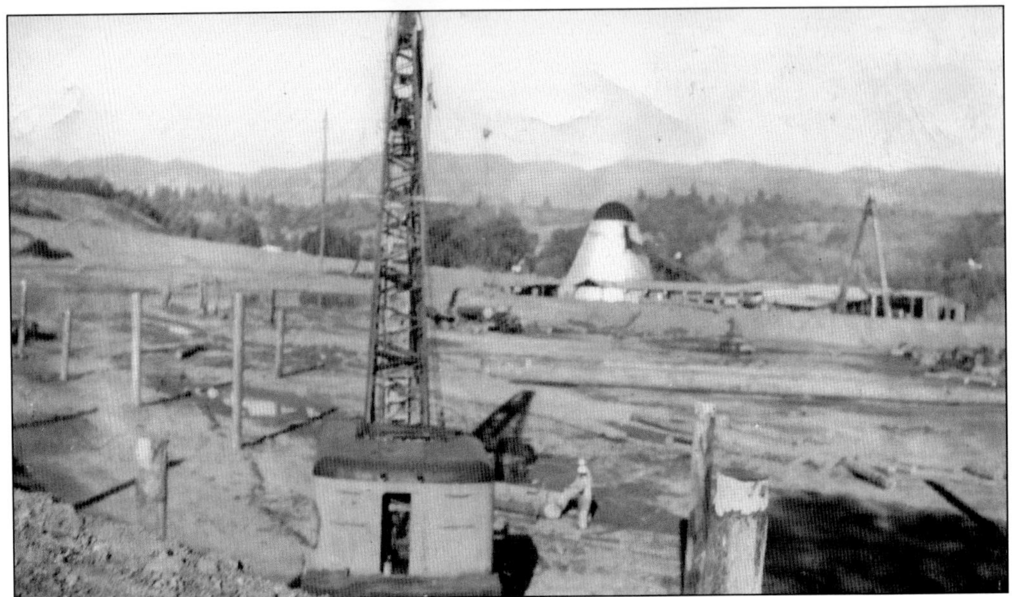

The Calpella plant had a crane for moving logs, in the foreground, and a teepee burner in the background. The teepee burned the scraps generated from the cutting of the logs into boards. These chips are now used in making particle board. (Courtesy of Lucille Rovera Neese and Susan Neese Mathis.)

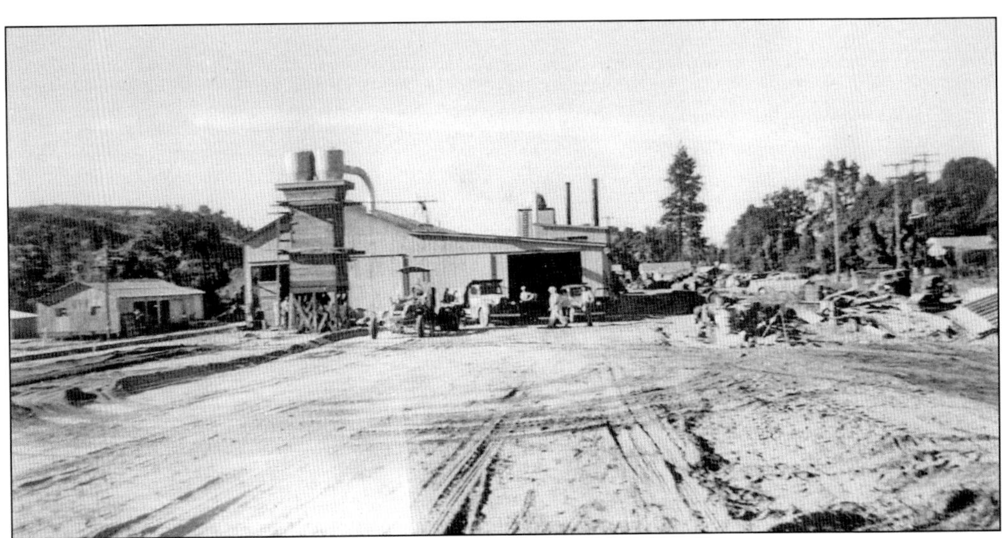

Gaetano Testa sold the land to the Calpella Plywood Mill in the 1930s; here the completed mill is shown in full operation on July 6, 1948. (Courtesy of the Testa family.)

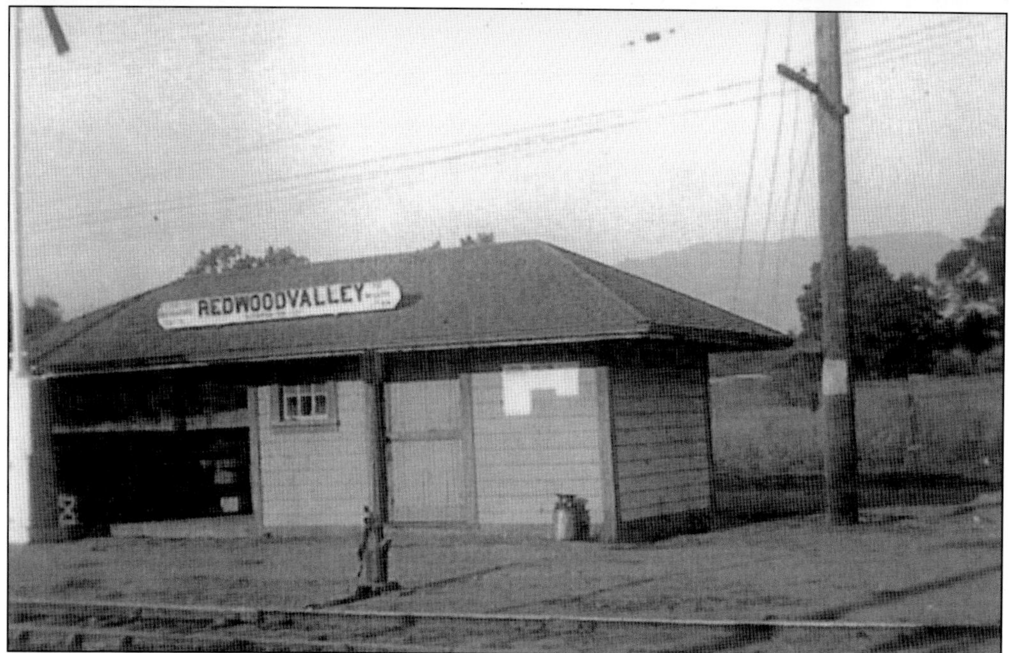

Shown here is the railway station at Redwood Valley, with its new sign, after the name had been changed back to Redwood Valley from Basil. It was a flag station, where the train would stop for passengers if it were flagged to stop. Helper engines were always added at the Edwood Valley Station to help the trains over Laughlin Mountain on the way to Willits.

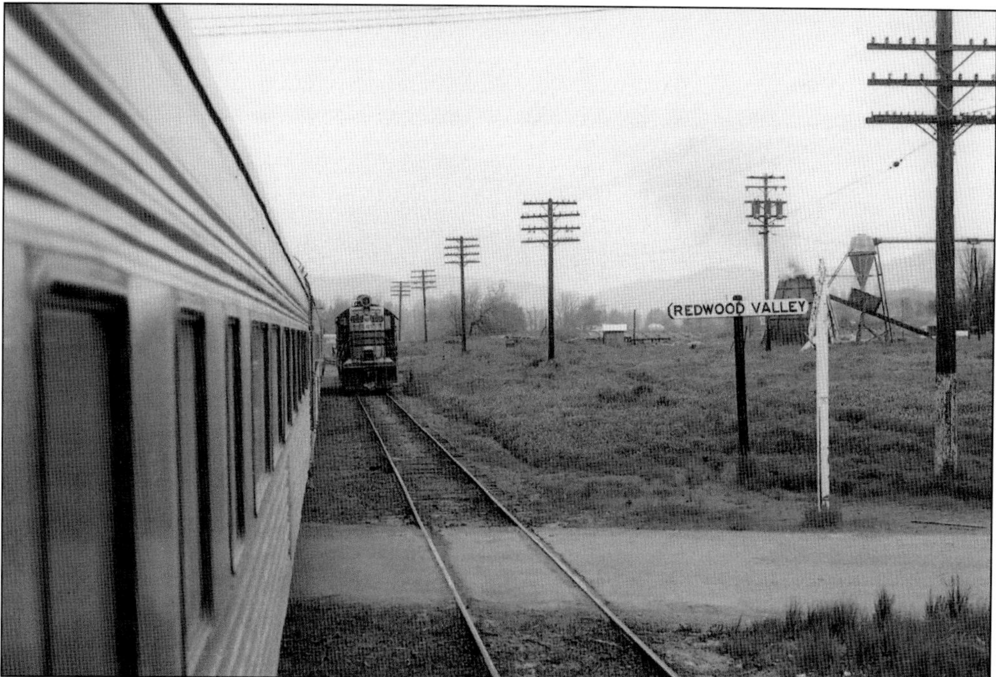

This is the view from the train as it approached the Redwood Valley Station heading north. One may view a teepee burner just to the right of the Redwood Valley sign. School Way is the dirt road in the foreground.

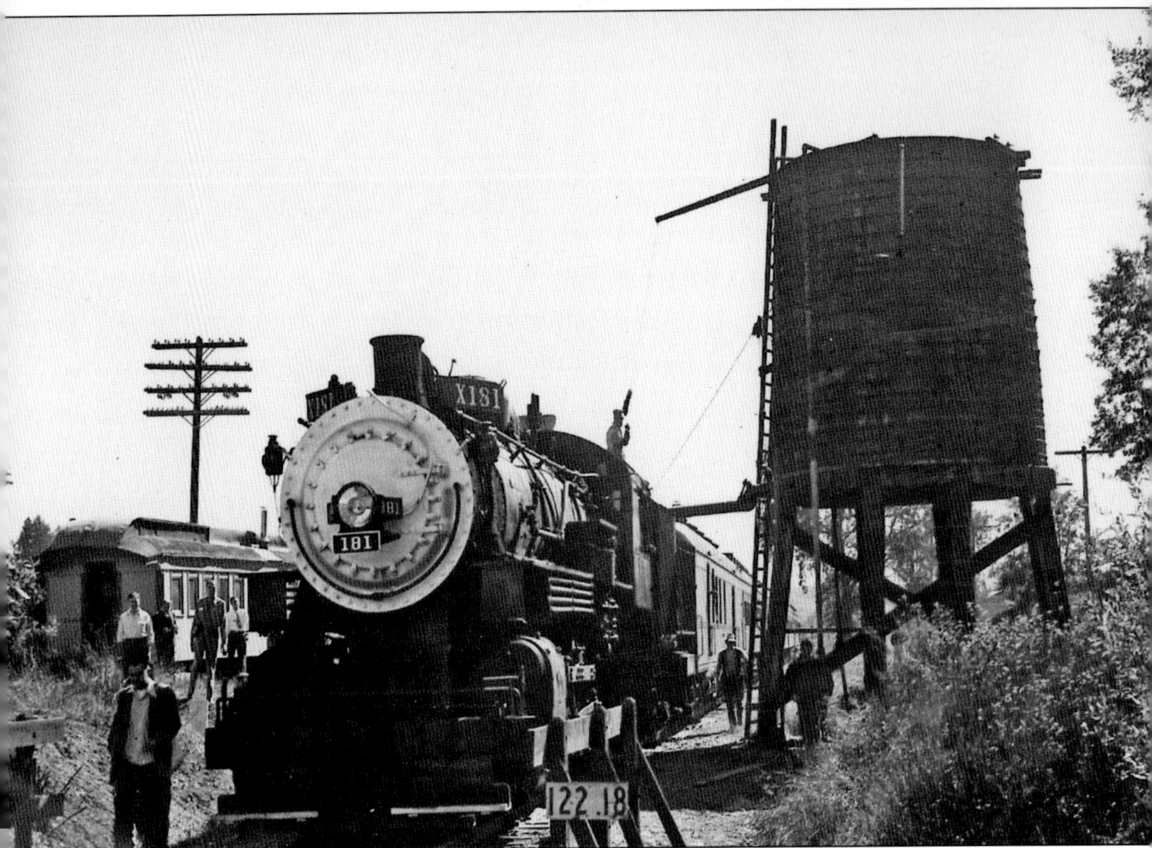

This October 11, 1947, photograph, taken by Arthur Lloyd, features Engine Extra 181 taking on water at the Laughlin Station, the other railway station located in Redwood Valley. An abandoned passenger car can be seen in the background.

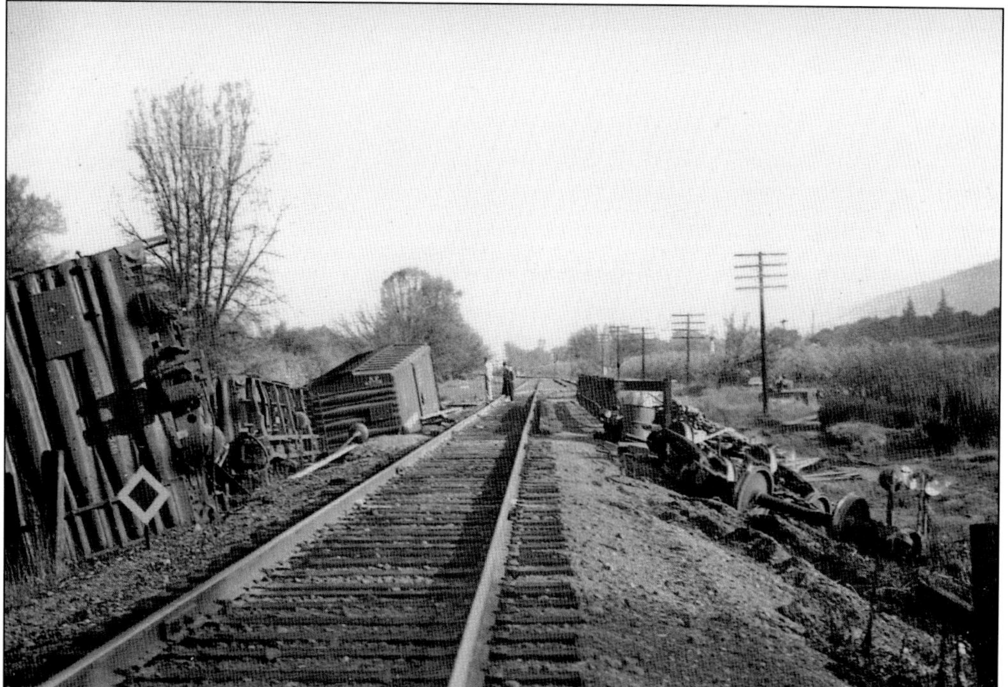

In 1959, there was a train wreck at the east switch in Redwood Valley. This photograph looks south along the tracks from School Way.

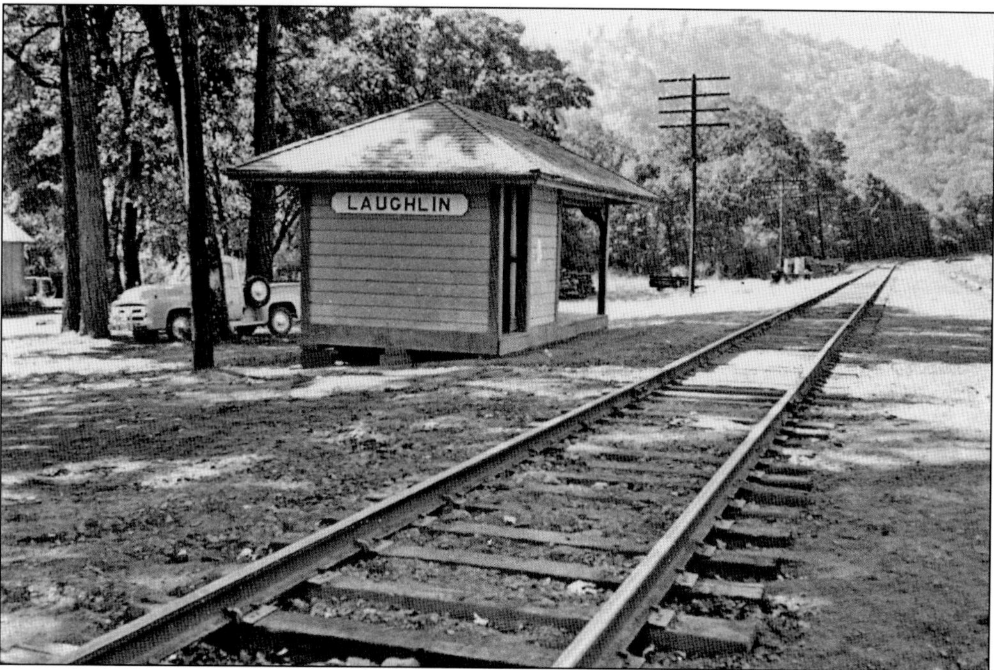

The Laughlin Depot area also contained a small store and a post office for a few years. The postmarks from Laughlin are very scarce and highly sought after by philatelists. Today, Laughlin Way runs just east of this station. Homewood Park, used by the early pioneers for picnics, was located adjacent to Laughlin Station.

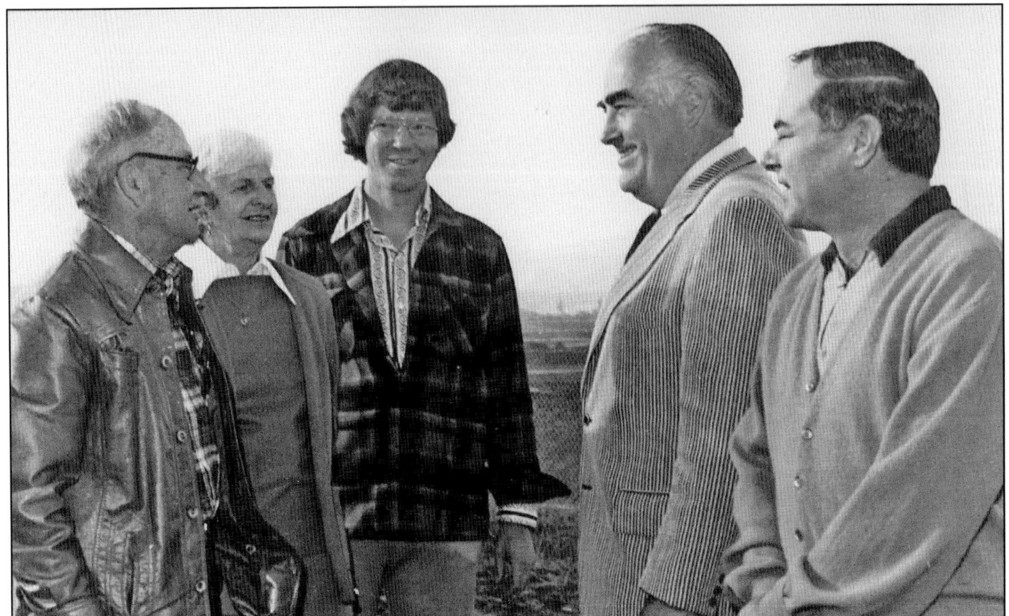

Pictured from left to right are Ernest Butow, chairman of the Board of Directors of the Redwood Valley County Water District (RVCWD); Ethel Jameson, secretary; John Wurschmidt, resident engineer, Tudor Engineering Company; Don Clausen, US House of Representatives; and Robert Brown, member of the RVCWD. All were instrumental in establishing the water district. (Courtesy of the RVCWD.)

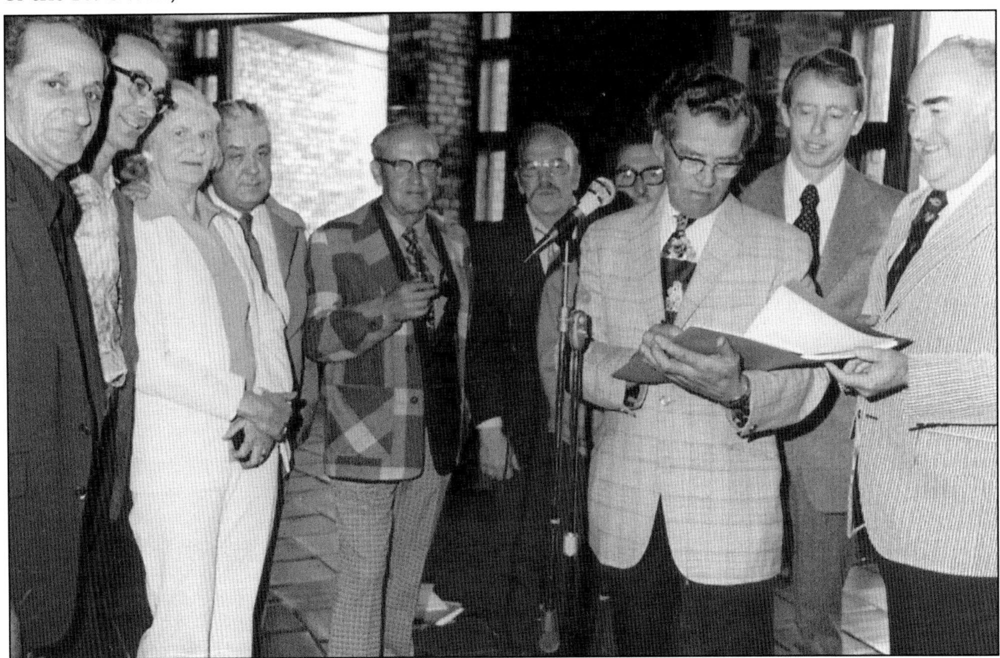

Present at the signing of the contract for the Redwood Valley Water Development Project in 1974 are, from left to right, Al Barbero, Mendocino County supervisor; Charles Barra; Ethel Jameson; Robert Vice; Ernest Butow; John Muir; Lewis Martinelli; Elvin Goodwin; Burgess Williams, Mendocino County supervisor; and Congressman Don Clausen. (Courtesy of the RVCWD.)

Seven

The Fire Department

Posters and letters were sent out on November 3, 1937, to the friends, neighbors, and residents of Redwood Valley proclaiming the need for the organization of a fire-protection district. The extent of the district was from the Mariposa Ranch to the north to Calpella in the south. It states, "It is a community hazard and the community must meet it. Every one for himself and his neighbor!"

The fire district originally met in the Redwood Valley Improvement Clubhouse on School Way. The Improvement Club was the legal head of the department until 1958, when the Redwood Valley Calpella Fire District was voted in. At its June 16, 1938, meeting, as the result of the community coming together, it approved the purchase of its first fire truck for the sum of $951. This engine is still part of the department today and provides rides to the public at the annual barbeque.

The original firehouse was located in the lot across from its present location and constructed of corrugated roofing that was obtained when the Redwood Valley Union Elementary School District took down one of its bus barns. In the 1950s, property was purchased in small segments and then a larger one from Les Stansell; this is where the department is located today. A new firehouse was constructed in 1990 and has state-of-the-art engines and equipment for the volunteers. This firehouse is dedicated to Delbert Phelps, fire chief from July 1978 until his retirement in 1995.

A special assessment for fire protection was passed on each parcel for $70. Additionally, the community supports its fire department every year when the dedicated and loyal volunteers put on a beef barbeque, a tradition that was started back in 1954 with a chicken feed.

The fire department is a shining example of what can happen when a community comes together; "Every one for himself and his neighbor!" Many personalities formed the foundation of this community enterprise: Les Stansell, Cyril Goudge, Tom L. Jameson, Delbert Phelps, and of course, the many employees and volunteers past and present.

Redwood Valley, Nov. 3rd, 1937

Friends, Neighbors,
Residents of Redwood Valley

Gentlemen:

As you must know, some of us have been trying to organize for the prevention and control of Fire in our district.

Fire is a terrible thing when it strikes, a hazard that we can only meet with preparation, co-operation and the proper equipment to fight it, - any day, any night, any place, your own property, your family's or your neighbors'.

Some of us under Chief Cy Goudge have volunteered to go any hour, day or night, to fight and help you without charge or cost, or pay of any kind.

To do this, we must have the means, the equipment to carry on. And if we have this equipment, we are promised the assistance of the Federal and State forces of the Forest Service.

At this date we have equipped ourselves with about 15 or 20 "back pumps" which are very efficient as far as they go, and we have in the treasury about $300 in cash.

We need a truck with a 300 or 500 gallon tank and pumping outfit, a chemical spray, fire axes, ladders and the usual tools necessary to meet any condition.

This outfit is going to cost in the neighborhood of $1250. We have arranged to house this equipment at or near the Charcoal Plant where the Chief is always on hand to receive telephone calls day or night and where the volunteers will speed on call, this call will be by siren or bell that can be heard over the Valley.

To raise $1250 we can ask only ourselves to contribute, and if each of us will do our part, - no matter how small, - we can raise it.

It is time for every one to do his best, no one can shirk or pass the buck to his neighbor. It is a community hazard and the community must meet it. Every one for himself and for his neighbor.

The district as we have it mapped out will extend from Mrs. Long's "Rancho Mariposa" on the North to and including Calpella on the South.

Some of us will start the list with a contribution of $25. Many others can and will match this sum. Many of us cannot pay so much, but all of us can pay something. F. A. Howland of Redwood Valley and J. A. Waldteufel of Ukiah will accept and receipt for any payment you make. There are no deductions, no charges, no commissions, every cent goes into the pot.

This briefly is the story, and now we pass it on to the residents and property owners of our Valley with confidence that the conditions warrant the effort and that we will all rise to meet it.

We are a good, tight little community, no better exists in the County, no other will scrap for their own quicker than we will, nor fail to protect what we have worked so hard for.

Do not delay and then forget it. If you do, then we must call on you, which means time, effort, and expense that you are putting up to your committee and for which they receive nothing.

Make your checks payable to "REDWOOD VALLEY FIRE CONTROL," and leave or mail them to F. A. Howland, Redwood Valley or to J. A. Waldteufel, Ukiah, **AND DO IT NOW.**

W. K. FORD, *President*
V. H. SOROLA, *Finnish Colony*
CY GOUDGE, *Chief*
J. A. WALDTEUFEL, *Secretary*

The 1937 letter and handbill sent out to the friends, neighbors, and residents of Redwood Valley called for the formation of a fire protection district: "Every one for himself and for his neighbor." It went on to say that some "would start the fund with a contribution of $25. Many of us cannot pay so much but all of us can pay something." The funds ($1,250) were raised within a few months, and the first engine was purchased. Notice the tack holes at the top where the handbill had been posted. It was signed by W.K. Ford (president), V.H. Sorola (Finnish colony), Cy Goudge, (chief), and J.A. Waldteufel (secretary). (Courtesy of the RVCVFD.)

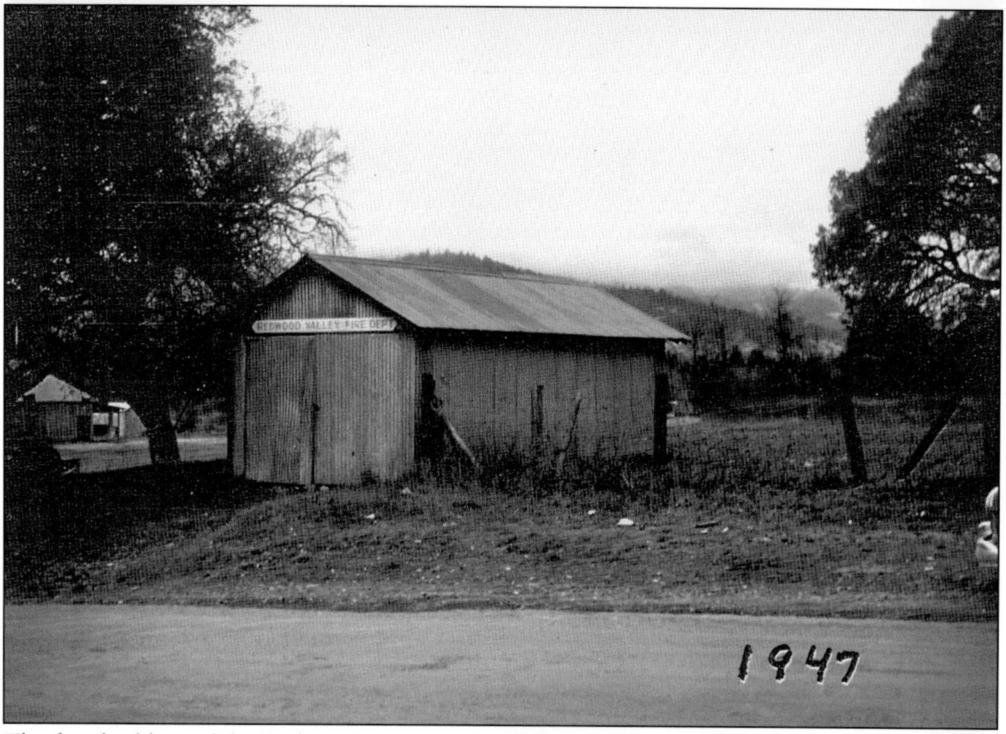

The first building of the Redwood Valley Fire Department (note that Calpella has not yet been included in the name) was located across the street from the present firehouse. It was constructed of corrugated roofing taken from a bus barn being torn down by the Redwood Valley School District. (Courtesy of the RVCVFD.)

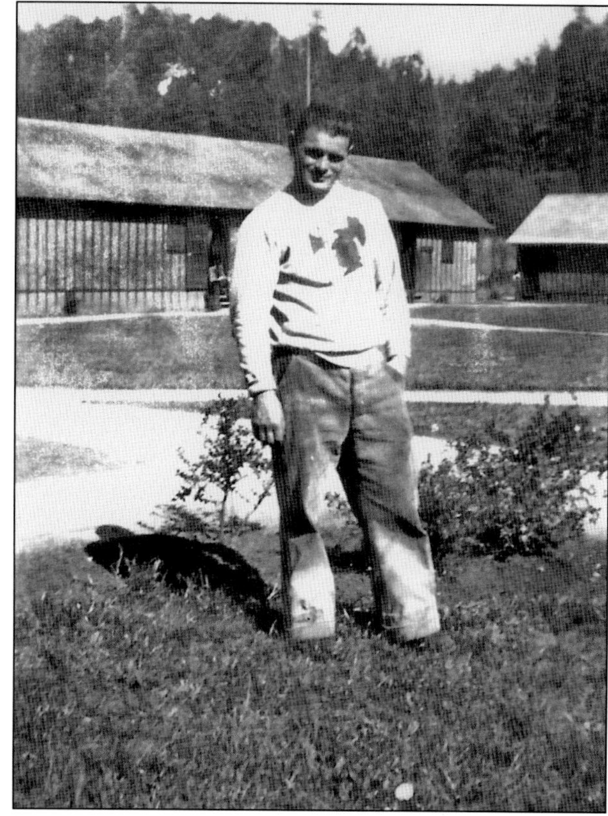

According to the minutes of the July 6, 1938, fire department board of directors meeting, Joe Borgna, pictured here, won out over Philo Phelps and William Hayes for the position of first driver in the fledgling department. He is shown in front of a Civilian Conservation Corps camp in 1939. (Courtesy of the RVCVFD.)

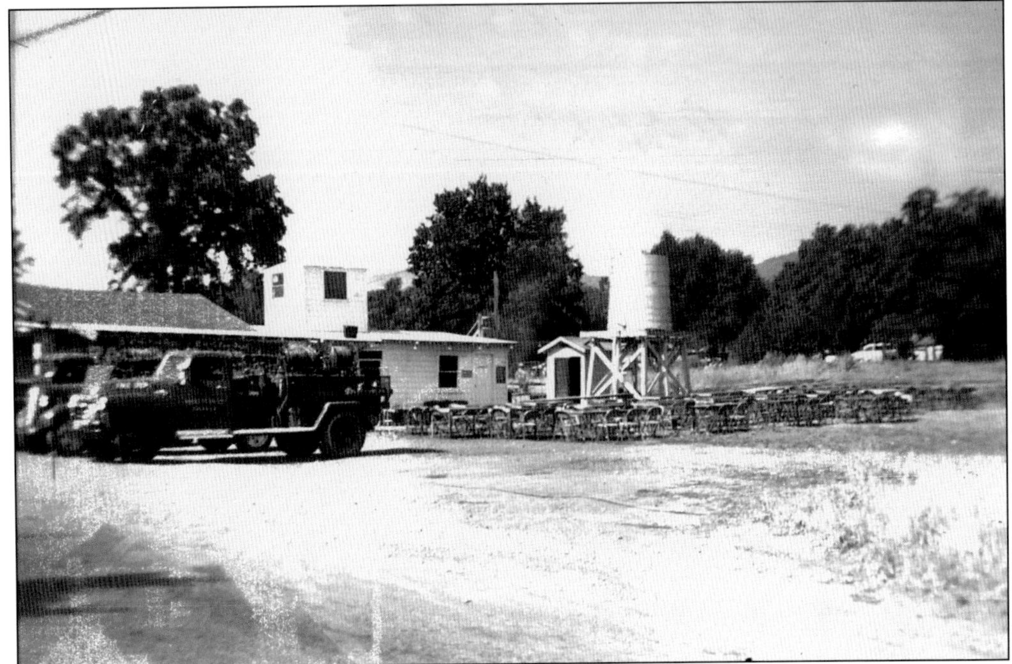

The first public barbeque was held in 1959. The barbeque has served as a successful fundraiser ever since. This photograph is from East Road, looking north. Picnic seating is in the forefront, the department's water tower in the back, and there is another tower to the left. This tower was used in a 1950s program called Ground Observer Corps, which spotted and reported aircraft. (Courtesy of the RVCVFD.)

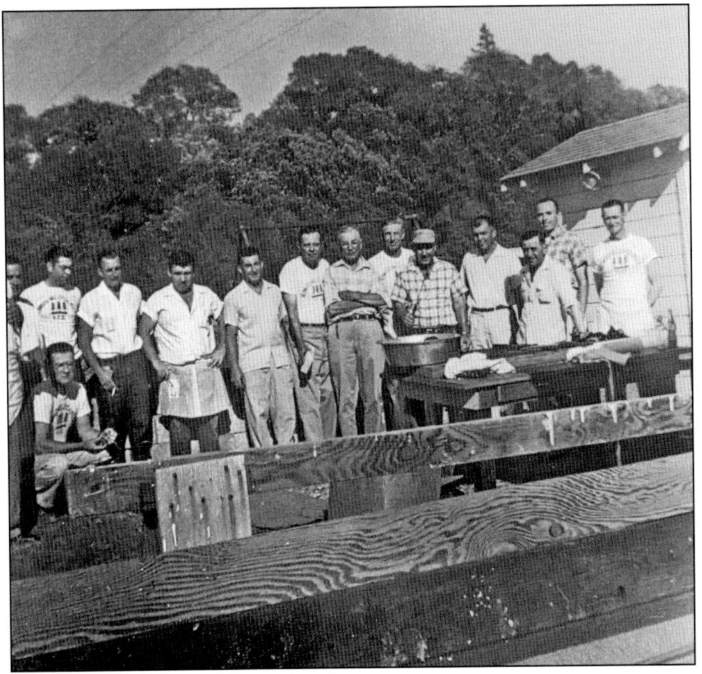

Pictured here is the department's barbeque committee; from left to right are Monk Myers (head), Arnold Ford, unidentified, Delbert Phelps (later chief), Lewis Martinelli (who is the last member from this image to continue working at the annual barbeque as of 2015), three unidentified volunteers, Domingo Deghi (with fork), four unidentified volunteers, and Fred Hand (kneeling). (Courtesy of the RVCVFD.)

Cyril Goudge was selected as the Redwood Valley Fire Department's first chief. The exact date this happened was sometime between June 18, 1939, and July 6, 1939; it unknown because there were no minutes taken at the meeting he was appointed. Goudge ran the local charcoal-making kilns north of School Way and near the railroad tracks. The first fire engine was parked there. (Courtesy of the RVCVFD.)

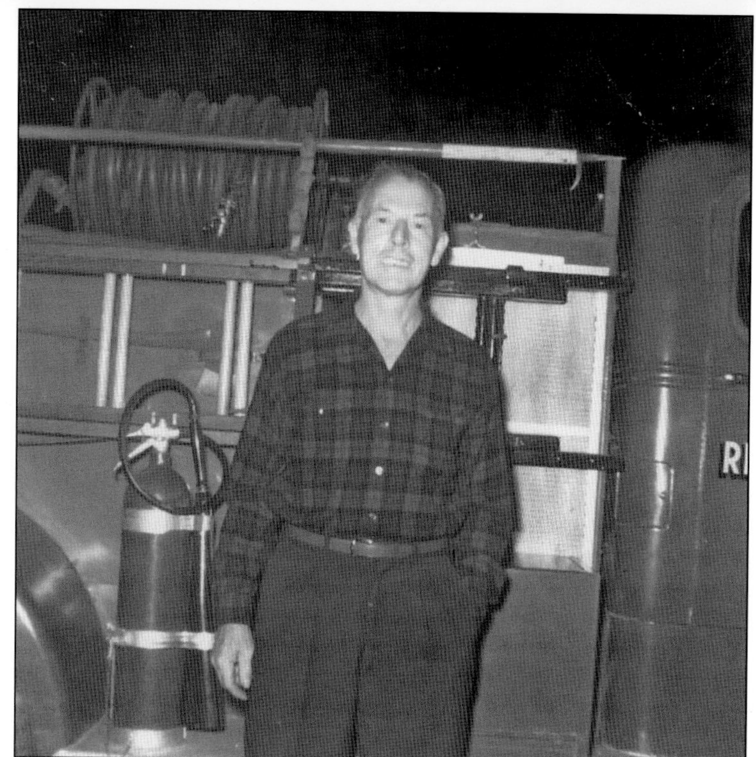

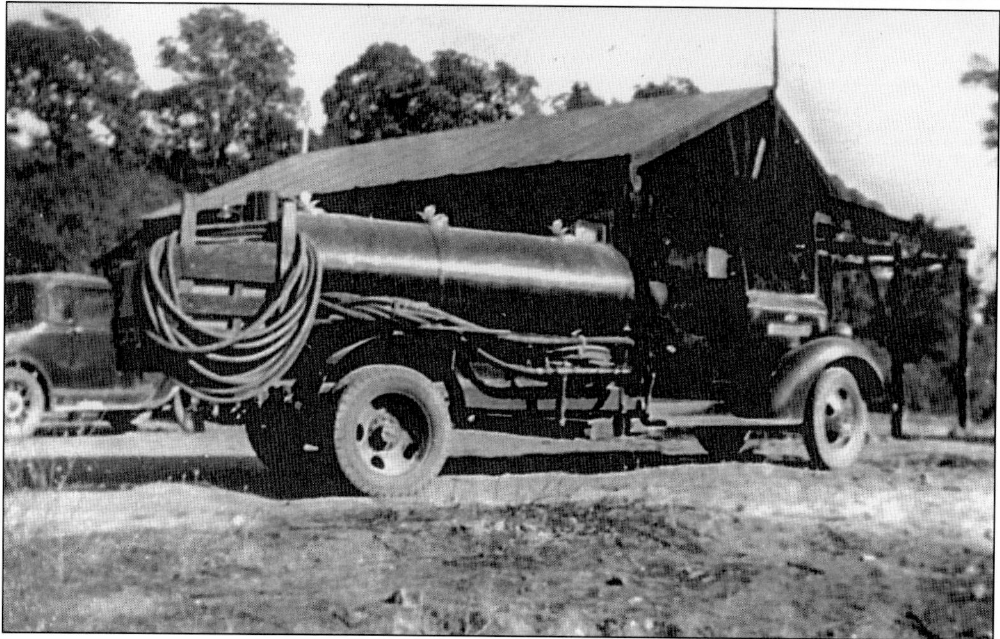

The department's first fire truck was a Chevrolet approved for purchased by the board of directors at its June 16, 1938, meeting in the amount of $951. In addition, a fire pump was approved by ranger Bruce Hufford to go along with the truck in an amount not to exceed $275. This photograph shows the fire truck in the area that is now the barbeque pit behind the firehouse. (Courtesy of the RVCVFD.)

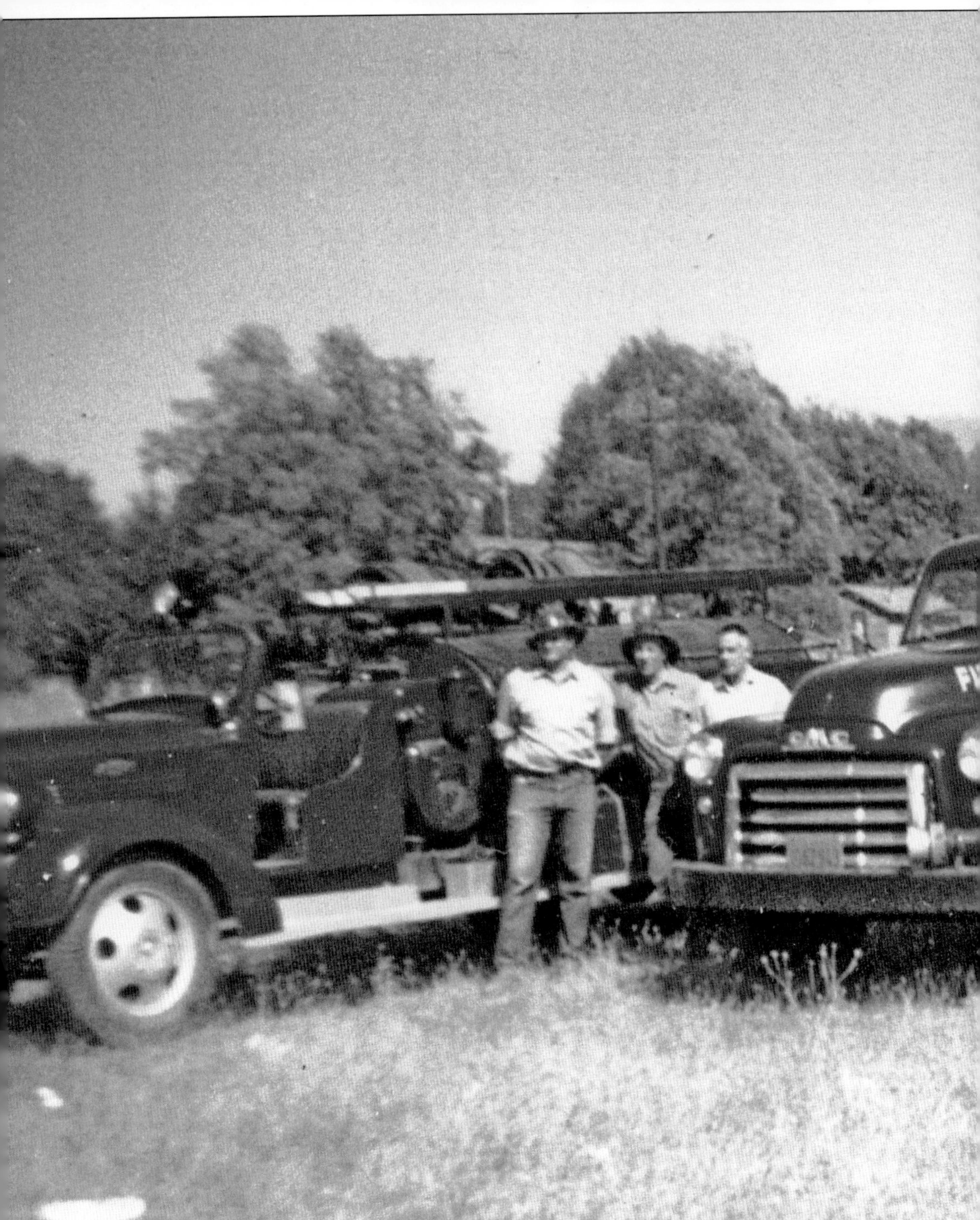

Proudly displayed at each public barbeque (here in 1959) are the departmental fire engines. The old first engine still provides rides for young and old alike during the annual cookout. As the population of the valley grew, so did the need for more fire-protection equipment. The citizens have always been supportive, including passing a special parcel assessment for the department.

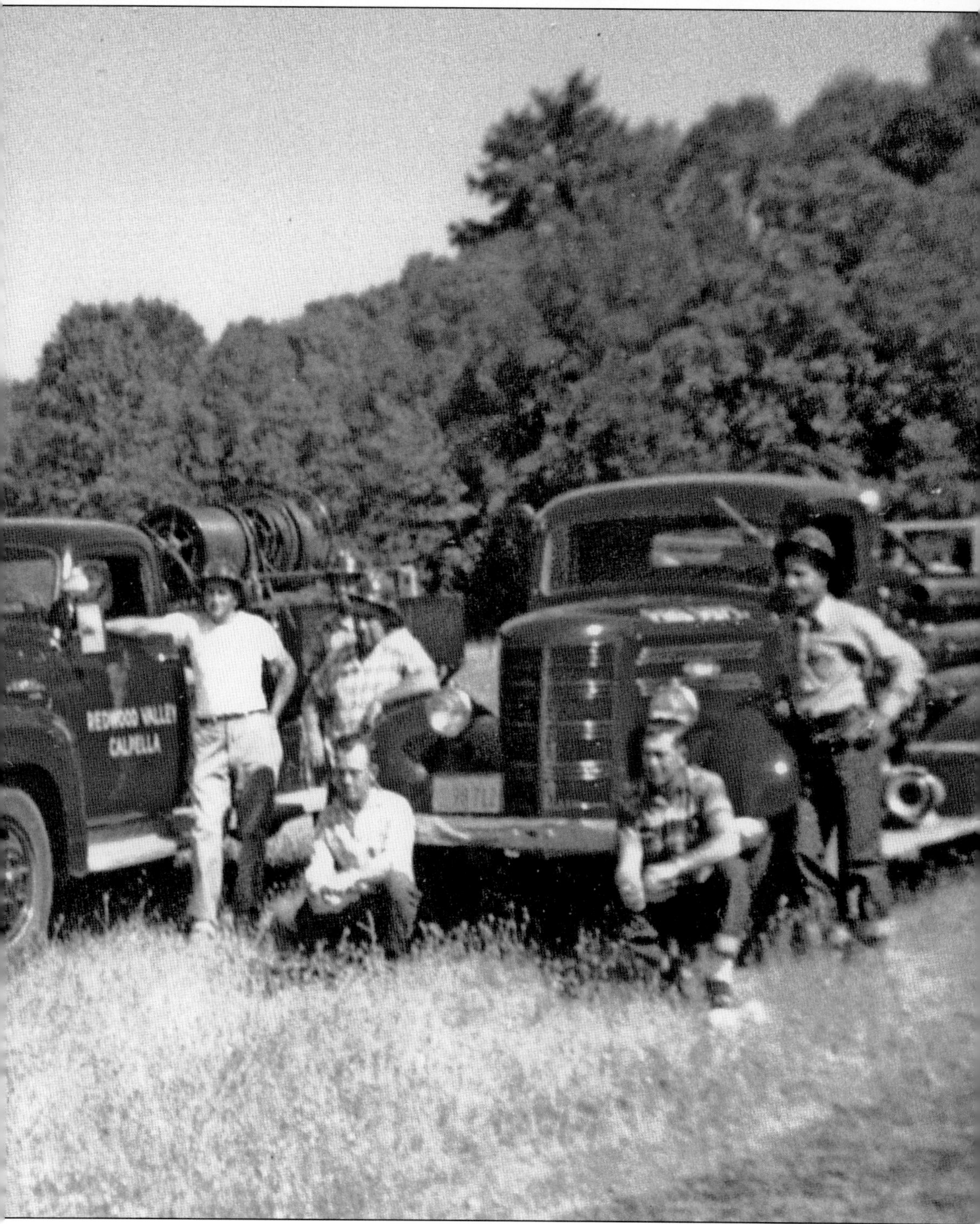

This photograph was taken in the field south of the firehouse. It shows the extent of the Redwood Valley Calpella Fire Department's fire engines and equipment. From left to right are Chief Tom Jameson, Lewis Martinelli, Monk Myers, unidentified, Joe Bishop, Delbert Phelps, Jim York, Arnold Ford, and Roy Adreveno. (Courtesy of the RVCVFD.)

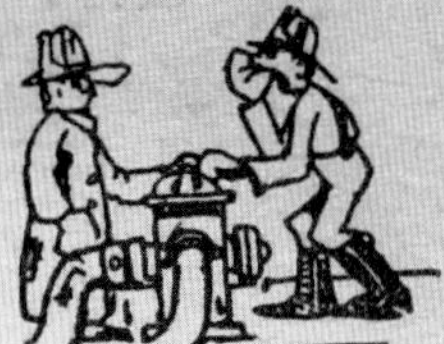

REDWOOD VALLEY-CALPELLA
VOLUNTEER FIREMEN

DINNER

SATURDAY, OCTOBER 27, 1956

REDWOOD VALLEY GRANGE HALL

5:30 to 9:00 P. M. Adults $1.50

No 497

This 1956 dinner ticket was sold to raise money for the fire department prior to the public barbeque. The dinner was served at the Grange hall, located on East Road. As the financial needs of the department increased, a decision was made to go public with the barbeque and dance. It annually raises thousands of dollars for improvements and equipment. (Courtesy of the RVCVFD.)

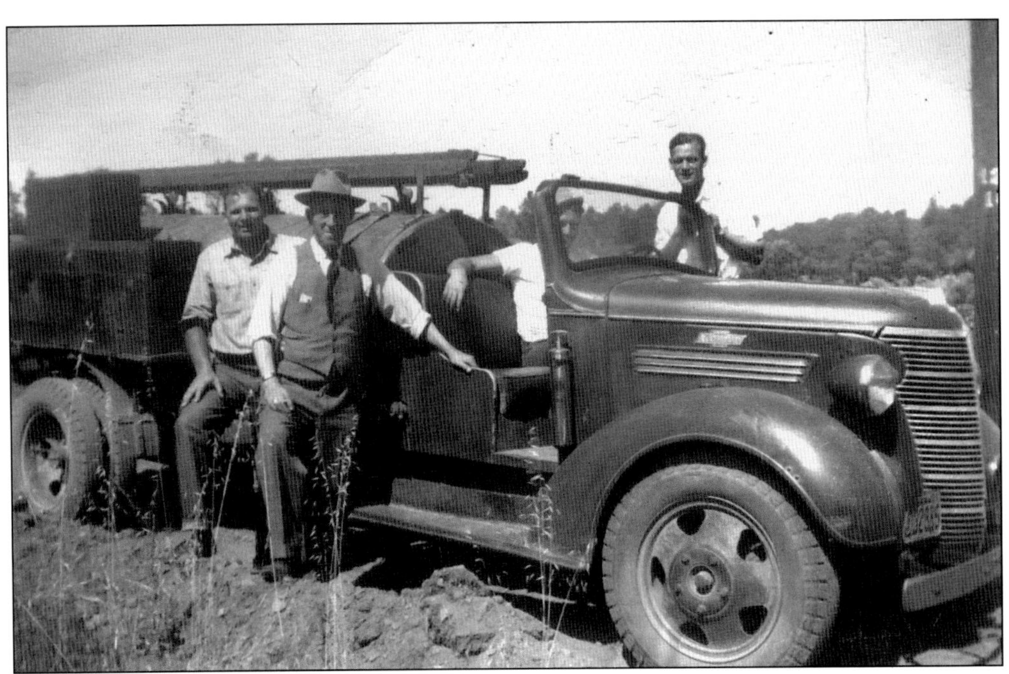

Still in use and pictured here is the original engine in 1949. Notice a ladder has been added above the water tank. Here is the crew that fight the fire at the Calpella Plywood Plant. From left to right are Tom Jameson, chief; Agent Dorking of the local railroad; Cy Goudge, the driver; and Gene Locatelli, acting as fireman. (Courtesy of the RVCVFD.)

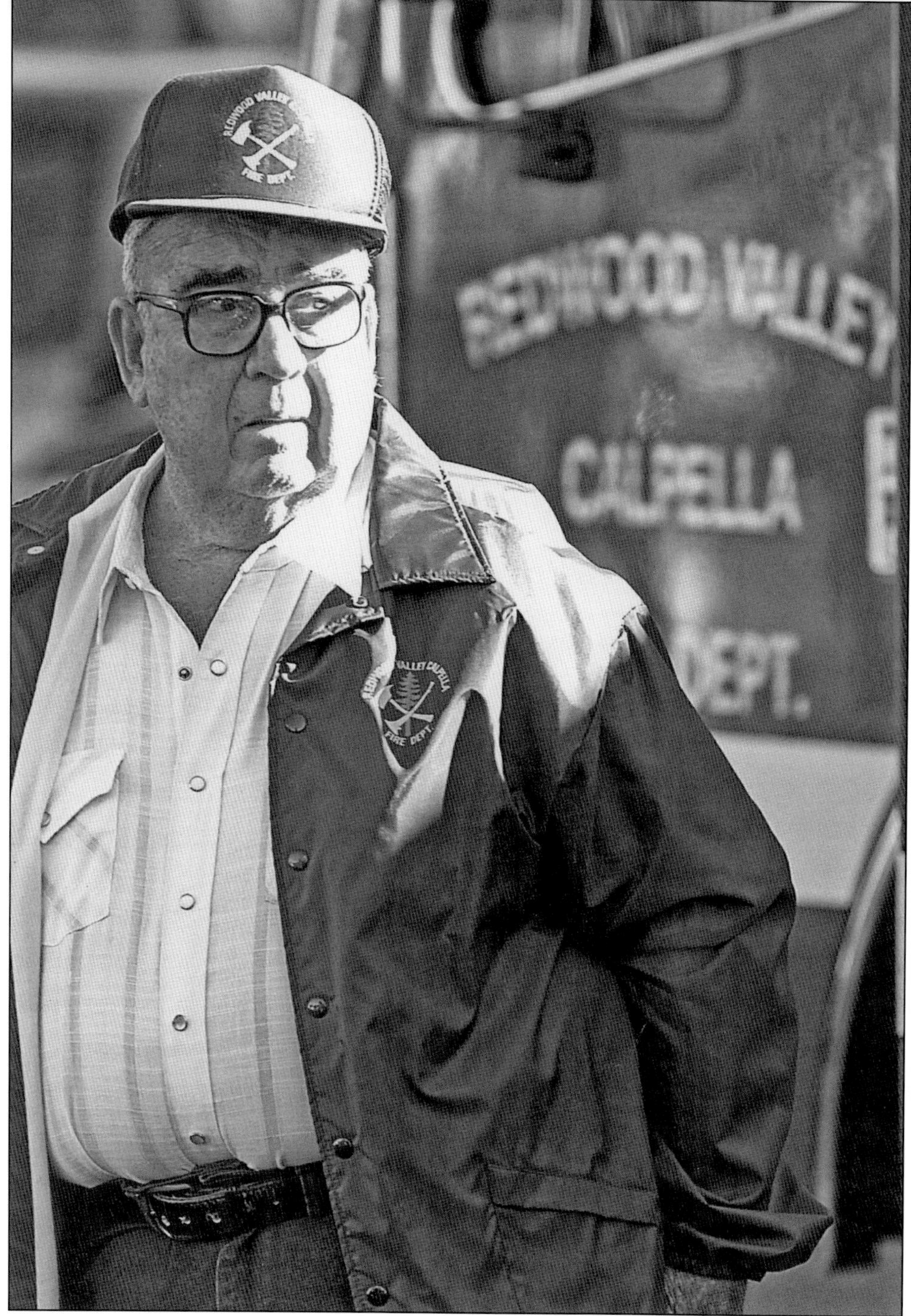

Pictured here is Delbert Phelps, born in a house across from the Redwood Valley Firehouse, which now bears his name. Phelps was a charter member of the Redwood Valley Calpella Volunteer Fire Department, which was established in 1953. "The Chief," as he was affectionately called, rose through the ranks to become fire chief in July 1978, a position he held until he retired on October 1, 1993. (Courtesy of the RVCVFD.)

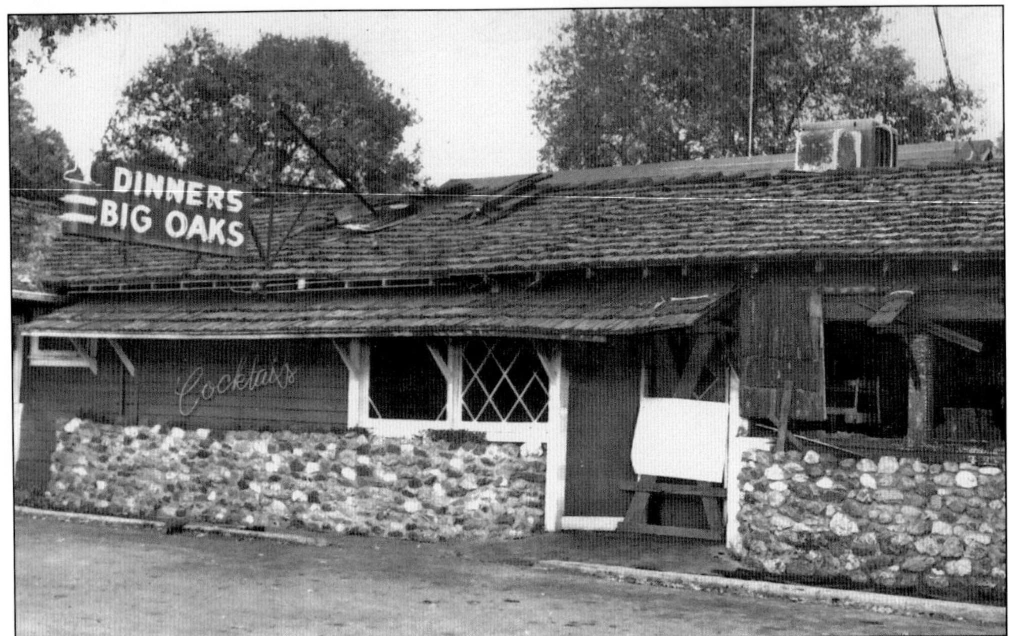

A popular local restaurant located at the north end of Calpella was the Big Oaks restaurant. Here, it is shown after being completely gutted by fire in 1966. According to volunteer fireman Lewis Martinelli, the main destruction occurred on the opposite side of building. This photograph was taken from North State Street. (Courtesy of the RVCVFD.)

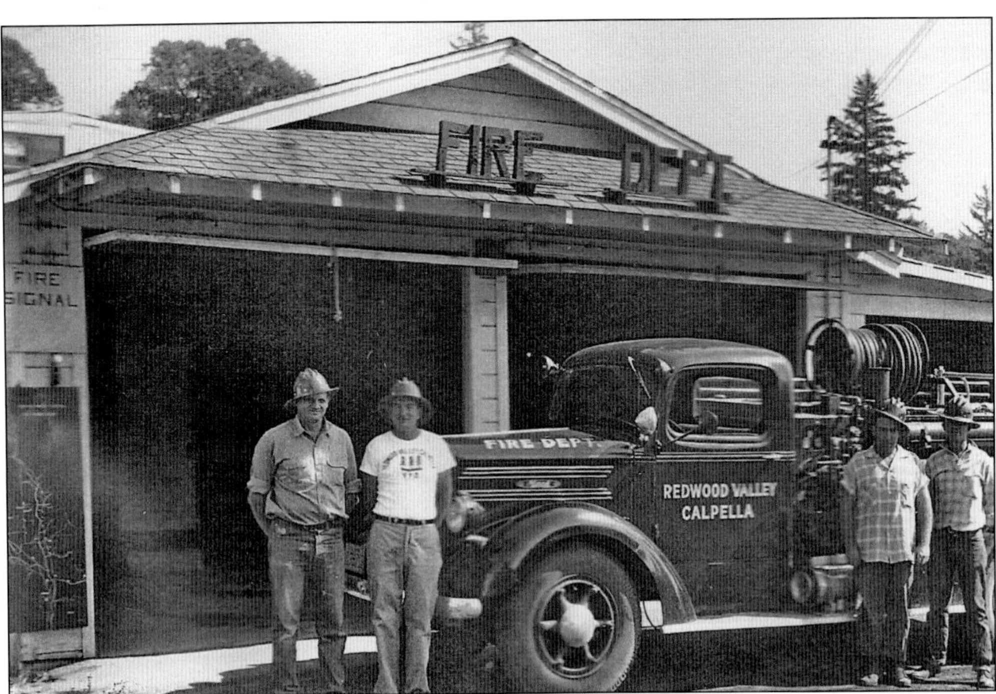

In this 1950s photograph, the officers of the RVCVFD are, from left to right, Tom Jameson (chief), Ed Hosheit (captain), Delbert Phelps (captain), and Jim York (assistant chief). (Courtesy of Linda Phelps-Wilson.)

Before the barbeque went public, the fire department held an annual turkey shoot to raise funds. Pictured here on November 11, 1956, are, from left to right, Rose Ricetti, Delbert Phelps, and Genevieve "Scrubby" Ricetti Tollini, who have come out to support the department. (Courtesy of Linda Phelps-Wilson.)

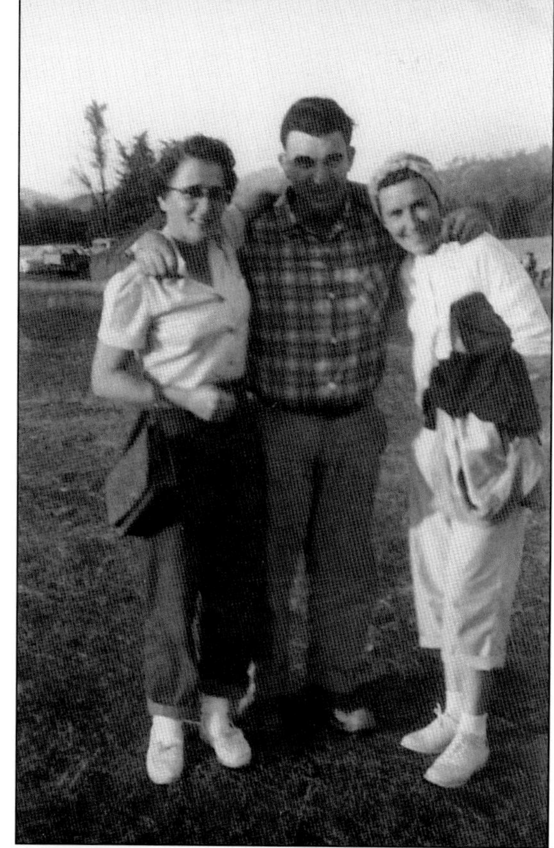

The turkey shoots were held on the Rawles and Ford Ranches and were family affairs. Everyone was invited to come out and cheer on the shooters. This November 1957 photograph features Nancy Ricetti (left) and David and Linda Phelps. (Courtesy of Linda Phelps-Wilson.)

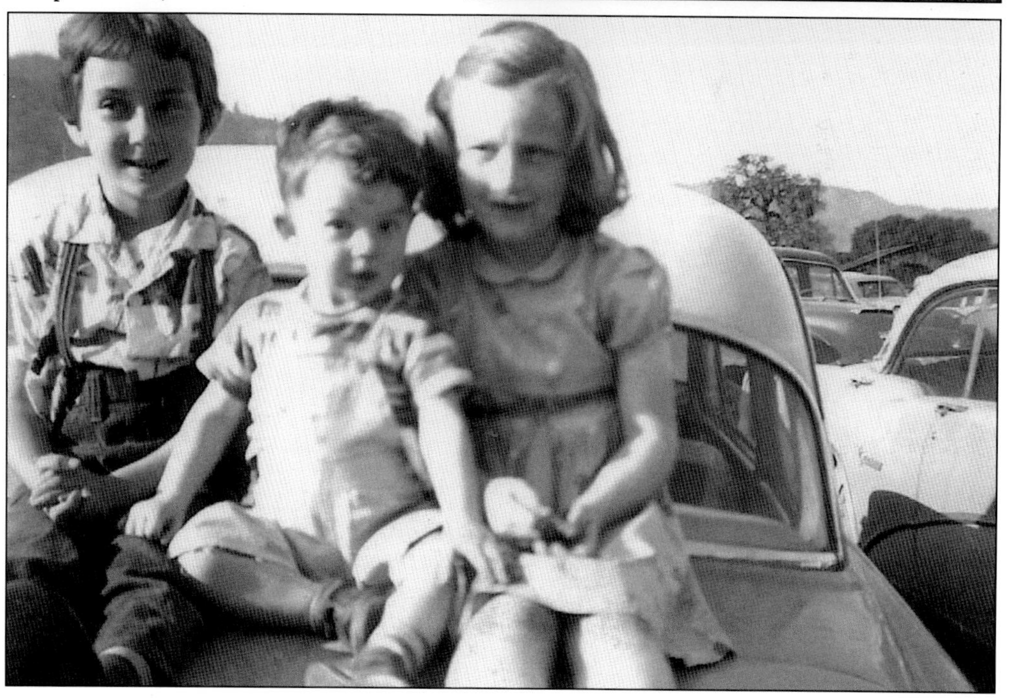

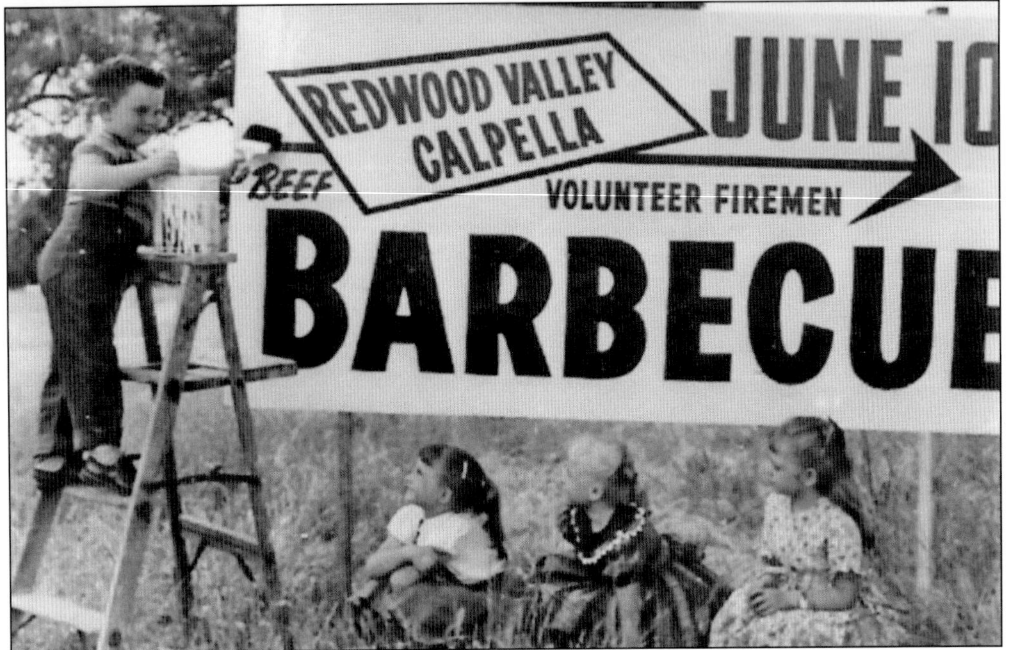

David Phelps (son of Chief Delbert Phelps), Nancy Jameson (daughter of the Chief Tom Jameson and granddaughter of T.M. Jameson), Janet Cundall (daughter of the pastor of the Redwood Valley Community Church) and Diana York (daughter of Assistant Chief Jim York) are helping to publicize the upcoming 1960 Redwood Valley Calpella Volunteer Firemen's barbeque. (Courtesy of Linda Phelps-Wilson.)

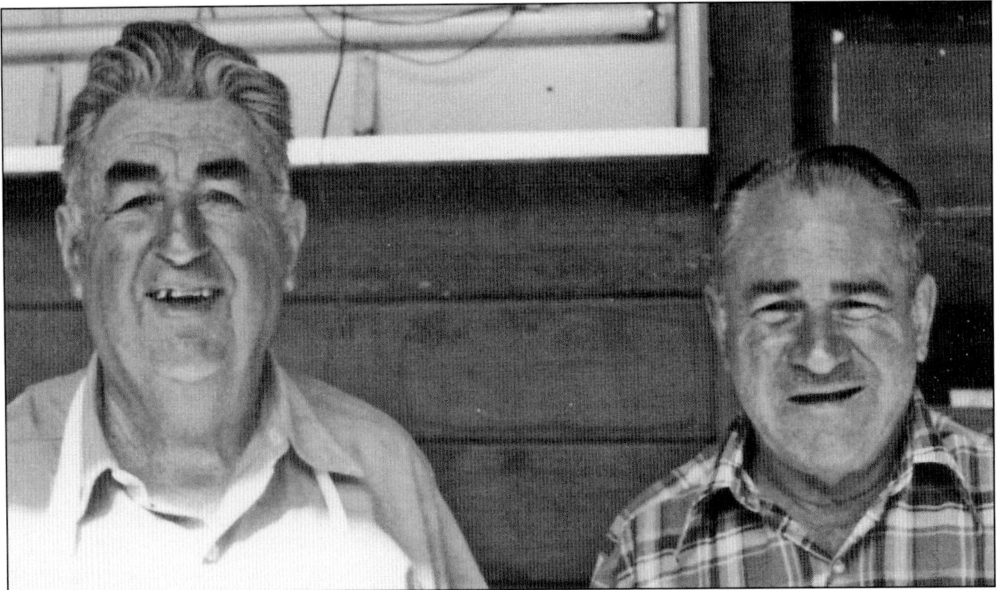

Pictured here on the left is Emil Poma, who has been seen throughout this book as a small baby, a schoolboy, young man, and now as an elder volunteer. Also shown is Hugo Graziano, a representative of the valley's Italian population and a grape grower on Road D, as well as the salad man at the barbeque. They were two steadfast volunteers at the annual event. (Courtesy of the RVCVFD.)

Eight

Redwood Valley Happenings

Over the years, the community of Redwood Valley has had numerous activities. The Grange has been a center of many events. Plays were put on for entertainment and to raise money for projects. It also hosts wedding receptions, breakfasts, *quinceañeras*, celebrations, and dances.

On May 23, 1941, an advertisement appeared in a Finnish-language newspaper in Superior, Wisconsin, inviting Finns to the Socialist Workers Organization of California's spring celebration on the Pekkala Farm in Redwood Valley, California. A community-wide May Day picnic used to be held at the Homewood Park.

Recently, 200 valley residents surprised the unofficial mayor, Ralph McDill, with a luncheon celebration when he retired after 55 years at the Redwood Valley Shopping Center.

The Redwood Riders sponsors the Black Bart Day parade. It started in 1960 and continues to this day with floats, fire trucks, horseback riders, folks on foot, and Black Bart winding its way through downtown. Each year, a community member is honored as Black Bart: Tom M. Jameson was the first; Leo Bleier Sr., Elbert Lane, Vic Soinila, Marty Moir, Ralph McDill, Delbert Phelps, and Ken Wilson have also reprised the role.

On July 19, 1984, a Brinks truck was robbed on the hill leaving Redwood Valley toward Lake Mendocino. The bandits fled with 10 to 15 bags of money; all were eventually captured, along with the loot.

November 20, 1978, will long be remembered in Redwood Valley as the day many of its friends and neighbors committed suicide in the jungle of Jonestown, Guyana. The local schoolteachers were especially hard hit as they read the names of their students on their television screens that day. On January 20, 2009, a local boy, Pastor Richard Warren, gave the prayer in Washington, DC, at Barack Obama's first inauguration.

A Taste of Redwood Valley, a wine-tasting event, takes place annually. All of the valley wineries are open for a weekend of enjoying the fruits of award-winning vineyards.

Rodeo events at the Jameson arena, horseback riding, fishing, hunting, hiking, camping, and crawdad fishing down at the river are enjoyed by all.

PROGRAM

10:00 A. M. Ball Game.

12:30 P. M. Auction of Baskets.

3:00 P. M.

Piano Solo — Miss Margaret Thompson

Reading — Miss Minnie Keller

Duet — Mrs F. Green and Mr. Fred Frank
Piano accompaniment - Miss Alice Strong

Recitation — Miss Marie Cagwin

Violin Solo — Mr. Kurt Schamber
Piano occompaniment - Miss Margaret Thompson

4:00 P. M. Races

Phone — Main 221

C. Hofman Co.
Department Store

Ukiah - - - - Calif.

MAY DAY PICNIC

GIVEN BY

Redwood Valley Improvement Club

Laughlin, California

May 11, 1912

This invitation was sent out announcing the 1912 May Day picnic at the Homewood Park at Laughlin. This was an annual event for many years sponsored by the Redwood Valley Improvement Club. The park is a beautiful stand of firs, which still exists today, but not as a park. The invitation contains this advice: "Reciprocity is the life of trade therefore patronize our advertisers." (Courtesy of Janet Marsh.)

S. T. Järjestön Californian alueen

KEVÄTJUHLAT

— vietetään —

Redwood Valleyssa, A. Pekkalan Farmilla

Toukok. 30-31 ja Kesäk. 1 p.

Monipuolinen, vaihteleva ja arvokas kulttuurellinen ohjelma. Yksityisiä numeroita tulee paikallisilta tovereilta ja ulkopuolisilta kuten:

RUNOJA, LAULUA, SOITTOA, Y. M., Y. M.

Ohjelmassa esiintyy m.m. San Franciscon ja Berkeleyn yhdistyneet sekakuorot.

—: Tanssia hyvällä soitolla :—

Ruokaa ja virvokkeita saatavana kohtuullisilla hinnoilla koko juhlien ajan.

TERVETULOA LÄHELTÄ JA KAUKAA ALUEEMME KEVÄTJUHLIIN!

—Californian aluekomitea.

Redwood Valley even sponsored a national event at the Finnish colony. On May 23, 1941, an advertisement appeared in a Finnish-language Superior, Wisconsin, newspaper inviting Finns from all over the country to the Socialist Workers Organization of California's spring celebration. The event was to be held on the Pekkala Farm in Redwood Valley, California. (Authors' collection.)

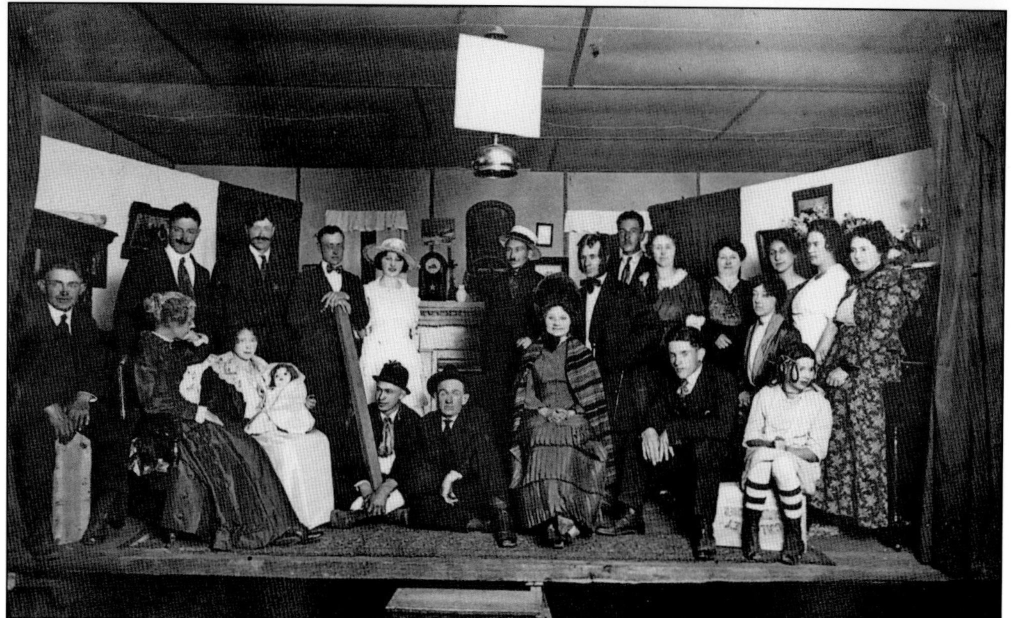

A 1922 play was put on to raise money for the Grange 382; identified from left to right are (first row) Merlin Tull, Laverne Kisler, Mrs. Ed Austin, John Tull, Ed Austin, Mrs. T.M. Jameson, Jack Goudge, Mrs. Collie McDonald, and Marion Jameson; (second row) Collie McDonald, Cy Goudge, Irwin Jones, Besmer DeVee, Robert Winsby, Fred Goudge Sr., Earl Sweet, Lucille Bednar, Mrs. Richards, and Mrs. Watson.

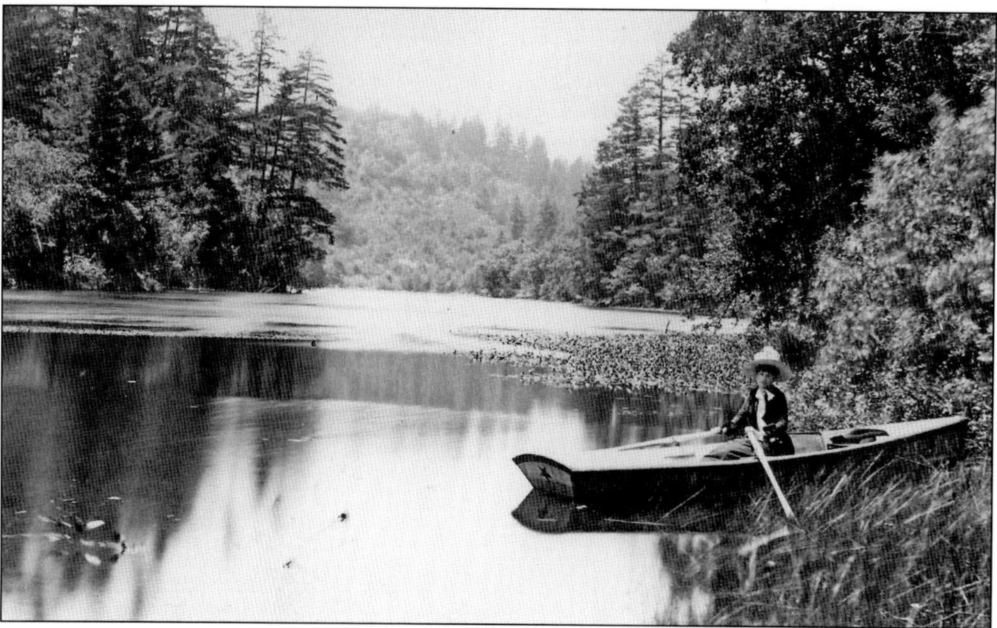

Leonard Lake is located to the southwest of Redwood Valley. At one time, it was a popular public destination for boating, fishing, and camping. The Grange spearheaded an attempt in the 1920s to have it set aside as a park for the general public. The $150,000 price tag was too much, and the effort failed. This A.O. Carpenter photograph is believed to be of Grace Carpenter boating on the lake. (Courtesy of Ed Bold.)

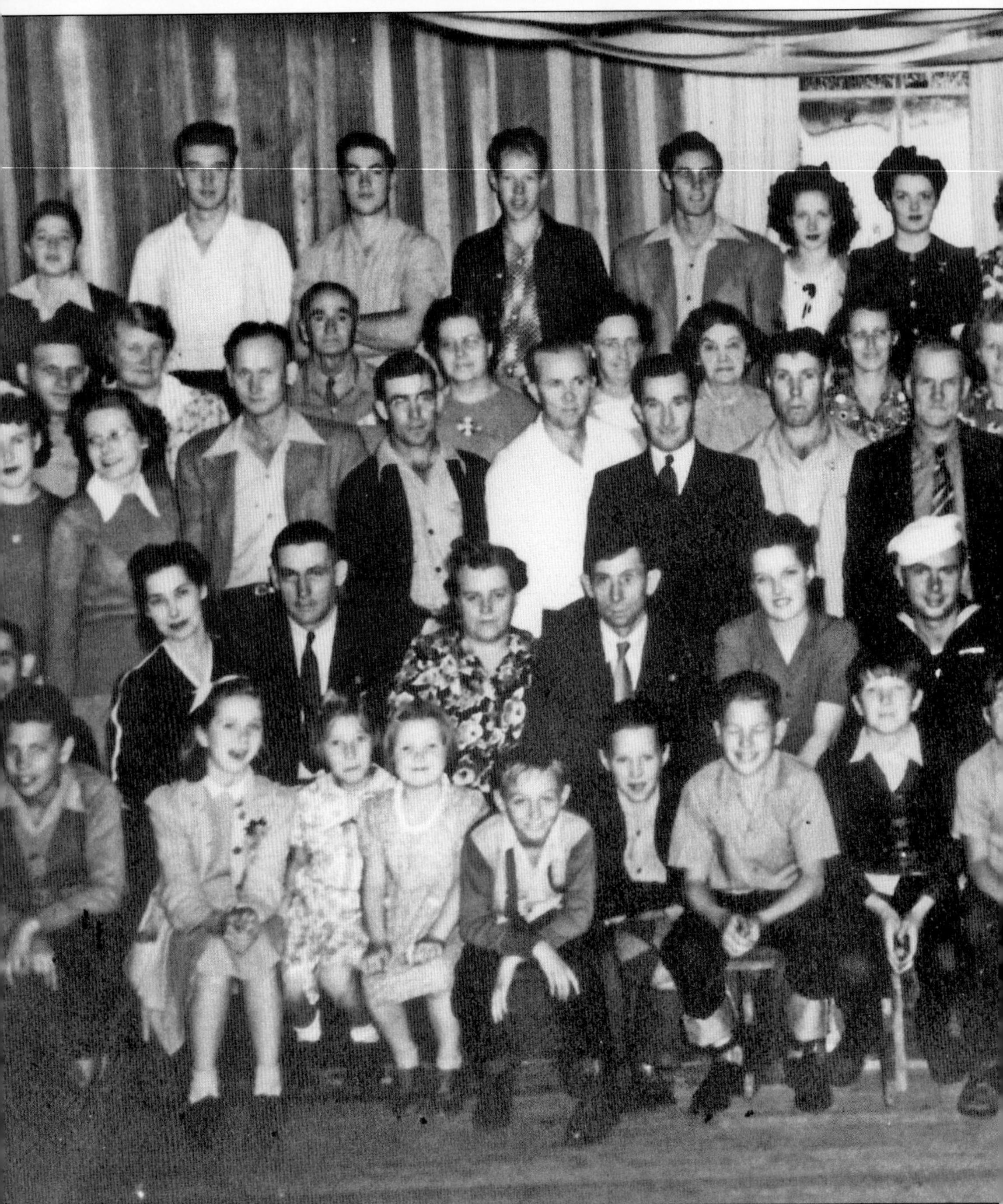

Shown here is the 1945 Harvest Celebration at the Redwood Valley Grange Hall. Many longtime residents were in attendance. From left to right are (first row) Oren Thompson, Janet Gillette, four unidentified, George Thompson, five unidentified, Arlene Gillette, Clarice Fernbach, Roselyn Lucchesi, unidentified, and Armando Lucchesi; (second row) five unidentified, Nora Morris, Ray Reed, and seven unidentified; (third row) Dora Weselsky, Mary June Scanlon, two unidentified, Roy Williams, Elbert Lane, two unidentified, Lloyd Yarbrough, Fred Bryne, unidentified, Don

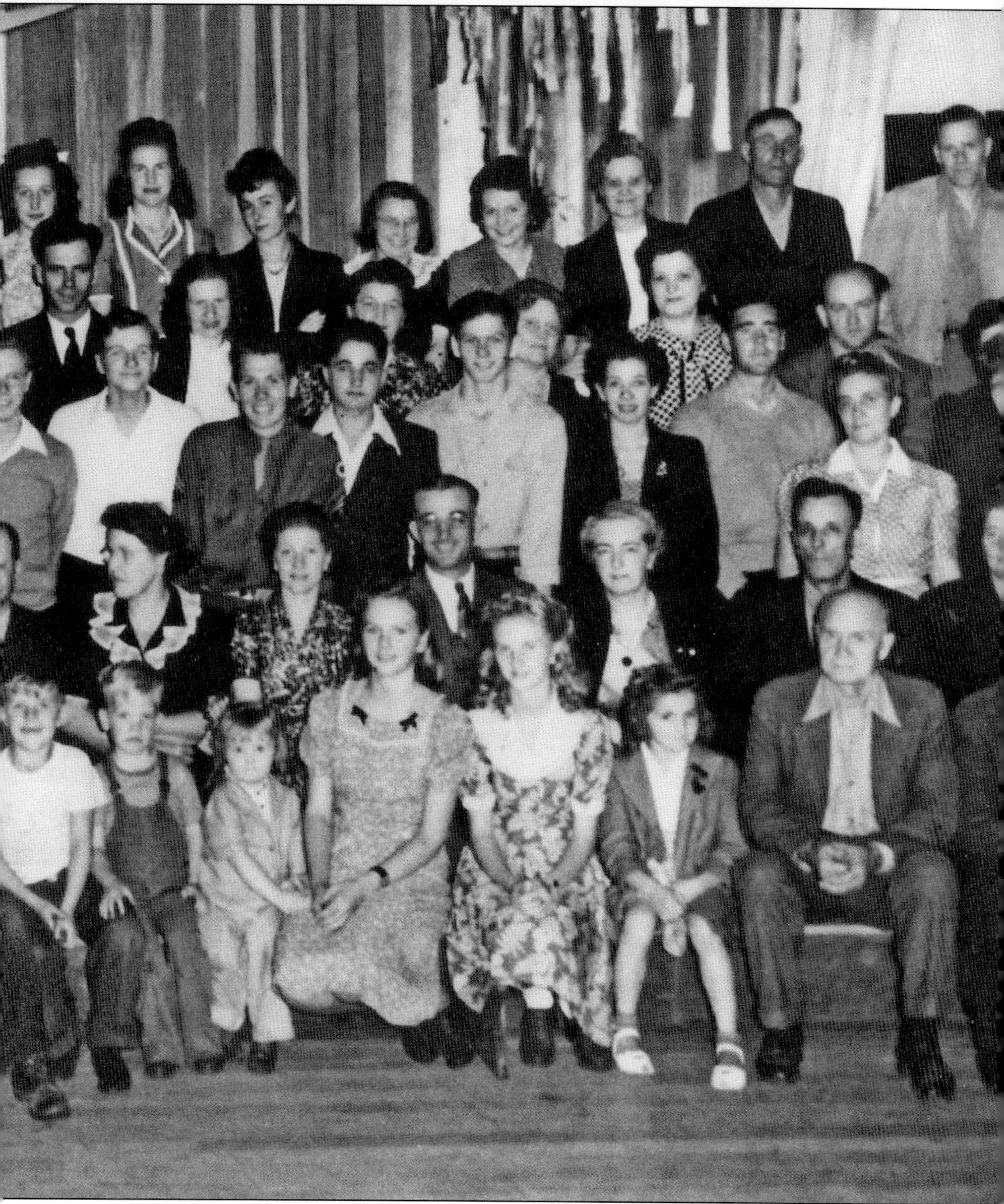

Hearn, Marston Gillette, Wilda Boyd Wood, Charles Wood, unidentified, and Jo Lane; (fourth row) Tom Jameson, Mrs. Fernbach, Harry Gillette, Ada Gillette, four unidentified, Doris Ford Pringle, John Pringle, four unidentified, Jack Simpson, and Virginia Simpson; (fifth row) Jimmy Goudge, JayLee Smith, Don Goudge, Charles Thompson, Angelo Marcheschi, Dorothy Boyd, Hazel Williams, Frances Wickstrom, Elaine Johnson, Rosalie Fernbach, Gen Ricetti, unidentified, Gladys Williams, and three unidentified. (Courtesy of F. Marston Gillette.)

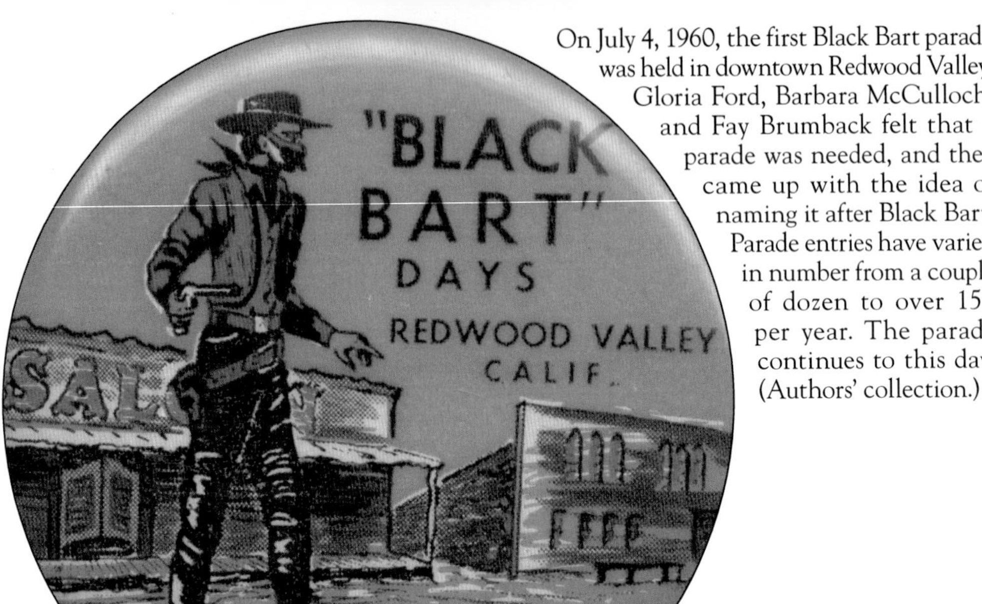

On July 4, 1960, the first Black Bart parade was held in downtown Redwood Valley. Gloria Ford, Barbara McCulloch, and Fay Brumback felt that a parade was needed, and they came up with the idea of naming it after Black Bart. Parade entries have varied in number from a couple of dozen to over 150 per year. The parade continues to this day. (Authors' collection.)

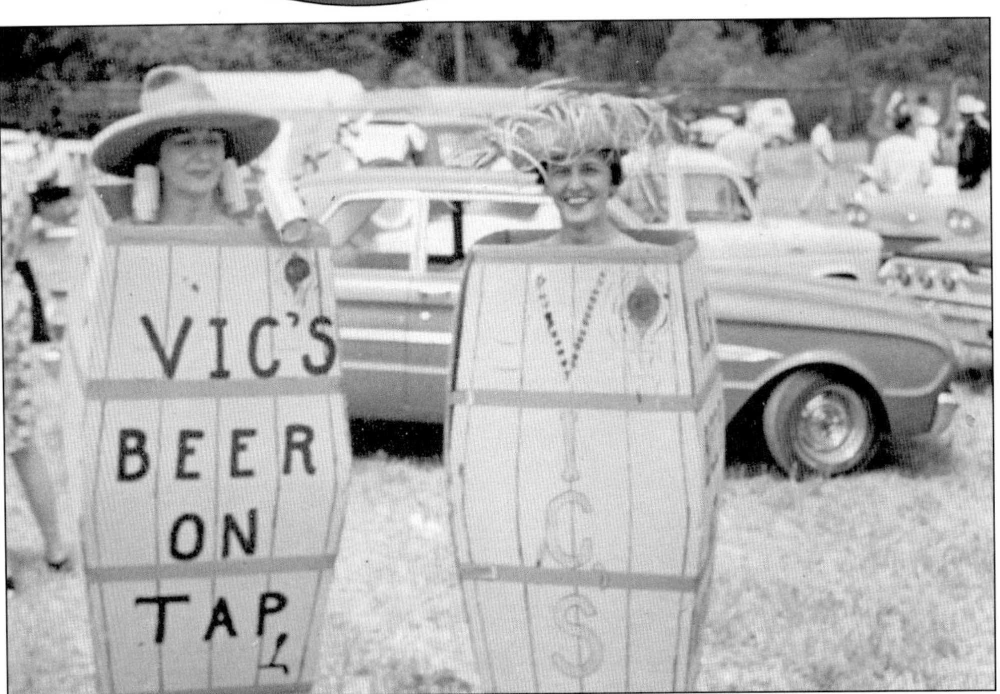

Many of the entries were on the humorous side and even a bit risqué. Vic's Place had some fun with this entry. Marselle Goodwin (left) is pictured with Alice Soinila in 1963. (Courtesy of Julie Soinila.)

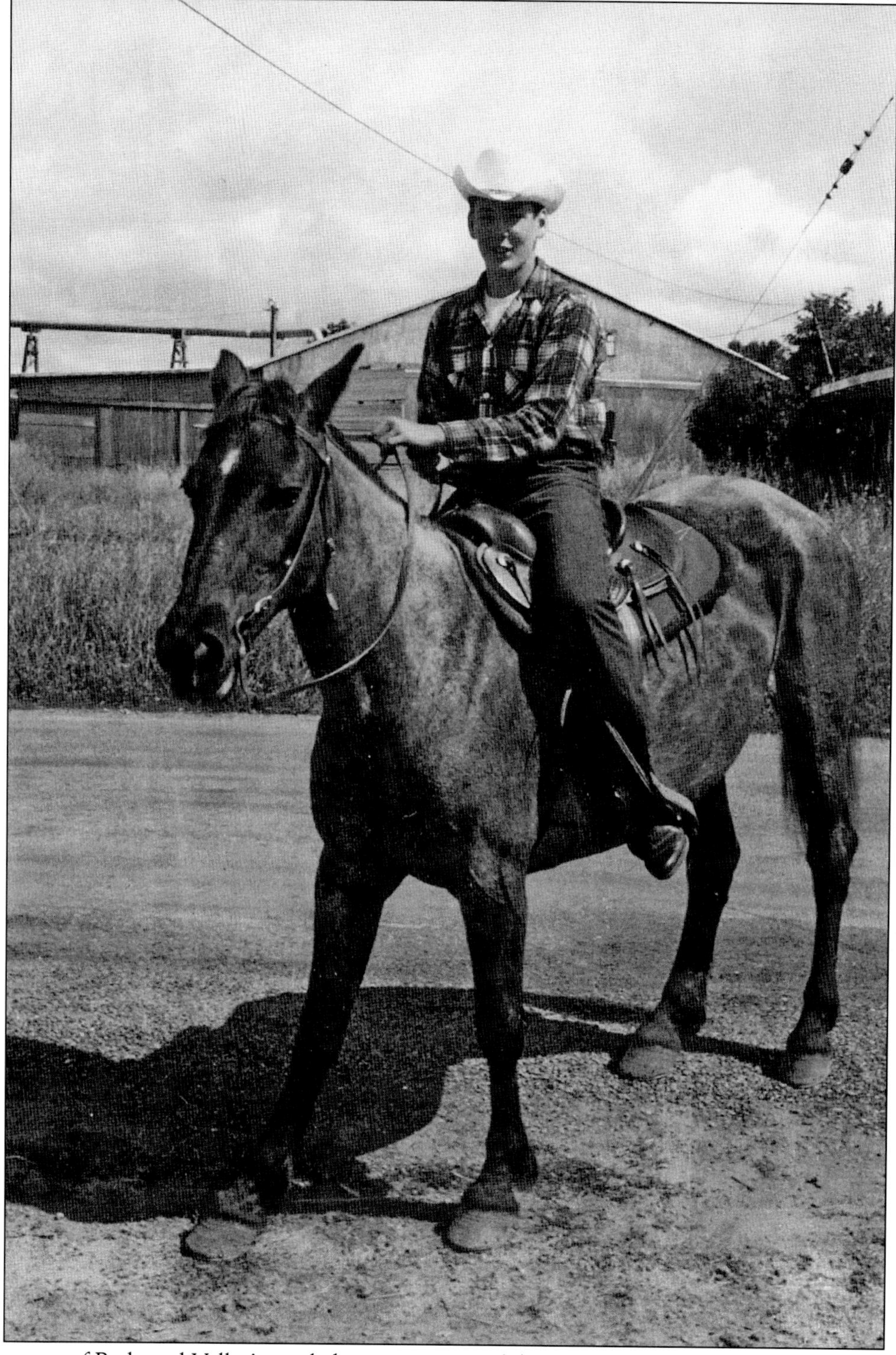

Because of Redwood Valley's rural character, many of the entries in the Black Bart Day parade are young people on their horses. Here, Gary Martinelli rides his horse Bluebird in the 1963 parade. (Authors' collection.)

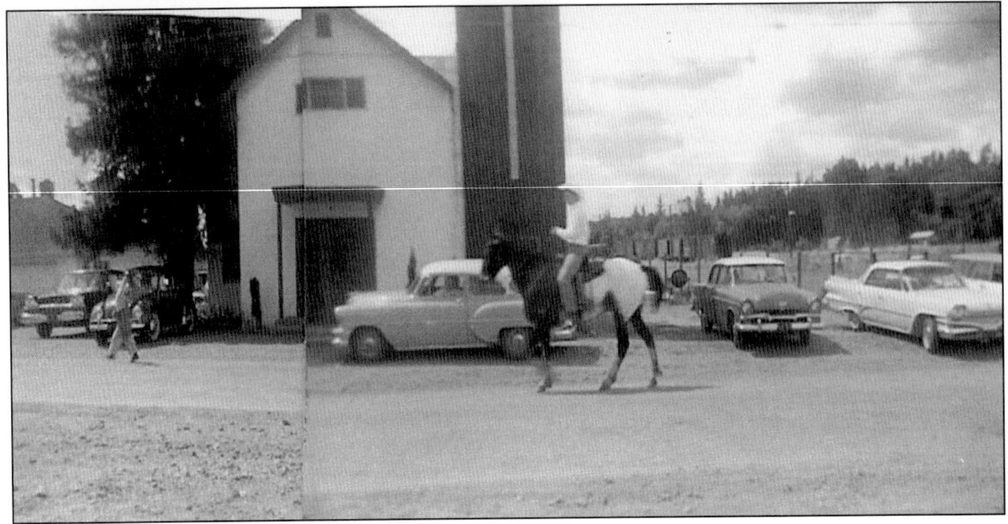

Lyle Hanks rides Chico in the 1963 Black Bart Day parade. Here, he is front of the Redwood Valley Community Church, with the railroad tracks and cars to the right. The redwood tree in this photograph is still standing. (Authors' collection.)

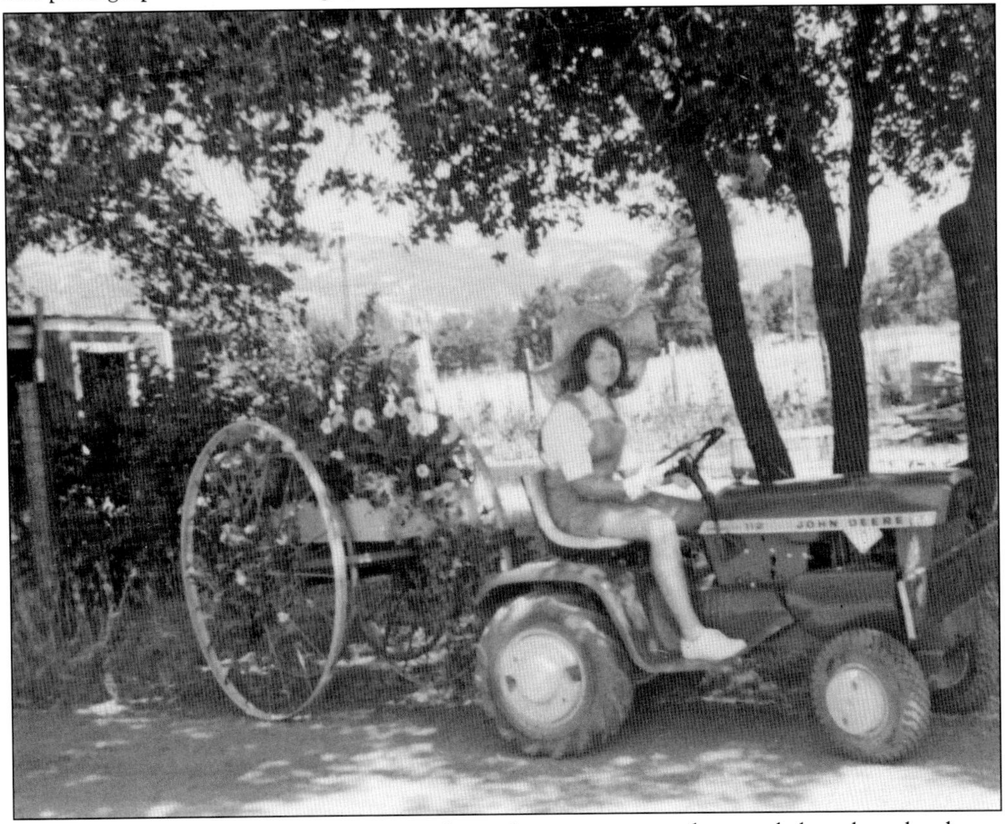

Each family and organization came up with an idea to enter into the parade based on the theme for that year. Dolores Martinelli of the Redwood Valley Garden Club helped decorate an old wagon, filled it with flowers, and then hooked it up to a John Deere garden tractor, which was driven by her daughter Linda. (Authors' collection.)

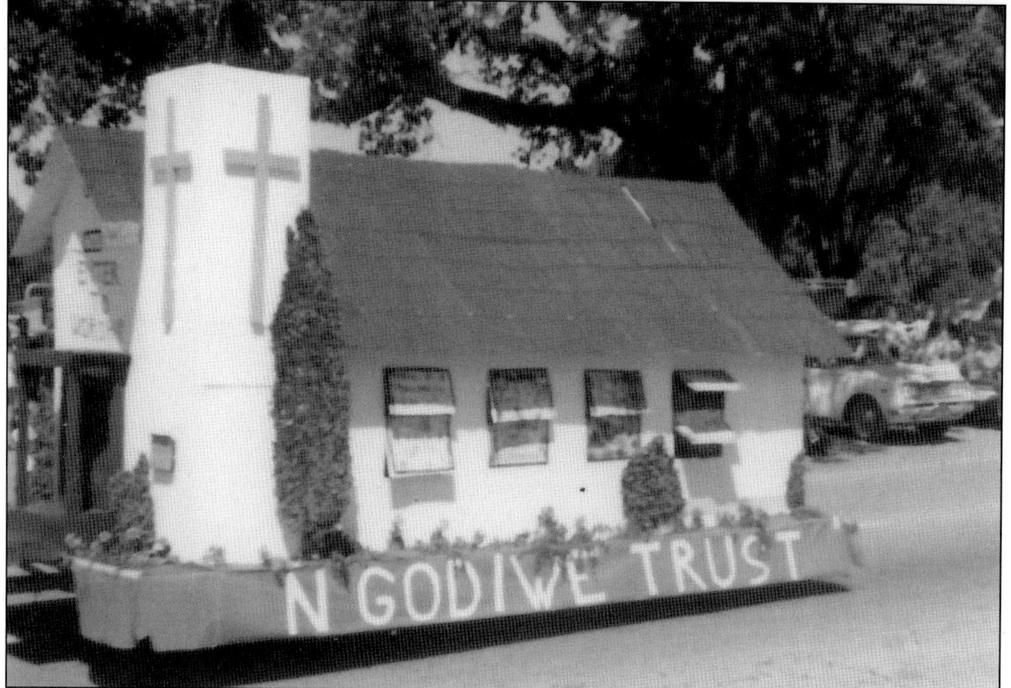

The local community church almost always had a float in the annual Black Bart festivities. This one was in 1970 and represents the church sanctuary, which was the original Redwood Valley Improvement Clubhouse with the tower that was added in the 1960s. There was one Sunday school room at the top of the tower. Apparently, some pranksters rearranged the slogan along the float's side. (Authors' collection.)

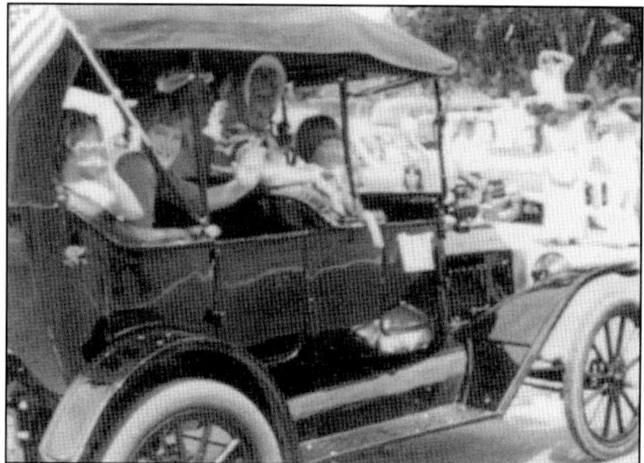

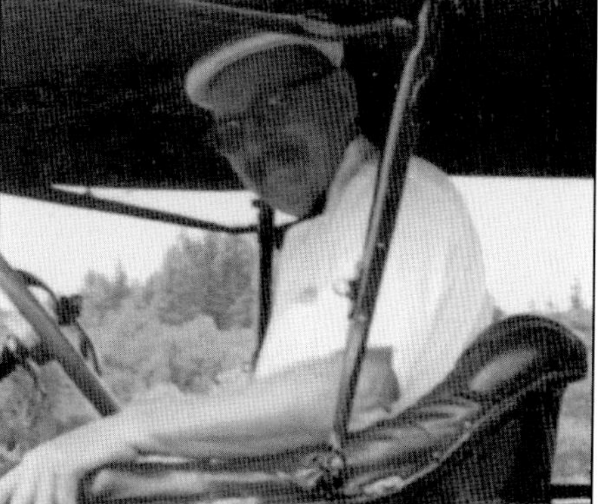

Shown here in the late 1970s is Vic Soinila serving as grand marshal while driving a Model T; Alice Soinila wears the bonnet. The close-up shows Vic wearing a fake mustache to look like a fellow who might be driving a Model T back in its heyday. (Courtesy of Julie Soinila.)

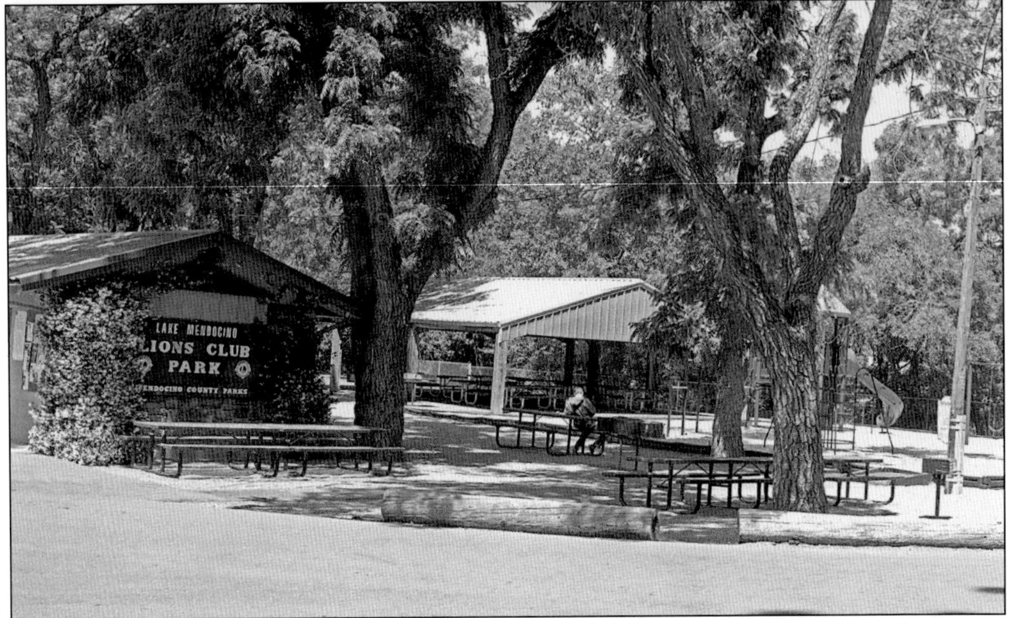

In 1961, the Lake Mendocino Lions Recreation Corporation created the park located along East Road in Redwood Valley. It includes three acres with a baseball field, restrooms, a sheltered picnic area, a small playground, and a large parking lot. Over the years, many improvements have been made. It is widely used throughout the year. Ball games, birthday parties, and a farmers' market regularly occur here. (Courtesy of Jim McCleary.)

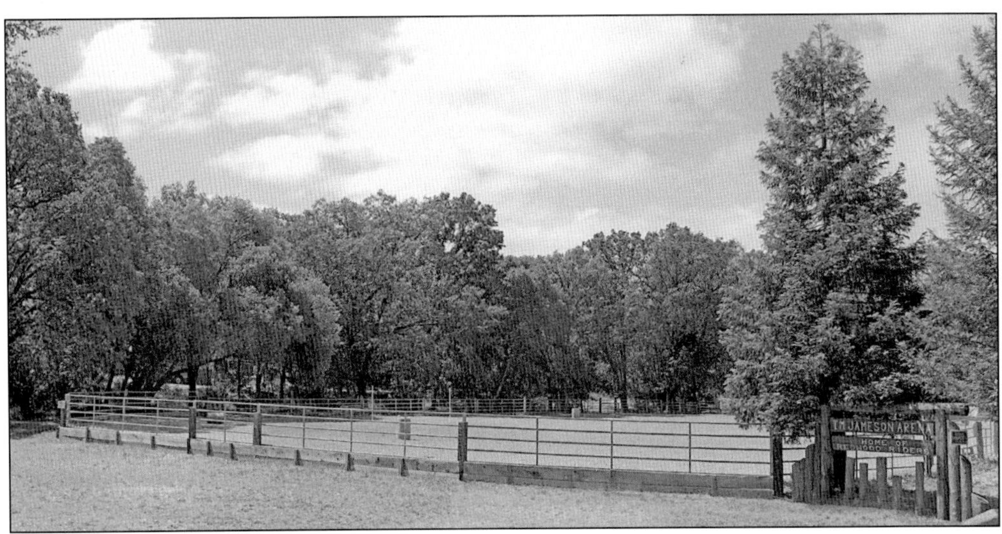

The Redwood Riders were founded in 1958 to create activities around the horses of members and their families. The Riders leased the property shown here from T.M. Jameson, who always expressed a desire to have a place for folks to ride their horses and promote Western riding. The Redwood Riders eventually purchased the land. (Courtesy of Jim McCleary.)

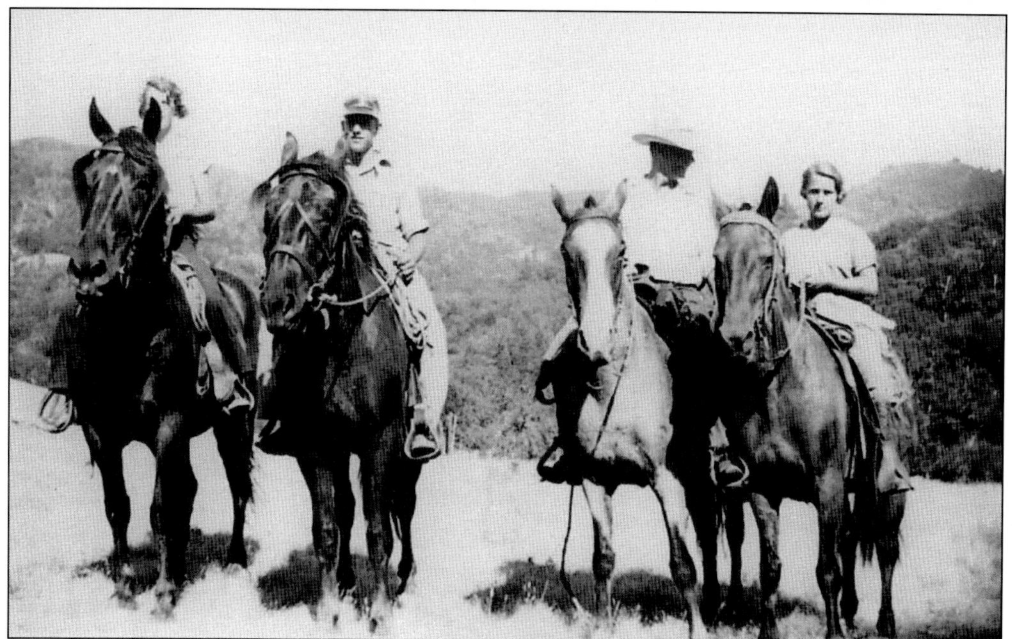

Horseback riding was part of everyday life on the Brown Ranch in 1933.

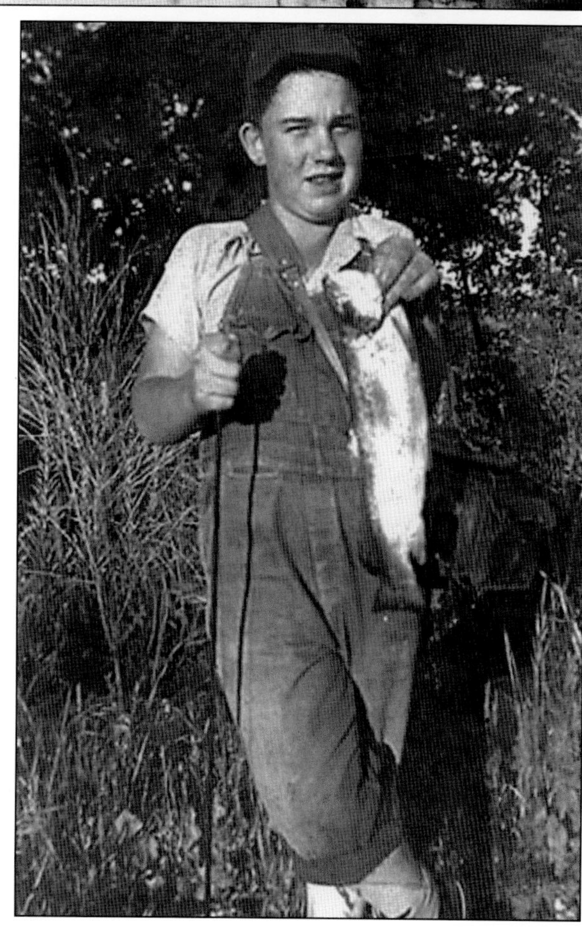

A teenaged Delbert Phelps is pictured here with a big one he caught in the waters of Leonard Lake. (Courtesy of Linda Phelps-Wilson.)

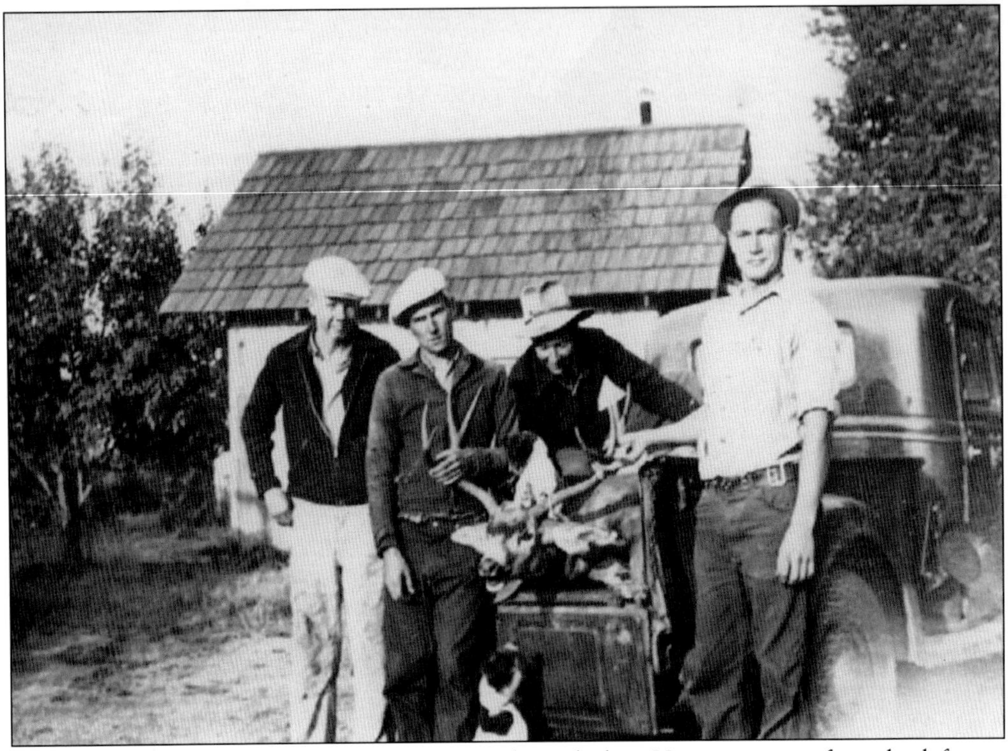

Redwood Valley had some very good hunting in the early days. Here is a group of men back from a successful hunt. From left to right are E. Leonard "Mike" Talso, John Ricetti, Bob "Red" Johnson, and Laurie Oman. (Courtesy of Marsha Johnson Isbester.)

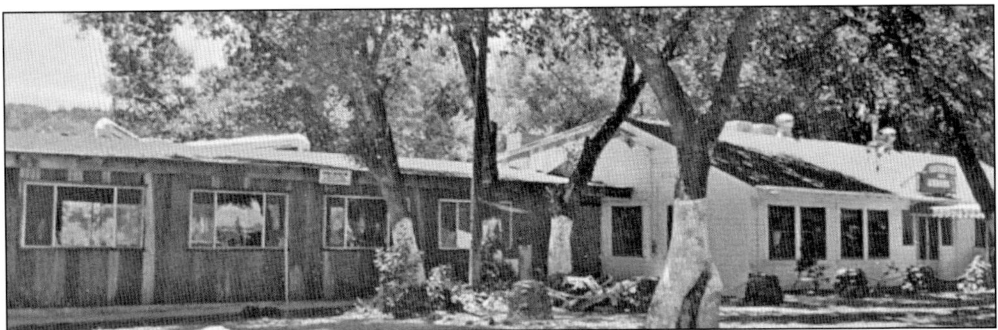

Shown here are the Duck Inn (left) and Southworth's Inn (right) before it became the Broiler. Southworth's was a Swedish smorgasbord. This inn was on Highway 101, a popular stopover for travelers on this section of the road. A rodeo grounds was located on the flats behind the restaurant and used until the Redwood Riders Arena was established.

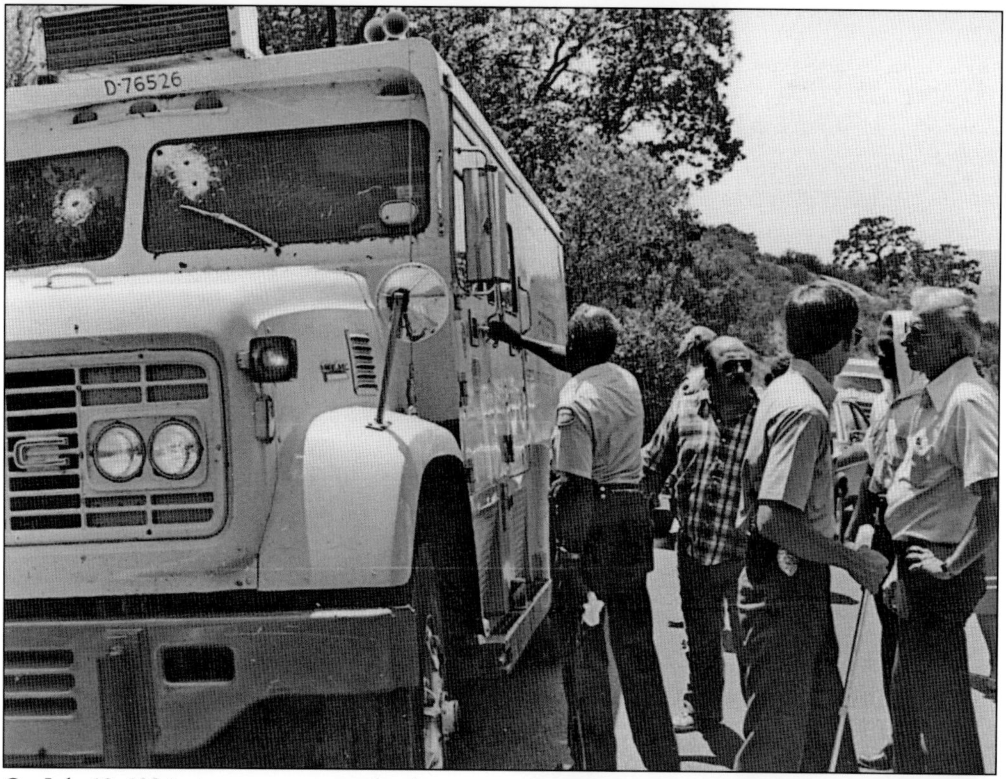

On July 19, 1984, six gunmen staged a daring robbery of a Brinks truck as it lumbered up the Highway 20 grade from Redwood Valley. Using two pickups, one slowing the Brinks truck in front and the other behind, they shot out the truck's windshield and made off with bags of money, having parked their getaway car at Calpella. Eventually, they were all were captured and jailed. (Courtesy of the *Ukiah Daily Journal*.)

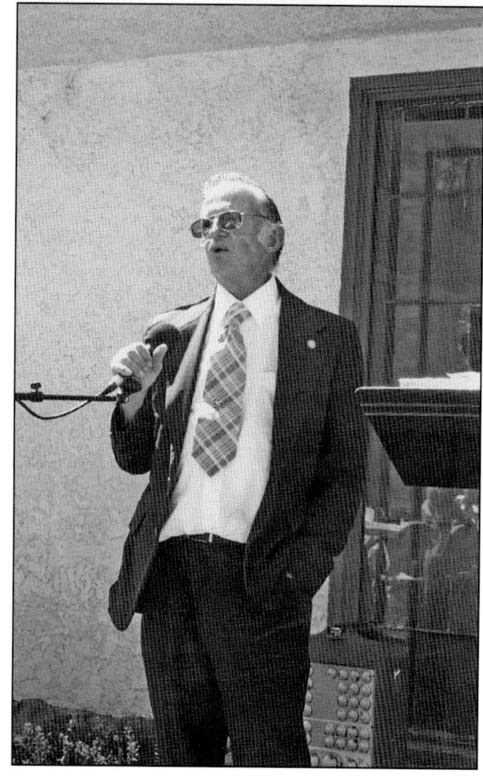

Ralph McDill addresses a crowd of over 200 friends as they help him celebrate his retirement after 55 years of employment at the Redwood Valley Shopping Center. McDill is known as the unofficial mayor of Redwood Valley. He first came to the valley in the 1950s and has lived and worked in the area ever since. (Authors' collection.)

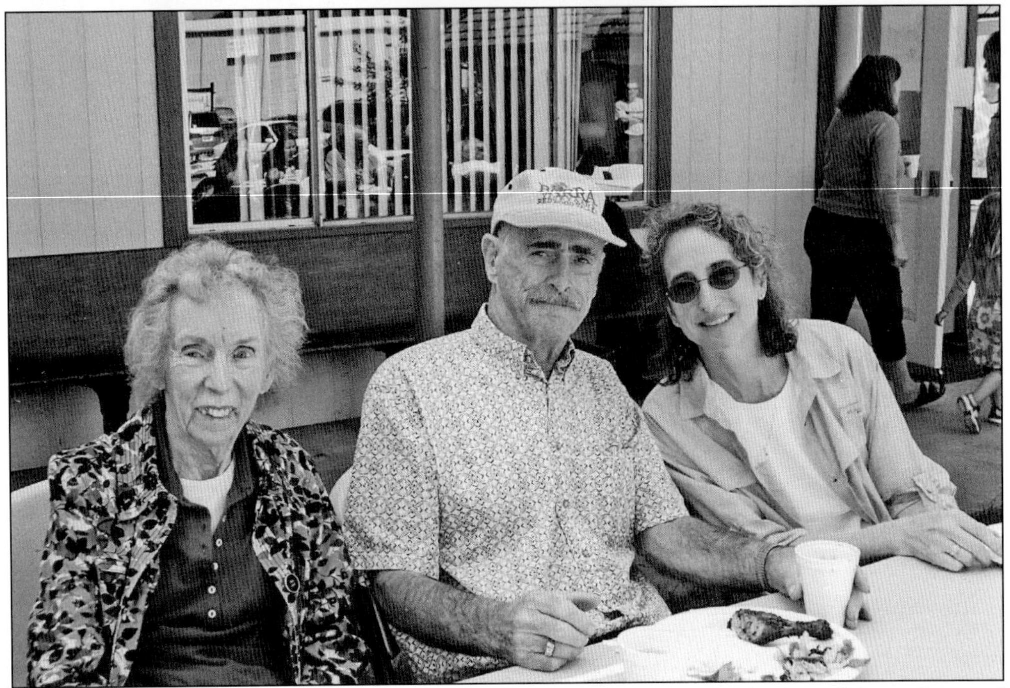

The late Bea Barra, Pete Barra, and Cyndi Barra Woskow were part of the crowd that celebrated Ralph McDill Day on August 28, 2010, at the Redwood Valley Community Church. Pete is a longtime resident of the valley and has been involved in the grape industry his entire life. (Authors' collection.)

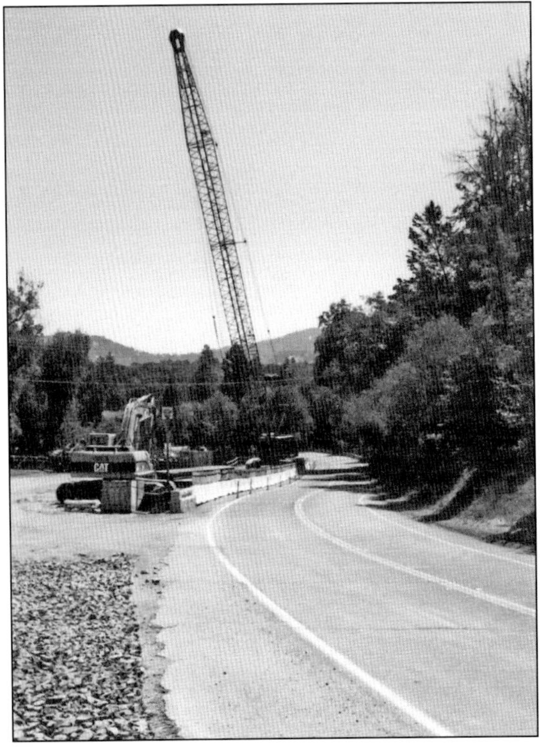

Progress continues on the new bridge being constructed at the Russian River crossing on School Way. It will be the fourth bridge at this location. Redwood Valley continues to grow. (Authors' collection.)

Here is this year's poster announcing another year and another barbeque. It is the 57th annual barbeque, held June 20, 2015. A Redwood Valley tradition, it shows that the community is looking out for itself and its neighbors. (Authors' collection.)

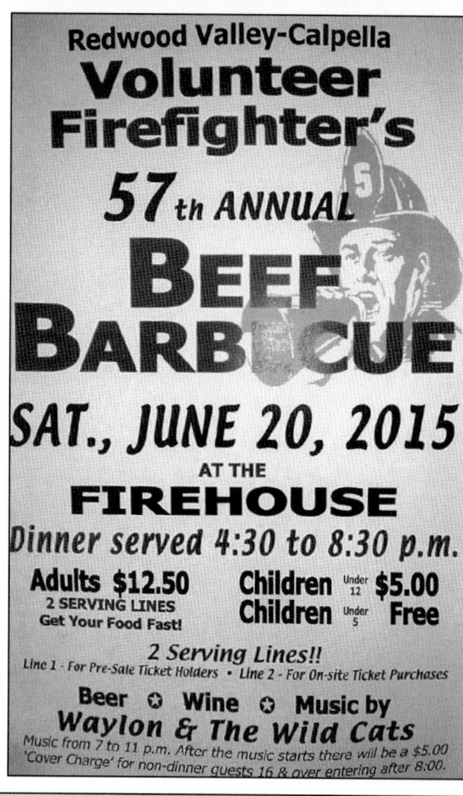

Here is a panoramic view of the beautiful and special place called Redwood Valley. (Courtesy of Wikipedia.)

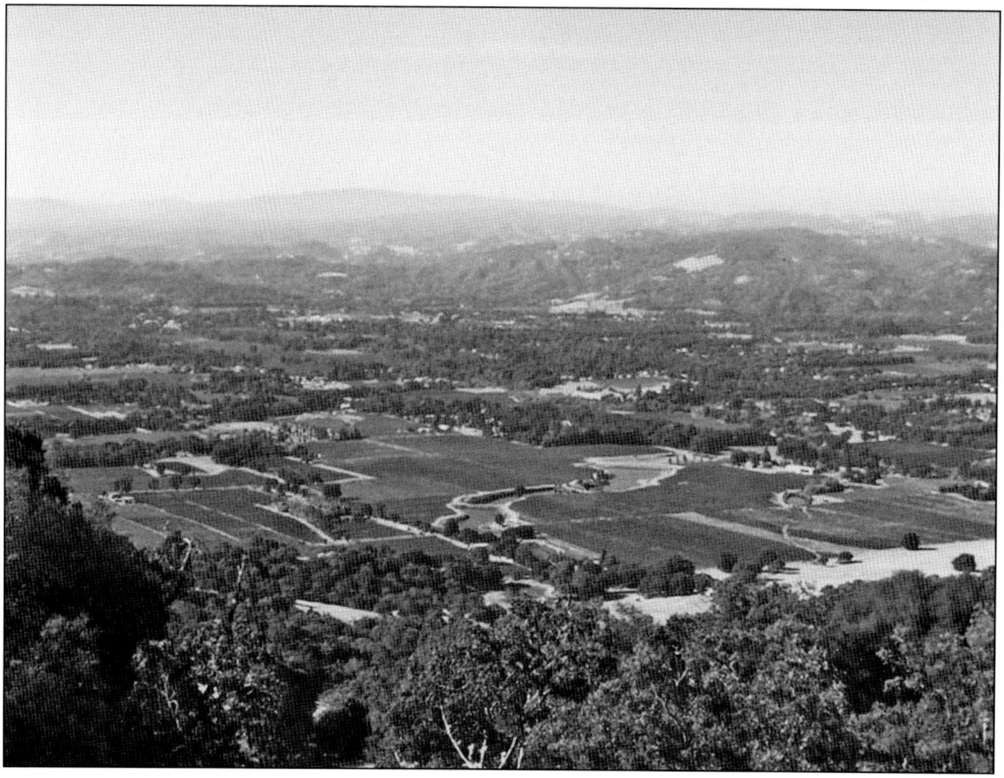